This book should be returned to any branch of the
Lancashire County Library on or before the date

3 0 JUL 2016

D0492987

PAPER TIGER

Xu Zhiyuan is a columnist for the *Financial Times Chinese* and former editor-in-chief of *Bloomberg Businessweek China*. He won the Excellence in Opinion writing SOPA award in 2008. His latest books include *A Stranger in Motherland* and *The Totalitarian Temptation*. He was also a visiting scholar at Cambridge and Berkeley.

PAPER TIGER

INSIDE THE REAL CHINA

XU ZHIYUAN

Translated from the Chinese by
Michelle Deeter and Nicky Harman

This book has been selected to receive financial assistance from English PEN's PEN Translates programme, supported by Arts Council England. English PEN exists to promote literature and our understanding of it, to uphold writers' freedoms around the world, to campaign against the persecution and imprisonment of writers for stating their views, and to promote the friendly cooperation of writers and the free exchange of ideas. www.englishpen.org

First published in 2015 by Head of Zeus Ltd

1 3 5 7 9 10 8 6 4 2

A CIP catalogue record for this book is available from the British Library.

ISBN (HB 9781781859780)
ISBN (XTPB 9781781859797)
ISBN (E 9781781859810)

Designed and typeset by e-type, Aintree, Liverpool

Printed and bound in Germany
by GGP Media GmbH, Pössneck

CONTENTS

THINGS SEEN AND THINGS THOUGHT

EARTHQUAKES AND GRAND OCCASIONS

FEAR AND FEARLESSNESS

ANGER AND ABSURDITY

PREFACE: CHOOSING TO BE AMBIVALENT

It was hard to write this preface, much harder than I expected.

This book is made up of a few dozen short essays. Some essays describe my travels throughout China and Asia, some are commentary on current events and some are descriptions of public figures. Most of the essays were written between 2007 and 2013, when the China model was extremely popular. In this book, I hope to show that behind the façade the China model is absurd, unjust and unsustainable.

In general I would call myself a liberal. I believe that if a government is not based on personal freedom, it is contemptible. Everything Beijing does is suspect and full of chicanery, no matter how much wealth or power it brings, no matter how much wonder it gives the average person. I have never believed in the concept of the China model. The economic miracle in China is the result of the hard work of the Chinese people and not the leadership in Beijing.

Most of these essays were originally published for Chinese media outlets based outside of Mainland China, specifically for *Yazhou Zhoukan* in Hong Kong and the Chinese edition of the *Financial Times* in London. Still, I have never considered myself to be a dissident writer.

I am afraid of being pigeonholed and having to make a definitive judgment on China when there are so many grey areas. China's story is a strange and complicated one. There are countless examples of political stagnation, violations of human rights, and the suppression of individual voices. But at the same time, I have seen economic and technological reforms that not only turned China into a modern nation but also made its society more open and diverse. People care more about protecting individual rights and young people are much more open-minded. All in all, I am very optimistic about China's future. The sclerotic political system and the strength of the steadily progressing society are in fierce competition, but I think the latter will ultimately be victorious.

In the past two years, however, my optimistic outlook has been tried and tested. I never expected to see my country to go backwards like this. Not only have the rulers of China launched an unprecedented crackdown on their own citizens, they are trying to revive Communist ideology even though it has been proven to be completely ineffective. As political commentator Timothy Garton Ash puts it, Xi Jinping is 'trying to steer a complex economy and society through difficult times by top-down changes, led and controlled by a purged, disciplined and reinvigorated Leninist party'.*

I have known too many friends who have been put behind bars. Some of them have made only the mildest of criticisms of the regime and yet their works have been banned. That means I am not able to publish books in Mainland China for the time being.

But that is not the whole story. As a miasma of oppression, fear and silence continues to spread, society has been engulfed by a wave of entrepreneurship and consumerism. Huge companies dominate the market and swarms of young people are leaving home to start their own businesses. Chinese consumers are flocking to cities around the world to see their sights and to shop. China appears to be a land full of opportunity.

My own life is filled with these contradictions. I am a writer

---

* http://www.theguardian.com/commentisfree/2015/jun/01/war-peace-depend-china-domestic-success

who is unable to publish in my own country, and yet my friends and I have successfully raised venture capital to start our own social media company. It seems that I have been oppressed and given a rare opportunity at the same time. I doubt that the intellectuals based in Warsaw, Prague and East Berlin during the era of Soviet domination, who were never given a chance freely to express themselves, would ever have dreamed that such an opportunity could exist in a one-party state. My counterparts in present-day Yangon, would, I suspect, be similarly surprised.

My publisher and I chose the subtitle 'Inside the real China' to emphasize the fact that, unlike outside observers, I come from China, and my commentary is (perhaps) more authoritative. But I suspect that there are disadvantages to this as well. An insider is like a fish in a fishbowl, unable to see the exact shape of its surroundings even though those surroundings are perfectly clear to everyone else. Ultimately we are all like blind men feeling an elephant; we cannot fully understand the way China is changing.

I cannot provide a clear-cut prediction on China's future. But my instinct says that China's party-state power is stronger than I imagine. Moreover, a majority of Chinese people believe in and rely on this power. No intellectual, no entrepreneur, no human rights activist, no dissatisfied worker or farmer can pose a serious challenge to this party-state power. As a result, the current China model will continue for a long time.

I wish I had more courage and optimism in terms of the ability of the people to overcome this totalitarian regime. Unfortunately I cannot hide my hesitancy, my evasiveness, or my confusion. Compared to my friends who are writers and lawyers and have been forced to leave the country or are detained for their views, I am embarrassed to think of how ambivalent my views are.

THE FACE OF CHINA

SPECULATORS IN A FRENZY

20 October 2007

The people flooding the stock market in China today are not white-collar workers from the city or financial experts. Everybody buys stock – university students, farmers, vendors, even the old lady down the road. Ordinary people have no confidence in society, so they rest all their hopes on the security that a huge amount of money can bring.

S he carried *Elliott Wave Principle: The Key to Stock Market Profits* and a biography of Warren Buffett in her book bag. She was searching the shelves of a bookstore trying to find a textbook on probabilities. I understand what my friend was doing. At school, she always said that maths gave her a headache. She had studied some accounting but still couldn't get the hang of a profit and loss sheet. When it came to the Chinese economy and the corporate world, not only did she lack a complete understanding, most of her ideas were wrong.

'Everyone at the table was talking about stock,' she said, recounting her experience of a reunion with some friends, trying and not succeeding to hold back her excitement. 'It seemed like everyone was making a ridiculous amount of money.' She had heard a number of stories of the fortunes made from investment, all of which ran along similar lines. A young graduate who was earning only 4,000 yuan (£260) a month decided to take the 200,000 yuan (£13,000) that his family had given him to buy a house and invest it in stock. In a couple of months he had earned 700,000 yuan (£46,000). After hearing so many stories like this, she wanted to set up a trading account. In the past few months, between 20,000 and 30,000 new stock trading accounts had opened every day. She still regretted having joined the game later than everyone else. The people flooding the stock market in China today are not white-collar workers from the city or financial experts. Everybody buys stock – university students, farmers, vendors, even the old lady down the road. Everyone's business seems to be booming all over China, and people mortgage their cars and homes or take out a loan to buy stock. On average, the market is still surging, but many people don't even understand what P/E (price-earnings ratio) means.

A parody of the song 'March of the Volunteers'* is very popular online, and the changed words go like this:

Wake up, you without accounts
Put all your assets in the tempting market
The Chinese people are in their richest moment
Everyone is excited and shouting
Go up! Go up! Go up!
We have one heart
We are all risking being conned
Earn on, earn on, earn on!

Sitting in a Starbucks in Beijing, I tried to use the example of the stock market crash on Wall Street in 1929 to bring her back to her senses. If even a shoeshine boy could talk about stocks, doesn't that signify that disaster is on the horizon? At precisely

* Originally heard in the anti-Japanese film *Children of Troubled Times* (1935), 'The March of the Volunteers' was selected to be the national anthem in 1949. The original words are 'Arise, we who refuse to be slaves; | With our very flesh and blood | let us build our new Great Wall! | The peoples of China are at their most critical time, | Everybody must roar defiance. | Arise! Arise! Arise! | Millions of hearts with one mind, | Brave the enemy's gunfire, March on! | Brave the enemy's gunfire, March on! | March on! March on, on!'

that moment, two middle-aged men sitting behind me spoke loudly. One said, 'Are you sure you want to go on with this? I feel like we're just helping the government to overheat the market.' Everyone knew what he was talking about: in 2008, before the start of the Beijing Olympics, the government would surely keep the stock market afloat, because a stock market crash and the resulting social chaos was not something they could afford to let happen.

For the past several months, society has seemed to be as calm as everyone expected. 'What do people worry about apart from stocks?' a business reporter asked me seriously. 'At our editor's meeting, nobody was even interested in reporting on interview topics, because nobody knew what was worth covering except for the Olympics and the stock market.'

According to my memory, this was the third money-related mania in China. The first was an Internet bubble in 1999. Back then, everyone in the cafés were talking about venture capitalism and dot-com firms. But the influence of these phenomena on society was limited because it was concentrated in universities, the IT industry and the media. Most of the money came from investors on Wall Street. In some ways it was an enlightening experience for China's business world and culture. We used other people's dollars and two years of time to help an entire generation of young Chinese people understand modern business, advanced technology, and the rules of the game in finance. The second mania was the real-estate bubble in Shanghai in 2004. Shanghai was bigger than Hong Kong in terms of landmass, and the average income of a Shanghai resident was lower than that of a Hongkonger; still, for some inexplicable reason Shanghai's real estate trends started to copy Hong Kong. Reverently, as if waiting for their favourite band to start playing at a concert, crowds of people waited in line to buy houses. The next day they would sell the houses for a profit. Within a very short time, the skyrocketing house prices made it impossible for a young person to save up and buy a house. But there were endless rumours that the cleverest people had earned a lifetime of money after selling houses a few times. The bubble was confined to a relatively small area and prices were too high to be sustainable.

This time, the stock prices had been rising for over a year, and the potential impact was greater than ever before. Opening a trading account was much easier than writing a business plan or paying a deposit on a house. Plus, everyone seemed to be making money, so why wouldn't the average person join in? Another key factor was that the people were completely confident with the capability and intentions of their government; they thought the government would never let the stock markets crash, at least not before the Olympics, and that was still a year away.

With confidence levels running incredibly high, anything seemed possible. In April 2006, Tianjin World Magnetic Card Co., Ltd. announced that it could not release a quarterly statement, and instead of punishing the company for not being forthright, the market ignored this red flag and the company's stock price doubled. In early 2007, Anhui KOYO Group announced that it was receiving government subsidies of 55 million yuan (£3.6 million) from the Suzhou city government in order to plug up losses incurred in 2006, but the company magically turned a profit and was no longer at risk of delisting.

It is unclear whether there were people manipulating those events. Still, many people buying stock in China believed that the price of the stock had no correlation to the listed company's business performance. China looks like it is filled with paradoxes: its performance in the macroeconomy is good, but individual firms are performing horrendously. In the same way, some listed companies reported insignificant profits, yet their stock prices continued to rise.

Even if you try to explain things away with the 'complexities of Chinese society' argument, the latest events are still incredible.

One billion people had worked feverishly for thirty years. In the process, they polluted countless mountains valleys and rivers, breathed in filthy air, mined all the coal from the ground and sacrificed lives unnecessarily. They abandoned the basic limits of reason and took advantage of the global division of labour, borrowed a number of different technologies, and produced a huge amount of wealth. Unfortunately, that wealth is not being used appropriately. China has not created a better education system, or an environment that encourages businesses to innovate. It has not even created a reliable welfare system. As a result, ordinary people are even more reckless in their opportunistic investing. They lack confidence in society, so they rest all their hopes on the security that a huge amount of money can bring. More than anything, they hope that taking these risks will benefit them. That was exactly why my friend in the café thought the stock market crash in the US in 1929 was not applicable to her.

THE PEOPLE BEHIND THE GLASS CURTAIN

2 December 2007

They are the elite strata of Chinese society, with cautious but haughty expressions on their faces. When they speak, they mix English and Chinese with ease. They live in offices inside glass curtains, coolly sizing up their home country from behind the windows. They are like a group of people without roots, proud of the fact that they are not connected to the land. They are unwilling to transform their wealth and education into wider social improvements.

B y the time I entered the restaurant, the beef was sizzling on the grill. They weren't drinking because they had an afternoon meeting to prepare for. After some small talk, they started to talk about the election in the US. Would

Hillary Clinton become the Democratic candidate and win the election? They moved on to exchange rumours and classified information about Chinese officials. These friends of mine graduated from some of the best-known universities in the world. They work for multinational companies or for state-owned financial institutions and spend significant portions of their lives on aeroplanes. The friend sitting across from me is going to Africa next week; the bank she works for is expanding its business there.

The restaurant is located on Financial Street in Beijing. When the ambitious plans for Financial Street were first announced ten years ago, the old residential buildings were demolished and cold steel bars were set in place as foundations for giant glass plazas. At the time, Beijing dreamed that someday its financial district would equal Wall Street in New York, the City in London, or Central in Hong Kong.

Turning from the gridlocked West Second Ring Road onto Financial Street, I am shocked by the sight in front of me. Immense glass buildings reflect a silvery light, each one separated by generous expanses of green grass. The streets are clean and the restaurants and cafés give off an aura of leisure in the warm sunlight. On the exterior of a gigantic Lane Crawford store, the indifferent faces of models wearing Dior perfume gaze at passers-by. From Monday to Friday at midday, crowds of people wearing immaculate black suits and dresses walk past. Each one has a cautious yet superior expression on their face, each one carries a Blackberry smartphone, and when they speak they mix English and Chinese with ease.

On the weekends, all the bankers disappear and the district empties. It then becomes a meeting place for fashionable twenty-somethings. They love the floor-to-ceiling windows, which they use to flaunt themselves. They are obsessed with being seen by others. They often sit in the seats by the windows to daydream.

Compared to the messy and noisy Chinese society that surrounds it, the Financial Street district is like a surrealist painting. It reminds me of the calendar pictures of pristine stately homes that poor families hang up on their walls. Those who work there are part of the upper crust of Chinese society, and they tempt everyone else with their luxurious lifestyles.

My friends live inside office buildings covered in one-way mirrors, so that the people on the inside can look out, and the people on the outside see brightly reflected light. Their main tasks are to manage information and capital. Money has never been so abstract – millions of yuan (tens of thousands of pounds) pass through their hands, and some of the transactions are executed by a few taps on a keyboard.

Talking about money, yearning to have money, and hating money – in the past few years, these three themes have become more and more widely discussed in Chinese society. As the stock market heats up and the price of all kinds of goods steadily increases, more and more billionaires are being minted. As more companies celebrate record-breaking initial public offerings, feelings of insanity and oppression increase. People are going insane trying to accumulate staggering amounts of money in short periods of time; simultaneously people feel oppressed because the only thing anyone ever talks about is money.

One of my friend's most important tasks is helping Chinese firms with overseas listings on stock markets. I can't tell exactly what their work is. Every time I read a prospectus for a public tender in the newspaper I feel utterly confused. I still remember the names of those all-star companies: Morgan Stanley, Merrill Lynch, Citigroup, Goldman Sachs and UBS. These companies are repeatedly linked in various ways with Chinese state-owned and private enterprises. Then they reveal their great ambitions in New York, London and Hong Kong. After raising enormous amounts of capital, they make the headlines in newspapers everywhere.

The size of my friends' salaries are truly shocking. In the past, jobs in the oil and automobile industries paid the most. Now, financial companies pay more than everyone else, and young people are eager to be recruited. The career options of university graduates epitomize the changes in Chinese society: twenty-two-year-old graduates who speak English fluently, think on their feet, and are lucky enough to be recruited by a multinational bank could expect to earn 1,000,000 yuan (£70,000) (140,000 USD) per year. Meanwhile, most of their fellow graduates have to work overtime just to earn 4,000 yuan (£260) each month.

I have mixed emotions when chatting with the elite of this era. They are knowledgeable about lots of financial terms, Ivy League universities, the top 500 companies in the world, and the people who grace the covers of English-language magazines. They talk about the US presidential election so passionately you would almost think they have a vote. They are part of an exclusive global elite. They share the same language and tastes, and are proud of their whirlwind lifestyle that takes them to New York one day and to Paris the next. In a world that redistributes wealth according to information and mobility, they are ahead of the rest. Yet they are difficult to engage in deep conversation. Accustomed as they are to jumping from one idea to the next, they often talk as if they were processing mind-boggling amounts of data; touching on various topics and staying busy, but never having a connecting thread of logic or a deeper emotional attachment to any part of the conversation.

They are not interested in their homeland. China is frequently conflated with China concepts stocks,* whose main

---

* China concepts stock is the stock of a company whose earnings or assets have significant activities in China. They trade on different stock exchanges such as the Hong Kong exchange, where they are called H-Shares or 'red chip' stocks.

purpose is to set prices on the market. They are a rootless people, not connected to the land beneath their feet, and proud of the fact. They coolly size up their home country from behind the one-way glass, and the people on the outside cannot look back at them.

They are the elite. They received the best education, benefited from China's prosperous economy, and have managed to push past traditional cultural and geographical boundaries. Yet at the same time, they are too clinical. It doesn't matter if they are squeezing international capital or capital from state monopolies, they know how to cooperate with the right forces to become successful and maintain their comfortable lifestyle. Unfortunately, they are unwilling to leave their protective bubble or to transform their wealth and education into wider social improvements.

THE DREAM OF A LOST COUNTRY BOY

25 January 2009

He went missing on 14 September last year. He left a slip of paper in his dormitory copied from the Daoist foundational text, the *Zhuangzi*: 'For the whole of one's life, one toils, yet never sees the fruits of one's labour. To be exhausted and without a refuge, to fear poverty and not have an escape, to crave success and be denied its fulfilment, to have no career and no way to support one's parents, is that not a great sorrow? People say, "It is not death" but is that an advantage?'

His name was Luo Lian. He was only twenty-four and he grew up in a village in Hunan province. He was the only son and had three sisters. Five years ago, after completing secondary school, he had decided not to take the college entrance examination, partly because his marks were not very good but perhaps also because it would have been too stressful. Soon after making that decision, he followed his older sister into the heart of the manufacturing industry in Guangdong province. Countless young people come here in search of opportunity. Over the course of two years, he worked in different factories but he always stayed in the city of Foshan. His colleagues found him to be taciturn and introverted.

For two months, nobody besides his sister and a few workmates even knew he was missing. If it weren't for his distant cousin, a reporter in a news agency, his story might have disappeared forever just like he did. Young people just like him can be found all over the Pearl River Delta – workers on the assembly line whose facial features are blurred and whose comings and goings go unnoticed. In late November, Luo Lian's cousin, Shi Feike, memorialized him on a blog which was later published by *Southern Metropolis Daily*. The article generated a huge response because of Luo's dramatic inner conflict and because the story touched a nerve in people across China.

He was a quiet migrant worker who had never gone to university and who contemplated the *Zhuangzi* in his free time. When life was tough, he used to copy quotations from it and other books into his journal: 'The earth is generous and loving and so should a noble person act, with virtuous actions and an appreciation for all beings' and 'Life is great because of dreams, changed because of study, and successful because of action.'

Even though nobody knew much about him, they called him a dreamer because of the quotations in his journal. As a result, the fate of twenty-four-year-old Luo Lian is filled with symbolism. He was a humble migrant worker who came to the city looking for hope; an idealistic youth trying to resist reality.

His fate signifies that the opportunities for someone to change their destiny are diminishing and that idealism will inevitably fail. It also symbolizes the vulnerability of individuals who have nothing to rely on and no one to confide in.

His death has stirred emotions that have been locked up in people's hearts for a long time. The gap between rich and poor is widening and the distribution of benefits is less and less fluid. At the same time that social mobility is weakening, society's values are becoming more and more homogenized. As material wealth becomes the exclusive measuring stick for success, everyone competes on a perilous, narrow wooden bridge. Social systems are becoming dehumanized. As a result, individuals cannot understand the complexities of the system, they cannot express themselves, and, most of all, they do not know how to protect themselves. As the world becomes more and more materialistic, people find that they no longer have space in their heads to think about spiritual things.

His melancholy and defeat represent the feelings of a large group of people, and he has become a symbol of depression and disillusionment for society. This burst of emotion is timely, as China is approaching a historical turning point. Thirty years of economic development have helped a great number of people escape from poverty, but now the economy faces new problems. Meanwhile, the social costs behind economic growth are going largely unnoticed. The youth and strength of people like Luo are like wood that a steam boiler consumes to keep burning. People see that the boiler propels the massive train of the economy, but they ignore the fuel – human lives. More importantly, the widespread enthusiasm about economic growth is rapidly decreasing. When Shi Feike returned to his hometown in Hunan he noticed something, 'I don't know when the change started but something was different. Success stories of people who moved to the city for work and returned with riches to build a house and open a store have gradually been replaced by unhappy stories of people who have constantly faced both natural and man-made disasters.' This chaotic and cruel society is both mentally and physically draining for people.

In a sense, Luo Lian's story is an extension of Nora's and of Pan Xiao's.* Eighteen years ago, debates over 'what happened after Nora left home' appealed to educated youths across China. Most people used the play to attack family institutions and traditions, which were the two main elements restricting the freedom of Chinese youth at the time. Thirty years ago, when Pan Xiao asked why people's lives were becoming more and more restricted, China was trapped in a spiritual vacuum. After enduring years of political struggle, the people wanted to free themselves from suffering and oppression, but they did not know where to begin. Luo faced a different situation: a new economic and social reality. His is the age of social Darwinism and materialism, a time when political and economic power are becoming ever more tightly interwoven, and when the average person feels weak and helpless.

These three cases demonstrate the relationship between the fate of individuals and the fate of society as a whole. When confronting their fate, people very easily oscillate from one extreme to the other. At first they are voiceless and swallowed by the larger community. Then, once their voice has been heard, it receives a sympathetic response and others are more than willing to put all the blame on the system and the society, as if the individual is a passive victim.

* Author's note: Nora is the main character in *A Doll's House* (1879), by the Norwegian playwright Henrik Ibsen. The book sparked discussion in China in the 1920s, and Nora was viewed as a symbol of women who betrayed traditional family norms in that era. Pan Xiao wrote a letter to the editor of *China Youth Daily* in the early 1980s deploring the fact that young people's opportunities were becoming more and more restricted, which sparked a national debate about future opportunities for the young.

But after widespread discussion of 'Nora's departure', we all realized that even if someone could overcome all of the oppression exerted by the family, the government, and society, that person would not necessarily live a better life afterwards. It was even possible that that person would go from hope to disillusionment. Ultimately, it is not possible to blame all of one's personal tragedies on the outside world.

The same is true for Luo. On the one hand, we hope that society can be introspective and finally pay attention to individuals who have been ignored; we hope that we can admit to the illness plaguing our society. On the other, we have to remind ourselves that we will never be capable of creating a system or a society that will allow every person to feel happy and satisfied with their lives, so that everyone can be free from suffering. In other words, we need to refrain from explaining all personal tragedies as symptoms of a sick society, no matter how tempting that may be.

THE STORY OF A VILLAGE OFFICIAL

3 May 2009

He won the election because the villagers were dissatisfied with the incumbent and wanted a fresh face. Once he took office, he realized that managing a village was far more complicated than running a factory. The relationships in a factory were clear-cut, with the client on one side and the workers on the other – economics decided the rules of the game. But as a village leader, he faced a world with many more variables.

Chen Pengxi said he liked rural sociology best because it was a pragmatic subject and it was applicable to his work. He never imagined that he would have to step

15

into a classroom again after completing technical secondary school twenty years ago. But, beginning in March 2009, Chen went every weekend to a school of economics and management in the Shantou city centre. He was part of the first class of students to complete a national programme which encouraged village officials to study at university. The three-year course at Shantou University was specifically designed for village officials.

In May 2008, at the age of thirty-eight, Chen was elected village leader of Longtou village in the Longhu district of Shantou, in Guangdong province. The village's history can be traced back to the Jiajing reign (1521–67) of the Ming dynasty, when the residents of Wuyixiang village, Putian county, Fujian province, moved there. Endless rows of spirit tablets in the ancestral hall proudly mark the unbroken vitality of this clan.

When Chen was born in 1970, the ancestral halls which had been maintained for generations were condemned as relics belonging to the 'four olds'. They were to be abandoned not revered. Since the People's Republic of China was established in 1949, the village, which formerly enjoyed autonomy, had been subjected to multiple rounds of reform. The communes replaced the peasant economy. The roles of landowner and tenant were abolished and the focus of moral authority and power was transferred from the ancestral hall to the Party Committee office. For some people, these changes brought hope; for others, disaster.

Chen's grandfather worked in the rice business between Wuhu and Shantou, and was once the richest man in the village. Then he was labelled a capitalist and lost his life and property at the height of the disastrous Cultural Revolution. Chen understood from a very young age that he was in one of the Five Black Categories, an enemy of the Revolution who was shunned by society. He worked at a number of temporary jobs, including as a carpenter and a construction worker. Then he discovered that he liked working in the textile industry, and in the mid-1990s he started his own business. Orders from Russia and Eastern Europe helped his business grow.

For the next ten years he was just like all the other small business owners dotted around the south eastern coast of China: conscientious, shrewd, clever and devoted to his enterprise. Then an event in the spring of 2005 changed the course of his life. He was in Tongxiang, Zhejiang province, having just completed a big deal, when someone phoned to tell him that his father had died.

Filled with grief and regret, he sold his factory and dismissed his employees within half an hour of hearing the news. How could he not have been at his father's bedside at the crucial moment? No matter how much money he earned, his way of life was now meaningless to him.

He returned to Longtou village, where nothing he did held his interest, until two years later when a retired Party secretary encouraged him to run in the village elections. At first he had no interest because he thought his father would not have approved. After all, his father had suffered greatly and was unable to forgive the government for what it had done.

After persistent persuasion from the Party secretary, Chen gradually changed his mind. The village needed someone like him as a leader – someone with real-world experience, someone with a head for business, someone who could get things done. And becoming a village official might help him find meaning in life again.

The four-storey office building in which he worked as village leader was a reminder of the wide range of duties covered by the village cadre. The ground floor was often used for mediating the latest dispute in the village. The first floor was used by the family planning office which was responsible for implementing the one-child policy; they had a difficult job given that so many families wanted to have a son. The second floor included meeting rooms and the offices of the village Party secretary and the village leader; every time their superiors came to do an observation they would begin their visit here. The third floor housed the office of the village militia. Finally, the fourth floor was let to a state-owned telecommunications company.

Primary education, family planning, family disputes, running water and land use planning for companies were among the many issues that Chen began facing on a daily basis. His chief concerns were the gap between the rich and the poor and the loss of cohesion in the village community. Being at the lowest level of administrative government was tricky. Officials there didn't have as much authority as they had had when everyone lived in communes, since they no longer controlled all the political and economic resources. As a result, the villagers paid little attention to their orders. They were required to implement the policies handed down from Beijing and could not negotiate with the town cadre. At the same time, the one-dimensional economic reform encouraged government officials to distort public services until they benefited the government, as if the officials were running an enterprise and not serving the people.

For example, they had problems with expansion plans for the village primary school. Six years ago, the town-level government had wanted to combine it with the school in the neighbouring village to accommodate pupils from both villages. It agreed to provide 800,000 yuan (£80,000) in funding for a new building. The school was built but the funding never arrived; Chen's first task was to try and chase down the money. When asked what he gained from being an official for one year, he smiled and said, 'I don't have a short temper anymore.' This year he has made ambitious plans to improve all the roads in the village and build a new farmer's market to tackle the village's financial problems.

Chen felt strongly that his previous knowledge was insufficient to enable him to tackle the complicated issues that a village official has to. The course at Shantou University has given him an opportunity to think carefully about the problems he faces. All the people on his course are cadres from villages in the area, who feel similar anxiety and confusion, despite their range of ages. The course material might not be immediately applicable but at least it helps him consider his problems from a different perspective. Communicating with people who have a similar background provides him with comfort and inspiration. Most importantly, he hopes that the experience, combined with the diploma, will help him to develop a broader social network so that the next time he needs to negotiate with a higher level of government he will have more of a voice. Like other cadres, he is aware of the fact that personal connections are vital to any public affairs project. He also knows that if he ever leaves office, these connections will be extremely beneficial to him.

History is full of ironies. The Communist Party depended on individuals and local organizations to gradually build up its power. Now it has to deal with the incompetence and corruption of those organizations. Providing university education for village officials seems like a feasible solution, but ultimately it is little more than a symbolic gesture. Can Chen Pengxi – or any of the low-level village officials – ensure the sustainable development of their village? If it is impossible to protect the basic autonomy of the villages, no matter how expertly the village officials attempt to apply the theories of administration and management they have recently learned, then the invasive, top-down bureaucracy will continue to operate unchecked.

LEARNING HOW TO BECOME A FREE PERSON

1 November 2009

He said that the greatest advantage of living abroad was 'learning how to become a free person'. China was like a play unfolding on a faraway stage, a play that he didn't have to grapple with at the moment. One must learn how to become a free person – his tone was calm but resolute. For a moment, the statement invaded the easy-going atmosphere of the restaurant serving Hunan cuisine. Seconds later, it was drowned out by the noisy surroundings.

We hadn't seen each other for at least two years. Back then, we were in a strip club on Lockhart Road in Hong Kong, drinking Tiger beer and watching tanned and voluptuous women swerve their hips. He worked at a foundation based in New York then. We talked about George Soros and his open society theory all night.

He was the same age as I was, and a graduate of Fudan University. He had started his career in journalism in the 1990s and soon became famous for writing excellent opinion pieces. Five years ago, he became the editor-in-chief of an up-and-coming international newspaper from southern China. Then one political report forced the newspaper to close unexpectedly, signifying the arrival of tight media control after a brief period of relaxed policies in 2001.

He went to the US to study and lived there for three years. He occasionally told me about the books he was reading. He particularly enjoyed one by Joseph Ellis called *Founding Brothers: The Revolutionary Generation* because it expertly combined a storytelling style with historical analysis. He said that while in America he had become an observer of the events happening in his homeland. He watched the seasons change, found a place to live, installed a satellite dish, and composed a CV in English.

'The best thing that I got out of those three years,' he said, 'was learning how to become a free person.' I knew what he meant: as a reporter with a ten-year career, he was in the same situation as many Chinese. He had struggled with China's system and ideology. Even if reporters decided to oppose the establishment and to dedicate their careers to extricating themselves from the system and its limitations, they fell into another trap. Because all of their thoughts and actions revolved around opposition, they started off pursuing an end to oppression but ended up enslaved to other types of limitations.

In New York, he experienced unrestricted freedom. Still, China seemed to have a hold on him that persisted throughout his life. Every so often he would rush over to Chinatown, stay for half an hour, and leave again. He couldn't stand the chaos and disorder. He finally exhaled when he arrived in the clean and orderly neighbourhood of Little Italy. He worked for a Chinese news agency in New York, but found the pettiness and narrow-mindedness difficult to endure.

Last year he returned to Shanghai. New York was spacious, full of resources, and could offer a variety of intellectually stimulating events. Even so, he was unable to find himself there. Surprisingly, he had the same problem in Shanghai. In the course of a year he switched jobs three times, from an Internet company to a magazine to another newspaper. 'It doesn't make any difference,' he said. He felt his new job was just as flawed as the others. 'There are too many restrictions. You can't say this, you can't mention that.'

He was wearing a loose white jumper. After a bottle of liquor, our conversation became increasingly animated. We talked about great Chinese writers like Lin Yutang and Hu Shi and discussed a variety of publications from the *New Yorker* to the *Atlantic*. Gradually I noticed a deep melancholy in his words. He had seen the world outside of China so he knew that there was a vast gulf between China and the rest of the world. He was also aware of the gulf between our generation and the generation that had lived under the Republic of China. 'They were tremendous people, but they were living at a time when tradition was replaced by modernity. Our generation grew up when the country was trying to sever its ties with traditional culture and build a new republic. We didn't learn any common sense until we were adults.'

His rueful thoughts were out of place in Shanghai's lively nightlife. The leaves of the poetic Chinese parasol trees had fallen and the bars on Julu Road were open. Their twinkling neon lights made people feel excited and weak with desire at the same time.

The scene is a metaphor for China: thinking tends to be negative and is always oppressed, while pleasures of the body are relaxing and enticing. Like two sides of a coin, they create a society that has mutated into something completely absurd. We also mentioned Liu Xiaobo's detention and the manifesto that he had written, 'Charter 08'. The official media coverage of the detention has been deliberately overshadowed by a huge blast of coverage for the thirty-year anniversary of Deng Xiaoping's Reform and Opening Up policy. Thirty years on, everyone still knows all about the Household Responsibility System, first implemented in Xiaogang village, and the 3rd Plenary Session of the 11th Central Committee of the Communist Party of China, but nobody is talking about the Xidan Democracy Wall* and the most famous dissident to post an essay there, Wei Jingsheng. The younger generation know all about Deng Xiaoping's 'Southern Tour' in 1992, but

---

* The Xidan Democracy Wall was a long brick wall on Xidan street in the Xicheng district of Beijing which, from late 1978, became a focus for statements of democratic dissent.

little about the tragedy that had happened three years prior to it at Tiananmen Square. These events represent the rise and fall of the government's power and set China's tragedies in motion.

Does that mean we should blindly criticize the stupidity of this age or the ugliness of this system? If the system collapsed suddenly, would that mean the arrival of a new world? Would people live peacefully and happily in it?

A truly free person should not surrender to historical tradition and social systems, blaming all their misfortunes on them. In the same vein, a free person should not put all their hopes on a completely new system, because that would only cause hopelessness without end. Sixty years ago, a generation of people had high hopes. When those hopes went unfulfilled, that generation felt a deep sense of loss.

We are all mild people; we don't have the courage or the endurance to become warriors. Living in this system, we feel a strong sense of oppression and are weighed down by anxiety. I'm not sure which method is more effective or important: expressing your dissent, or trying to promote freedom and fairness in your own little world. As far as I can tell, it's a choice determined by one's personality.

We parted at the end of the street in the middle of the night, each filled with our own hopes and difficulties. The year was ending, but these old questions would follow us into the new year. It seemed that nobody could find a precise answer for any of them. Some of us probably assumed that we were the masters of our fate, when in reality we were only observers. We assumed we were free, when we were more like puppets controlled by an unseen force.

DISPUTES BETWEEN THE DISSENTERS

24 January 2010

In May 1989, Liu Xiaobo mentioned Wei Jingsheng in an article discussing the death of Hu Yaobang.* According to Liu, Chinese intellectuals revealed their hypocrisy and slave mentality by showing empathy for Hu's death and relative indifference towards Wei's situation.

There had been an outpouring of grief following Hu's death, each mourner-servant desperately hoping he could become an enlightened ruler. By contrast, Wei had made huge personal sacrifices in the name of democracy, human rights and freedom by writing 'The Fifth Modernization', which suggested that the government should consider adding democracy to its stated modernization goals of industry, agriculture, national defence, and science and technology. He had been imprisoned for ten years, and yet very few people paid attention.

Twenty years later I read in the *International Herald Tribune* that Wei had beseeched US President Barack Obama to put pressure on the Chinese government to release Liu, who had been sentenced to eleven years of imprisonment.

The way that Wei and Liu helped each other at different points in their lives seemed like a cycle in history. In twenty years, China had swung from one extreme to the other, and all the way back again. The Tiananmen Square protests changed the image of China which Deng Xiaoping had been carefully crafting. The new image abandoned Karl Marx and embraced

---

* Hu Yaobang (1915–89) was a reform-minded General Secretary of the Chinese Communist Party (1982–87) who was forced to resign by senior members of the Party on the grounds that he had been too lenient with student protesters.

Adam Smith; it replaced violent totalitarian government with economic development. Compared to the Soviet empire, China was benign and promising. Surely it would develop according to Western standards sooner or later? Such a rosy vision was destroyed by the fresh blood spilled on Tiananmen Square. China was still the same old China, and whenever the regime felt its monopoly on power threatened, it would use cruel and violent measures to regain it, without thinking twice.

Gradually, this image of a 'tyrannical China' was forgotten as it used its market influence and economic growth to conquer the world. A new hope bubbled forth: surely the market economy, a growing middle class, a technological revolution and the forces of globalization would change China? Ultimately, the country *would* assimilate into the existing world order. For a second time, the world discovered that things did not work as it expected. Liu Xiaobo's eleven-year imprisonment, and the smearing of the Nobel Prize by the Chinese government propaganda machine, more effectively communicated the real nature of the regime than any other actions.

At the same time, Wei Jingsheng changed his opinion. In an article written for *Cronache di Liberal*, an Italian daily newspaper, he attacked the Nobel Peace Prize Committee and Liu Xiaobo himself, writing,

If a participant in the Tiananmen Square protest is sent to prison and eventually lowers his head and repents to the authoritarian government, we can forgive him and understand his suffering. Still, we would not call him a role model for young people. We would not teach the next generation about him. If that person not only repents but abets the murderer of civilians by spreading lies on that government's television programme and by saying that he had not seen people dying at Tiananmen Square, then we would have a hard time forgiving him. That's because he would have made himself into an accomplice. If after his release, that person is unable to handle the trauma he sustained in prison and continues to use language more vile than that of the Communist Party to defame the movement; if he says the movement was spun out of lies and tricked the people, then this person has run out of moral credit.

After describing Liu Xiaobo in three hypotheticals, Wei not only denied that he deserved a Nobel Prize, but branded him unethical.

This was a truly surprising and heart-rending event. The article is reminiscent of another event that happened ten years earlier. When Wei Jingsheng arrived in Washington, a dissident who was already in the US, Wang Xizhe, shouted abuse at him in public. Wang's anger and frustration stemmed from a question that he could not answer. Why had Wei garnered so much attention and become a hero while Wang had received so little attention, despite the fact that he had opposed the system ruled by the Communist Party for much longer? The concepts of ambition and jealousy had become mixed up with democracy and human rights.

The incident reaffirmed the pessimists' opinions of China's progress towards democracy: if all the dissidents were fighting among themselves, then they were merely products of the totalitarian regime. Their language and their actions were just an extension of the regime, and it was highly doubtful that they could build a new China. When pessimists sneered and showed contempt for the infighting dissidents, they frequently lacked sufficient empathy for the horrifying experiences that the dissidents had faced.

Liberals often wonder why China has not produced someone like Solzhenitsyn or Mandela, but those who know of the way that China conducts thought reform, and the inhumane conditions people face in prison, can usually understand why the dissidents often become so extreme. Their wounds are deeper than people can imagine, and they often lacked the mental strength to recover from them. Like caged animals, they are filled with a desire to fight but feel confused and impotent at the same time. The government had taken away their freedom of expression and freedom of assembly while they lived in China. Apart from sending a signal by committing suicide, they had no way to act on their ideals. Once they gained freedom abroad, then all their ties with China were cut, making them people without roots.

Perhaps this is what real life is like. Wei, Liu and Wang, and many other lesser-known dissidents do not act like the heroes in fairy tales – each one has his tragic flaws. Infighting and mutual denunciation is all part of the long and arduous process of dissent. Sometimes the process does not lead to the result that we anticipate. If we truly intend to build a better future, then understanding the faults and complexities of human beings is the first step. But this first step shouldn't diminish our praise for individual heroes, no matter whether they are Wei Jingsheng, Liu Xiaobo or someone else. They had the courage to stand up for their principles, even if only for that moment.

THE FROG AT THE BOTTOM OF THE WELL

26 January 2010

The rise of a major power is made up of thousands of details; like dispatching troops, mining mountains, building trading ports and skyscrapers, and most importantly entering the hearts and minds of the people without anyone noticing.

'They looked down on us ten years ago. Now they are afraid of us. Just wait and see how they treat us ten years from now,' a guy sitting at the table next to mine bragged to his friends in the café of a Beijing Friendship Hotel.

The newly renovated Friendship Hotel boasted bright lights and plush carpets, destroying the old stereotype of the Friendship Hotel as a privileged space isolated from mainstream society.

Beneath China's dazzling exterior, the pace of change in the 1990s and 2000s was actually much slower than most people had anticipated. During the Qing dynasty, the government pushed foreigners outside of Canton's (present-day Guangzhou) city walls, only allowing them to live between the city wall and the river. During Mao's era, embassy districts and Friendship Hotels were the only windows through which foreigners could connect with China.

This seems to be deep in the past now. Non-Chinese are allowed to travel all over the country and are no longer restricted to Friendship Hotels and other designated areas. Chinese people no longer need special travel documents and foreign exchange in order to visit Friendship Hotels. After years of self-abasement, China now feels self-important. Not only is it holding its head higher, it has plans to rule the world.

What does China rely on to rule the world? The people sitting at the next table represented China's elite class – they drank the finest tea and ordered the largest fruit platter on the menu. To judge from snippets of their conversation, most of them were from Ordos, a city in Inner Mongolia with a booming economy thanks to its energy production. They all had crew cuts. Their bloated faces and greyish skin suggested that their lives of endless cigarettes, alcohol and general immoderation, were taking a toll. The speaker seemed a little older. His face was plumper and his hair was thinner than the rest. Still, he was the most self-confident, with the satisfaction of a Beijing local who had grown up in the city and understood that the world was at his feet. His conversation moved from the wife of the chairman of Datang Electronics, to the niece of the CEO of Huadian International, to a property sale about to happen on Jinbao Street, to a stock transaction worth 700 million yuan (£63 million), to a partnership with a major Japanese company.

His words were startling – they clearly showed that he was part of the elite: he referred to huge sums of money, vast real estate projects and companies monopolized by state interests were all on his lips. It became clear that he had an extensive personal network that included many important people. Impressively, his contacts included not just Chinese but people from all over the world.

I read parts of the latest issue of *Foreign Affairs* after listening to his conversation. China expert Elizabeth Economy described China's new role on the international stage as a 'game changer'. Deng Xiaoping made it a policy for China to keep a low profile ('Hide brightness, cherish obscurity'), but his stance has gradually lost its effect. China is about to directly challenge the global order. 'China's impact on the rest of the world has, in many respects, been unintentional – the result of revolutions within the country. As the Chinese people have changed how they live and how they manage their economy, they have had a profound impact on the rest of the world.'

To a large extent, the main strategy of the Chinese government has remained unchanged for over thirty years: promote economic growth and political stability. China has wanted to become a benefactor of the existing international order – it never intended to challenge the status quo. Still, the outcome was inevitable. China, with its vast population, had to rely on the international market in order to meet domestic demand in the long run. Its skyrocketing demand for energy and raw materials combined with its rapidly expanding economy has had a lasting impact on the world economy. The economic changes naturally had knock-on effects on politics and society.

China has supported dictatorships in Africa and selectively increased the sale of goods in the European market. In a nutshell, it has used its economic influence to create political influence. At the same time it has leveraged its undervalued currency and cheap labour to create a competitive advantage that is still changing the political and economic structure of the world today.

Neither the elites sitting in the Friendship Hotel nor the highest level politicians are fully aware of their country's influence. China is like a slow-witted giant whose eyes are covered and heart is missing. It is unable to reflect on its actions and does not understand the principles behind, or even the scope of, its actions. It is unaware that it will inevitably affect a large number of regions. It is hoping to achieve the status and glory of a major power, but it is totally unaware of the responsibility such a role entails.

To some extent, these elite people, and indeed China, are like the bullfrog in the ancient Chinese proverb. Sitting at the bottom of a well, the frog assumed wrongly that the sky was small and limited. Its size gave it pie in the sky dreams. Even if it became a much larger frog, it would still be sitting at the bottom of a well.

THE VICTORY OF THE MASSES

10 May 2010

Approximately thirty years ago, when French students were asked who they admired most, they didn't pick Sartre but Coluche, a comedian who was famous for using irony as well as offensive language. The times had changed, and the idealism and dreams of changing the world that were fashionable in the Sixties had made way for the disillusionment and narrowly defined individualism of the Seventies. Irony became a mood for an entire generation. All anyone cared about was your 'stance', not the specific content of your ideas.

Everyone in China is talking about the young writer Han Han. He seems to be the people's last hope when everything is becoming increasingly oppressive and perplexing. Many older intellectuals claim that he is clear-headed and the media say he is 'the leader of his generation' and 'the person of the year'. Young people think he is cool and has deep things to say. In 2010, Han Han was named by *Time* magazine as one of the 100 most influential people in the world. Liu Xiaobo, who had spent eleven years of his life in prison after writing 'Charter 08', a manifesto on democratic values, did not make the cut.

Nobody can deny Han Han's charm. He is a champion racing driver, a bestselling novelist, a young rebel and an off-the-cuff satirist, all rolled into one. He has managed not to sell out either to the government or to any corporations. And he has accomplished all this at the age of twenty-seven. People are especially obsessed with his blog, which pokes fun at the idiocies and injustices in Chinese society and by some counts is the most-read blog in the world. The majority of Han Han's posts have to do with the arrogant and bureaucratic political system. He is not only sarcastic, he also strives to create new meaning, even though Han himself is not sure exactly what that meaning is.

Considering that he is so young, it seems that his talents are more than adequate. He has already become the nicest, smartest celebrity we know. The only problem is, many people, including those who claim to be deep thinkers, put him on a pedestal that Han himself is unwilling to stand on. People claim he is the hero of his generation and a symbol of the power of thought as well as of opposition to the regime.

But that's not who he is. The more people claim that he should have this identity, the more it becomes clear that this is an era of shouting people, of idiocy, frailty and cowardice. In some respects, Han's success was not his own, but that of the emerging era of the masses.

One could make the argument that all prominent people are going to have something in common with the era in which they live, but a clear trend is forming: fame and influence is no longer related to a person's character or their talents. In the West, this is the era of Paris Hilton and Susan Boyle. They are famous either because everyone knows their name or simply because they aren't afraid to act foolishly on television. In contrast, in China it is the era of singer Li Yuchun, winner of a singing competition called 'Super Girl' and comedian Xiao Shenyang. People rooted for them because they had under-stated personalities or they were self-deprecating.

Han Han is different from Li Yuchun and Xiao Shenyang, but the same force has pushed him onto the stage. He is a product of today's celebrity culture and success culture, and he fits the modern expectation to be good at many things but expert at none. He can race cars, write and perform. He also subconsciously recognizes the strengthening anti-intellectual trend in China, and his writing is plain. He writes about topics that aren't too deep, in a style that is easy to understand, and he never mentions facts that you might not know. His ironic and provocative style makes him sound witty. He knows what he can get away with, and he never says anything that offends the government. If he is anxious or confused, he never shows it. He is so cool.

Not surprisingly, talking about Han Han soothes the mind like a massage. While talking about him, you bathe in youth, the ultimate cool, success and wit. You feel like you have joined some kind of protest, but the action is totally safe and does not require any intellectual or moral sacrifices. Nobody hesitates to talk about him. In short, he is the ideal consumer good.

But is there anything in the world that is absolutely perfect? Comparing Han Han to Liu Xiaobo is neither fair nor fully appropriate. Still, the opposing attitudes that the public has towards these two individuals provides an excellent example of the characteristics of his generation. The reason why people never talk about Liu Xiaobo is that they are forbidden to speak of him in public spaces; just mentioning him is risky. Yet being collectively silent or ignoring the issue implies that we have no interest in true freedom or true resistance. It shows that we are afraid. We would have to pay a price if we wanted true freedom. Freedom requires not just resistance but a clear argument, which in turn requires intellectual and emotional maturity. We would have to be ready to deal with the consequences of our decisions.

The enthusiastic praise for Han Han is a sign that society refuses to pay the price for true freedom. Every time we delight in a few sound bites of satire, we deceive ourselves into thinking that we have contributed to the dissolution of this abhorrent system of power. In actuality, nothing has changed, and the satire just sugar-coats the reality.

Perhaps some people think that Han Han shouldn't be held accountable for his actions. He can put up a symbolic resistance on the fringe of things and then exit the stage as if he had just gone shopping at the market. Han has become an excuse for everyone. They enjoy his childish arguments and they enjoy showing off the pitiful pearls of wisdom those arguments produce.

In the end, the people will have to pay for their idiocy and cowardice. If they are unwilling to show interest in real achievements, to admire outstanding examples of moral courage, or to accept meaningful ideas, then they have no choice but to continue mucking around in a mud pit, complaining at each other and sharing their apathy. The number of mediocre people is so staggering as to create a surprising illusion: it seems like China has already changed the world. It's true that China *has* changed the world, but that is only due to its sheer size, not its admirable accomplishments. The insanity that Han Han has kicked off has revealed just how lifeless, pathetic and shallow this country is, despite its celebrated rise. A bright young person has spoken a few words of truth and has rattled the nerves of this era. Rather than calling this Han Han's success, it is more realistic to call this the success of the mediocre people, or the failure of a nation.

LOYAL TO THE PARTY

30 August 2010

In a series of critical essays entitled 'The Second Kind of Loyalty,' dissident writer Liu Binyan sparked debate across the country. The essays expounded on three kinds of loyalty. In the first kind, people did what they were told and never objected to a proposal. The second was that espoused by the protagonists in Liu's work, Chen Shizhong and Ni Yuxian: they were willing to make any sacrifice, however perilous, in order to uphold their principles. The third was the most dangerous to work with. People who showed it did not care about anything besides their personal interests. They would support one leader one day, but might pledge their loyalty to someone else the next.

'The Second Kind of Loyalty' was published in 1985, when China had not yet fully emerged from the shadow of the rule of Mao Zedong (Mao Tse-tung). People were still digging up facts and trying to discover the truth about what had happened. What could lead China to a series of disasters like the Anti-Rightist Movement, the Great Leap Forward, and the Cultural Revolution? Liu thought that moral degeneration was the source of China's series of tragedies. His solution was simple: he heaped praise on the two people mentioned in his essays. Liu's protagonists had written ten letters of accusation and nearly one million characters admonishing the Party. In spite of this criticism, they passionately supported the Communist Party and swore to be loyal to the death. They had the ability to challenge the bureaucratic system and social injustice, but they never realized that there was a problem with the system in the first place.

Most people still had at least some remnants of trust for the Communist Party of China, holding onto the belief that the Anti-Rightist Movement, the Great Leap Forward and the Cultural Revolution might have just been mishaps that could be expected along the path to communism. As long as the leaders could set things right in the end, the Party could restore itself and put China back on track.

Twenty-three years later, this dream has evaporated. The Party's idealist tendencies have completely vanished and both Party members and officials have become bribable business-men looking out for their own interests. They only believe in profit. Of course, they still need to put on a show of loyalty. In their official speeches, they reiterate their loyalty to the Party, the people and the country. Behind closed doors, it is more important to show their loyalty to a specific leader or faction, because personal connections are the only way to preserve one's status. Nobody has taken the time to resolve the obvious contradiction here; the frequent clashes between personal interests and Party interests go unquestioned. Worse still, national interests are routinely sacrificed for Party interests.

Even though the rules of the game are unwritten, an astute observer can occasionally see the game played out on big stages.

In a speech in August 2010, Li Rongrong formally announced his resignation from the State-owned Assets Supervision and Administration Commission.*

> I would like to thank the Party for the many years that it has trained me. I have worked up from the lowest levels to the central committees of the government. I have continued to mature, bit by bit, and my success is all thanks to the careful training of the Party. Mao Zedong thought nurtured me to become an adult; the Deng Xiaoping reforms inspired me to become a leader; the third generation of politicians urged me to become a senior cadre. I consider myself to be loyal to the president, loyal to the Party, loyal to my country and loyal to my career. I have no regrets about my decisions for the Party, my country or my career.

How can we best critique the speech given by sixty-six-year-old Li Rongrong? From the moment he took office in 2003, state-owned enterprises (SOEs), including those under his control, experienced a dramatic transformation. They quickly became the wealthiest and most powerful businesses in China. As a result, they were a symbol of China's rise. Nineteen of China's SOEs made the Forbes 500 list in 2008. Anyone who remembered the large number of SOEs that went bankrupt in the 1990s, and the dreadfully high rate of unemployment for workers was stunned by this transformation. In 1998, the annual profit of China's state-owned assets was 21.3 billion yuan (£2 billion). Ten years later, the monthly profit of those assets exceeded 100 billion yuan (£10 billion).

---

* The State-owned Assets Supervision and Administration Commission, or SASAC, is a government body which oversees and manages state-owned assets in China. It operates under the State Council and was created in 2003. Its mission is to promote Chinese state-owned enterprises, especially the largest and most important ones.

Did those bureaucratic, inept SOEs transform into competitive companies overnight? Both statistical reports and common sense suggest that the number of jobs and efficiency rates of SOEs are no match for private companies, and the only thing making them highly competitive is the fact that they monopolize their respective markets. Their rapid expansion was fuelled by unlimited cheap loans, their many problems were covered up by their immense scale, and their supreme power allowed them to shout over anyone who expressed doubts.

The expansion of SOEs has stifled the creativity of the private sector and distorted the principles of competition. In today's business world, power and relationships are dominant once again.

But Li Rongrong turned a blind eye to all that. He was perhaps a truly excellent member of the Communist Party, having both the capability and conviction that most officials lacked. He believed that as long as things could be regulated properly and they could avoid another mistake like the Great Leap Forward, a planned economy would still be highly effective. He might even have believed that he was a loyalist, because he helped SOEs have a lead in the market and provided economic support for the Communist Party's monopoly on power. Presumably he had never heard of the famous quote by Albert Einstein: 'Blind belief in authority is the greatest enemy of truth.' His arrogant efforts have ultimately hurt China's long-term interests. The monopolization of riches has strengthened China's power, but at the same time, made it corrupt, conceited and bigoted. Do all the loyal Li Rongrongs actually help the system?

A MODERN-DAY KONG RONG

5 September 2010

As the story goes, when Han dynasty scholar and politician Kong Rong was only four, he gave the bigger pears to his older brothers. When he was ten, he went to Luoyang with his father because he was hoping to see an official named Li Ying. Li was a leading scholar, and it was written in the history books that anyone who paid him a visit would become famous just by entering his halls. However, he did not accept visits from just anyone, and guests were required to be either eminent or related to him in some way. When Kong reached the gate of Li's estate, he told the guard that he was the son of a friend of Li's relative. Kong was brought to the hall, which was packed with guests. Li asked Kong to explain how they were related. Kong said that Confucius (Kongzi) was his ancestor, and that Laozi (surnamed Li) was Li's ancestor and Confucius's mentor.

No one could confirm or deny the validity of either of the ancestry claims, and Kong Rong went on to become the most illustrious child in Chinese history. The only person who even comes close to his level of childhood fame is Wang Bo of the Tang dynasty. When Wang was five, he wrote a well-known line of poetry, 'Wild mists veil the emerald stairs, The moon in flight heads toward the southern horizon.' Still, Wang's poem had less impact than this moral lesson for children, 'Four-year-old Rong/ gave the best pears to his elders/ the first thing you should learn/ is the proper way for younger people to relate to older people.' The moral was included in a collection of morals written in the Song dynasty called *Three Character Classic*. Eventually it became a primer which was read by generations of children.

Kong Rong became famous at the exact moment when all philosophies besides Confucianism were eschewed by society. People loved to hear Kong Rong's story, not only because he was precocious, but because he confirmed two prominent characteristics of Chinese scholars. First, he respected the moral order dictated by society. Even as a four-year-old boy, he knew what his place was in the family hierarchy, and he knew that it should take precedence over his natural inclinations, hence the story of the pears. Moreover he had an incredible ability for conversation, which seemed to be a way to resist the strict social order. In the world of words, scholars could find complete freedom, which was exhilarating, although it never resulted in any profound thought.

These two characteristics were also apparent in China's politics and society. The national social order had all the characteristics of the hierarchy of the family: at home, you respected your elders and your father; at the imperial court, you had to obey high level officials and especially the emperor. Filial piety and loyalty to one's government were closely related. The independent ego did not exist back then; individuals only had meaning within the context of a social network and moral norms. As Song dynasty scholar Zhu Xi said, 'Uphold the heavenly principles; extinguish heavenly desire.' These early scholars rarely used the wisdom of past generations to help them search for the true meaning of life or for a complete understanding of the world. Apart from espousing some theories on proper moral attitude, they played frivolous word games. They expected to change the world when, in reality, they were good for relaxing and discussing unimportant topics in good times, and were completely useless in times of crisis.

A child was capable of internalizing social values and completing his life journey before reaching the age of ten. Should he have been praised for that, or was it just more absurdity? Many people sigh that Chinese people are paradoxically worldly-wise and naïve. Furthermore, how can dynasties move from prosperity to decline in such a short time? Why is it that Chinese people are so hypocritical – all saint without and all devil within? Why is it that we always become tragic heroes when our country needs us and we are facing invaders? How is it possible that such a flourishing society never went on to develop the modern science and technology of the Industrial Revolution in the West?

Things haven't changed since the Han dynasty. The children of China are not like the children of other countries because they are required to assimilate social norms and learn the importance of order and obedience at an early age. Before the individual identities of Chinese children even have a chance to develop, they are told the correct path to follow. They are never given an opportunity to consider the possibilities they might have; the established set of social values is so inflexible that the only way out is to become a learned scholar. Knowledge does not have value by itself, it is only a means to an end. That end is either real political power or less tangible moral authority. During the Han dynasty, useful scientific endeavours like observing stars, discovering properties of flowing water, and developing new farming techniques were considered heresy. All scholars were supposed to serve the king, to talk about any topics they pleased, and to help establish a political and moral order. Individuals were never encouraged to develop their curiosity.

Twentieth-century China faced near-constant turmoil. Family, the bastion of society, disintegrated, and modern state power filled every nook and cranny. Kong Rong had been required to know about the seniority in his family, whereas the children of modern China had to understand social classes and the power of the state. They may have been freed from the confines of Confucian thought, but they were still not allowed to act like children: they were the Young Pioneers of China, they were the Little Red Guard. No one read *Three Character Classic* anymore. In its place, Chairman Mao's words appeared in the classroom, in homes and on the streets. Children were no longer the sons and daughters of humble parents; they were the future leaders of socialism. Child prodigies like Kong Rong and Wang Bo faded from memory; meanwhile, we focused our attention on *Little Soldier Zhang Ga* and the *Little Sisters of the Grassland*. Their childhoods were filled with fondness for their people, hatred for social stratification, and a deep love for the Party. When they grew up, they knew they wanted to be pillars of socialism.

When the Mao era ended, memories of both Kong Rong and the *Little Sisters of the Grassland* left us. The pressure and anxiety to succeed filled the void. All over China, small children's schoolbags were crammed with books. They studied English, played the piano, and took extra maths classes; otherwise they would lose the race to succeed before they had even reached the starting line. Some of them even dressed up in cute outfits and went to TV show castings, hoping to become famous overnight. They do not act anything like Kong Rong, who suppressed his desire to eat the bigger pears. Instead they act like little emperors and empresses, happily becoming the focal point of a family. Yet making them the focal point overestimates their importance, and they are unable to grow independently and discover themselves. They have to advance on the path that society has recognized as the correct route to success.

In this era, the Party and the government are our signs of success. They both have unlimited power, incredible wealth, and the undivided attention of the whole world. Naturally, standing on the side of your country means you are on the path to glory. Who would refuse to stand on the side of their country? Which is why, during the opening ceremony of the Beijing Olympics in 2008, nine-year-old Lin Miaoke stood centre stage at the Bird's Nest, smiling sweetly and lip-synching

'Ode to the Motherland'. As cute as a button, she embodied a splendid lie to the whole world. Two years later, when she received an award on a television show, she said, 'First of all I would like to thank my country,' then smiled brilliantly, as she had been taught.

She became the Kong Rong of her generation. Kong Rong gave the best pears to his brothers and Lin Miaoke thanked her country above all else. Then she smiled straight at the camera.

THE FACE OF THE SYSTEM

20 March 2011

The news was reporting on the National People's Congress and the National People's Political Consultative Conference, important meetings held in Beijing every March that are usually called the Two Meetings. Watching the faces of the politicians on my television screen I suddenly thought of Alexander Herzen, the lonely but perceptive Russian émigré, who believed that everything was contained in a face.

Herzen's description of the dictatorial Russian tsar Nicholas I was rather critical: 'The sharply retreating forehead and the lower jaw developed at the expense of skull were expressive of iron will and feeble intelligence, rather of cruelty than of sensuality.'* Then, 'the chief point in the face was the eyes, which were entirely without warmth, without a trace of mercy, wintry eyes.' When Herzen saw the excavated sculptures of important historical figures in Italy and thought of the history of the Roman empire he said that the fall of the

* *My Past and Thoughts: The Memoirs of Alexander Herzen* by Alexander Herzen.

empire was 'expressed in eyebrows, lips, foreheads'. A low forehead, an ugly face and sunken cheeks were the signs of both a corrupted physique and corrupted morals. Courtesans and emperors had these facial features as well. In the faces of military officials, on the other hand, he said that 'everything that makes a good citizen, everything human, has died out, and there is nothing left but the passion for domination'. As for monks and priests hungry for power, 'the mind is narrow and there is no heart at all'.

So, what about the faces captured on camera during the Two Meetings? Goodness, they all looked so similar – puffy, grim, and exceedingly depressed. They were mediocre in a way that was virtually infectious. It was as if someone had held a party and only invited brothers to attend. None of them looked kind. Behind the wooden, cautious expressions, you could see slickness, as if they were privy to plots and schemes. You could tell that they were proud too – they were unaccustomed to treating people equally, and they lived in a world of classes. They were exceedingly modest towards their superiors and unbearably proud towards subordinates. A feeling of emptiness exuded from their every pore. Whether they were silent or engaging in witty conversations, you could feel that they were opportunists through and through. They didn't believe in the value of anything apart from their selfish interests. They reminded me of the rats who tried to hide food in Kafka's novels, living in constant fear.

How can that be, when they are the most powerful group of people in the most populous country in the world? Their decisions affect a territory spanning nearly 4 million square miles (10 million km^2) and the lives of over 1.3 billion people. Besides managing a country on such a shocking scale, they say that they are the successors to the longest enduring civilization in the world. This civilization has fallen once before, but the politicians take credit for putting China back at centre stage.

Outsiders often marvel at their ability to unite such a vast region with so many different groups of people and achieve dazzling economic growth.

But if you watched their faces on the television screen or if you actually sat in the People's Hall, you would have found it difficult to associate them with China's achievements. China has been changing at a dizzying pace, and yet they are static. China is predicted to become the new leader of the world, but they are still repeating the same stock phrases. On the whole, China seems confident and even aggressive, but these politicians are frightened and worried about all kinds of conspiracies.

They are not dictators like the ones in textbooks – not a single one of them can change the course of history purely through willpower. They have lost their political ideals and zealous ideology. On the one hand, there are huge advantages to this. The course of the country is no longer controlled by violent, bad rulers on the far left or far right, and the people are less likely to fall into a collective hysteria. On the other hand, it could mean a slow death for China. A lifeless, ineffective system stifles every individual. Collective leadership means that no individual can be held accountable for a specific policy. Ideology has been eliminated and any remnants of beliefs and ideals buried. The desire for personal profit, which fills the void ideology has created, is even more unprincipled. The politicians have received a better education than most and have travelled outside of the country. They have been introduced to new words and new ideas, but they use these things to cover up their old, vile habits. They are all top-rate actors, incredibly sly and unscrupulous.

Yet at the same time, they are merely puppets; manipulated by their own short-lived fears and desires, thinking that besides naked power and profit, there is nothing else of worth in this entire world. They are incapable of seeing other possibilities in life, and they have no faith in themselves. They do not believe that they can change the current situation at all. All they can do is go with the flow – pursue the things that others pursue, fear the things that others fear, and worry about the things others worry about. It is nearly impossible for them to face their inner thoughts or even reflect on their actions. The only way for them to successfully claw their way to the top has been to extinguish their personalities and defeat their sense of right and wrong.

This has dire consequences for the country. China has become an unthinking animal, which cares about nothing but production and consumption. This is disastrous for the politicians as well. Not only have they squandered their opportunities to achieve great things, they have let their faces grow uglier and uglier, until they were no longer theirs, but ones shaped by the system. If they are truly the successors to Confucius's political philosophy, as they claim to be, desecrating the bodies given to them by their parents was the worst offence they could possibly have committed.

THE UNHAPPY NETIZENS

5 June 2011

After first trying with an egg, the young man threw a shoe and succeded in hitting his target – the father of the Great Firewall. He rushed out of the auditorium and a group of people helped him escape by obstructing the path of the security guards. At the entrance to the university, someone gave him a new pair of shoes. For that audacious action, the young man was recognized as a hero all over the Internet.

The attack had been publicized in advance. The principal of Beijing University of Posts and Telecommunications, Fang Binxing, was in Wuhan to give a speech. At fifty-one, he served as principal of the Chinese Academy of Engineering. But he was best known as the chief architect of China's Internet firewall, which led to the nickname the 'father of China's Great Firewall'. The firewall was a key part of Beijing's plans to tame the Internet. Echoing the strategy of the ancient dictators of China, who built the Great Wall to protect against intrusions from 'barbarians', the totalitarian government of modern China hoped to use a firewall to block out any 'inharmonious information'.

The current regime is both a symbol of vulnerability and of arrogance. It is vulnerable because it believes that one news report or social media website is enough to break up its monopoly on power. It is arrogant because it assumes that it can successfully prevent Chinese citizens from accessing parts of the Internet, something which is constantly updating, open, and in communication with the outside world. It also assumes, arrogantly, that it can use technology to solve all of its problems. It isn't as foolish as the leaders of the late Qing dynasty, who tore down a completed railway. Moreover its totalitarianism is not as complete as in past decades. For example, it does not block the people's ability to see or hear *anything* unorthodox; and it has stopped bamboozling them with politicians' quotations and articles from the 'two newspapers and one journal' – the *People's Daily, People's Liberation Army Daily* and *Hongqi Magazine*. Yet the current regime is still trying to turn China into a giant local area network, partially closed to the outside world, to create an unreal realm of information. It is still trying to eliminate people's critical thinking skills and make them into obedient followers. In a totalitarian system, people are not just people, they are the foundation of the country, the soldiers fighting for supremacy, the producers in the factory, the consumers in the markets which foreign investors are so keen on exploiting. People are functional units; they do not have the right to understand the way the world truly works. They are meant to live in a space isolated from the outside world, in which any information from it is carefully filtered.

This promising young academic at the Chinese Academy of Engineering had propelled the entire firewall project forward. Perhaps he never fully understood the consequences of his work. There were a lot of people like him living in the twentieth century. They called themselves technical experts to disguise their loathsome roles, and they made excuses for their actions, saying things like, 'I was just doing my job,' or 'I made sacrifices for my country.' Only on very rare occasions did they believe that. After experiencing the moral value crisis in China, they became extreme utilitarians, like so many other people in China. In their world, morals were non-existent. The only guiding principles were two Darwinian wills: to survive, and to defeat the competition. That is also the spirit of our generation, which admires unscrupulously shrewd behaviour.

The Great Firewall has been largely successful. The totalitarian government domesticated the market economy and tamed the wild technology known as the World Wide Web. The Great Firewall has become part of the Chinese model. A joke about the effects of the firewall goes something like this, 'Many have died and many have flourished in the past ten years. Baidu is strong and Google is dead. . . Twitter has died, and Facebook has been walled up. Renren happily travels to the hometowns, Ma Huateng is the King of Knockoffs. Sina microblog laughs while Twitter's tears turn into rivers.' China's Internet demonstrates how successful domestic companies can be when the Internet is closed off from the rest of the world.

At the exact moment when the totalitarian country celebrates another victory, a new crisis arises. Every generation wakes up to reality in a different way. For example, the Lin

Biao affair* shook the beliefs of the Red Army, forcing them to reconsider their principles. The young people in China who were born in the late 1980s and early 1990s have grown up in an age steeped in materialism; one far less political than in recent history. They had and still have a lot of space where they can hide, places where they do not have to face reality. But the brightest of the lot know exactly how the space in which they can move around is gradually being taken away. Their forums are shut down arbitrarily; their beloved Google has been forced out of China; and they are no longer allowed to upload pictures onto Facebook like other people their age.

Young people may be the suns around which their parents orbit, yet they too can feel discriminated against. So they look for their own way to protest. The announcement that Fang Binxing was going to deliver a speech at Wuhan University caused a tidal wave of a response on the blogosphere. Out of nowhere, a game promising rewards sprang up. People said that if anyone was brave enough to throw a shoe at Fang during his speech, that person would receive iPads, free food and shelter, and total devotion from girls. It was all in jest, of course.

Ever since the Grass Mud Horse phenomenon** was born, where sensitive topics are discussed using innocuous homonyms

* Lin Biao (1907–71) was a minister of defence in the 1950s. He became the chosen successor to Mao Zedong in 1969. He always defended Mao's policies and encouraged the army to embrace Maoist thought. In 1971, Lin died in a plane crash, allegedly after an unsuccessful coup and assassination attempt. The accident later became known as the 'Lin Biao affair' in China. There is still some scepticism regarding the Chinese explanation of Lin's death.

** The Grass Mud Horse (or Căonímǎ) is an Internet meme used as a form of symbolic defiance of Internet censorship in China. It plays on the Mandarin words 'cào nǐ mā', meaning 'fuck your mother'. The Grass Mud Horse is one of a number of mythical animals created in a hoax online encyclopedia article in early 2009, the names of which form obscene puns.

of commonly censored words, games have become young people's favourite way to protest. And why wouldn't they be? They are filled with laughter, they are spontaneous, and they do not include any sadness. Still, when on 19 May 2011, some people offered a reward for punishing Fang Binxing, nobody expected it to turn into real action. But within hours they were watching as someone actually pitched a shoe towards the target of their mockery. The shoe did not just express the displeasure of the youth who was restricted, it also sent a powerful message to people in positions of power similar to Fang: you need to be responsible for your actions or you will pay a price for your evil deeds. The shoe incident became a central topic on the Internet. It was shared and discussed, causing happiness for some and shame for others.

It is difficult to overestimate its significance. The shape of political protest changed, as many more people started to believe that uploading images and files and cracking jokes were legitimate ways to resist the government. It was a protest against the totalitarian system, one which was closed, proud, and made deliberate attempts to sever links between people. However, impromptu, passion-driven protests have a difficult time achieving real change. After the clever jokes erase the assumption of self-righteousness held by the powers-that-be, the jokesters themselves vanish. Theirs is a parasitic movement which does not provide an alternative way of running the country. The young generation believe that the most important protest hasn't even begun yet. They want to find a lasting system of values, way of communicating, and set of moral principles. Naturally, this represents a more fundamental challenge to the totalitarian government.

FATHER'S WARNING

30 July 2011

'Don't let your tongue run away with you,' my father said over the phone. He sounded tense, a mixture of concern and anger. He had just finished reading an article I had written about 'turning left', an ideological trend in China. I knew what he was trying to say; he was just worried about my safety. His generation experienced too many violent political movements, so he was much more sensitive to the fact that an individual's fate could change drastically after one essay, one sentence, even one careless action.

He was born in 1949, the same year as the People's Republic of China. He grew up in a village in northern Suzhou province. The Cultural Revolution cut his education short. He witnessed his own father, who was a member of the County Committee, being forced to wear a humiliating hat and walk through the streets. He joined the army when he was twenty, which was the best way to improve his lot in life as a young man from the countryside.

In 1983, my father hung up his military uniform after Deng Xiaoping confirmed plans to reduce the size of the military by one million. Fortunately, he managed to stay in Beijing. The army had changed his way of thinking and his preferences. Now he preferred order and hierarchy over individuality and was less tolerant of diversity. Instinctively, he was disgusted when students gathered at Tiananmen Square in the summer of 1989. He believed that they were disrupting the normal order of life. He applauded the wisdom of State Council spokesman Yuan Mu, who calmly responded to the students' questions and demands.

In the 1990s, the work unit to which he was assigned became a construction company, and it greatly benefited from a wave of construction projects promoting urbanization at the time. Like a number of city-dwelling families, we suddenly became much wealthier. By the turn of the century, my father owned his own car – something he could have never imagined as a young country boy.

I could tell that my father's personality had changed slightly. He loved to read books and the selection on our shelves ranged from *Jean-Christophe* by Romain Rolland to a Ming dynasty collection of short stories called *San Yan Er Pai* to books by Marxist historian Jian Bozan. My desire to become a writer was all thanks to that untidy collection of books. I heard others say my father was aloof; he rarely asked for help from others to get ahead. But I remembered in the late 1990s, at dinner, whenever he talked about the new construction projects he would mention which project manager earned a million yuan (£90,000) bonus, or which one of his colleagues had bought a new car.

One thing remained unchanged: my father always cared about my future. If I could get into Beijing's most prestigious university and find a good job, he would consider me successful. Ever since I was small, my father would tell me, 'Grown men never rest on their laurels.' It seemed that he was subconsciously encouraging me to escape the figurative prison that had trapped him. He liberated me from the clan lifestyle in Jiangsu province by moving to Beijing; he didn't want so many family members influencing my life choices. He even wished that I would break free of China's grasp. The best possible outcome would be if I could study and live permanently in America. We never went so far as to discuss what the purpose of all of this was. Perhaps constantly reaching for the next rung on the ladder was the course of his entire life. He would move from a village to a large city, he would go from being poor to being relatively wealthy, and although he never studied at university, he helped his son to go to Peking University.

He probably never imagined that he would have to worry about my safety, or that I would get wrapped up in politics and ideology. I never thought that would happen either. Even today I am unlikely to say that I have an interest in politics. I grew up in the 1990s, during a period of depoliticization. I was chiefly concerned with personal freedom, human dignity, and having plenty of options in life.

At one point I naïvely assumed that the era where politics ruled everything was firmly in the past. But in the past few years I have come to acknowledge the following reality. I had thought it would be possible to get away from the problems that haunted China, but there is no escape. If I seek human dignity, personal freedom and plenty of options in life, then I have no choice but to face the renewed expansion of the regime and the re-emphasis of communist ideology. My criticism of those things is not guided by a clear motivation, and I am not stirred by a moving and tragic desire to challenge totalitarianism. I just want to preserve the last shred of dignity that an intellectual (or indeed any healthy and well-rounded person) can possess: the ability to criticize. How can anyone stand by and watch the changes happening in China without saying a word?

I am not sure if my father has ever understood what I was trying to say in my articles. It is difficult for him to believe that an individual's right to enjoy free speech is just as important as his right to an adequate standard of living. But how can I judge him for that? No one in his generation enjoyed freedom of speech; even the right to an adequate standard of living was only possible at a very late stage. The few brave souls who tried to change the situation faced immense suffering. Sometimes he and I would talk about critics of the Cultural Revolution like Yu Luoke[*] and

---

[*] Yu Luoke wrote *On Family Background* in 1966, which criticized the Communist Party's blood lineage theory. It was popular with many people but the government disapproved of the content. In 1970 he was sentenced to death for his writing. He died aged twenty-seven.

Zhang Zhixin.* My father admired their courage but he did not want his son to take them as role models. Whenever I mentioned their names, he felt uncomfortable.

He felt uncomfortable because of a deep, gnawing fear. This fear follows him everywhere, so that he doesn't know how to express it. The fear is born of government persecution, daily political turbulence, and harsh living conditions. He always wanted me to be successful so I could avoid the cut-throat competition prevalent in the lowest classes of society. He hoped that I would live in the US so he could be sure that I was safe. The outcome of fear is a tendency towards high levels of utilitarianism. When dignity and freedoms are not dependable, the only thing that can be firmly grasped is material wealth.

This kind of fear does not always take the form we expect; often it appears in the form of admiration. My father was incredibly thankful for Deng Xiaoping, simply because he allowed the people of China to live relatively normal lives (normal in terms of material things, that is).

In order to preserve this ephemeral and incomplete sense of security, my father stands firmly on the side of the regime. He is afraid that any voices of dissent will disturb the peace. At this point, his thinking matches the propaganda disseminated by the regime almost perfectly.

Unfortunately, he has found that his own son has become a dissenting voice. As a result, he reacted the way the regime told him to react rather than by speaking from the heart. According to him, my article 'went too far', but I think he said that out of anxiety. It was the same attack that the totalitarian regime of forty years past had used against anti-revolutionaries, and

---

* Zhang Zhixin was opposed to Mao's personality cult during the Cultural Revolution. She was imprisoned for many years on a counter-revolutionary charge. After enduring brutal torture, she was executed by firing squad.

that the China Central Television reporters had used against the students who protested at Tiananmen Square. He said it out of love and concern for my wellbeing. Still, his words were combative because he was unable to remove the deep imprint given to him during that era.

I strongly believe my father's feelings are shared by many other fathers and other people all across China.

THE ELITE VOTE WITH THEIR FEET

9 October 2011

With its silk screens, paper lanterns and pictures of women hanging on white walls, it was clear that this restaurant was trying to create an atmosphere of old Beijing. The smell of zhajiangmian (fried noodles in soybean sauce) drifted in the air. In the past two decades, this kind of atmosphere has been gradually disappearing. Wide streets, giant skyscrapers and flashing advertisements are everywhere now. The signs of Beijing's long history are increasingly hard to find, as if Beijing were a brand new city.

I was sitting and talking at one of the tables with my friend. He was the manager of the restaurant, had just turned forty, and was a graduate of the famous Tsinghua University. The Tiananmen Square protest was the most important event in his life, as it was for many people of his generation. The demonstrations, seas of people, tanks and blood made him feel simultaneously excited and disillusioned.

When Deng Xiaoping restarted economic reforms in 1992, my friend was finally able to release his creativity and energy. He became a businessman. He worked in imports and exports, starred on a television shopping channel, and finally became rich after opening a chain of teahouses and restaurants. He owns at least a dozen other Beijing-style restaurants in different areas of the city.

He is not one of the famous entrepreneurs in China but he has earned enough money to allow him and his family to live a comfortable life. He spends his leisure time reading classic texts such as the *I Ching* and the *Zhuangzi* in a quest for spiritual and intellectual fulfilment. He has become very content with his lifestyle in the past few years. He has everything he ever wanted, and can also impress others by quoting ancient Chinese wisdom, making himself sound smarter.

In some respects he represents the spirit of the last twenty years. The Communist regime and the people reached an agreement: as long as the people did not challenge the regime's authority, the regime would give the people the freedom to make and spend money as they pleased.

He didn't want to talk about that today. He wanted to talk about the new life he was building for himself. He had just returned from Vancouver. He looked thinner, more tanned, healthier and more energized than before. Having nothing to do in Canada, he had spent each day soaking up the sun. He had bought a new apartment in the city centre and looked at a couple of secondary schools for his daughter. He was considering having her study in Canada in two years' time. Two years ago he had applied to Canada's immigrant investor programme. Since then he had constantly been going back and forth between Beijing and Vancouver.

'It was just like buying insurance. It protected my security and freedom,' he said, explaining his immigration decision. For the past four to five years, his feeling of insecurity had continued to grow.

This was all because of his work: as his business grew more important, he butted heads with bureaucratic organizations more and more often. Different agencies responsible for industry and commerce, prosecution and investigations, the fire department, and even the sub-district office had the right to interfere with his affairs at any time. All the energy initially unleashed by the market reforms had been swallowed up by the bureaucracy. The more wealth a Chinese business owner accumulated, the more afraid they became that it would all be expropriated. Chinese business owners were especially vulnerable to bureaucrats. Countless examples from the past sixty years showed that the government could arbitrarily seize personal property at any time.

The restaurant manager felt even more insecure when considering his daughter and her needs. Behind China's burgeoning economic growth were crises of the environment, education, food safety and morals. He was worried that his daughter would not grow up in a healthy environment, or have strong moral examples to follow; that she would breathe unclean air, drink unsafe milk, and learn the arts of lying and hypocrisy too early at school.

'I want to immigrate for my daughter's benefit,' he said. Still, it's true that my friend would be the first one to benefit from the immigration process. While living alone in Vancouver, the restaurant manager discovered aspects of his personality that had been hidden for many years. For a long time, he had not even realized how exhausting his work was. He was always busy dealing with the complicated interpersonal relationships that Chinese society demands. He enjoyed feeling successful, but his definition of success was very narrow. Now, living in a strange land, he had regained his personal freedom. He had realized that he wanted to travel around the world, learn how to scuba dive, and maybe someday learn how to speak and read English really well. He had found a new sense of self. In a way it sounded like an interesting paradox. He needed to separate himself from all the *uncertainties* existing in China – relating to political and social institutions – and at the same time he needed to free himself from several annoying *certainties* – the unchanging values and views China had given him.

What would he do in Vancouver? Would he open another noodle restaurant? He had not decided yet, but he already felt more confident than before.

He was a member of the latest wave of Chinese migrants. Ever since the nineteenth century, war, revolution, famine, and the search for riches have enticed Chinese people to move abroad. Unlike past waves, the new migrants are not villagers from Guangdong and Fujian province, nor international students. They are the brightest and richest people in Chinese society. They come from huge cities with the most opportunities, and they make up the middle class. The China that they are leaving is not weak, nor is it being humiliated by foreign powers. Far from it. China is wealthier than ever before and people believe that it may become the next world leader. These migrants not only created this wealth, but also benefited the most from it.

Their departure reveals the darker side of China's rise.

Even while the country becomes stronger, individuals feel more and more vulnerable. China can launch a spaceship and bring about an economic miracle, but it cannot provide individuals with basic security. In response, people use their feet to express a vote of no confidence. Even the most successful elites are no longer capable of changing the political or social institutions, so their only choice is to flee. That way they can preserve their last bit of personal security and their freedom.

Perhaps this is an important step in an ancient country's process of self-renewal. If at least some of these migrants can have an experience like my friend, rediscovering both the world and themselves, they may be able to bring new ideas and new drive to China.

THE ANXIETY OF THE YOUTHS IN OUTER PROVINCES

11 September 2011

The stale air hung in the dimly lit room. The air conditioning rattled noisily. Beer, coffee and bowls of peanuts were arranged on small tables with plastic table covers. About six or seven young people sat around him. They were all about twenty-five years old and they had just started working in journalism.

He soon took control of the conversation. His small stature and unremarkable looks belied a penetrating voice. High-pitched and a little hoarse, it carried a worldliness and impishness that boys sometimes put on to make others think they are sophisticated and have seen the world.

He claimed that he never went to classes when he was at university – some second-rate institution in Nanchang – and that people thought he was weird. All of the buildings at that institution were made of red brick, and people told the following story to explain that. A former president of the university had toured several universities in Great Britain, and the most important thing he had learned was that all the prestigious ones were built of red brick. Nanchang may have successfully replicated the Victorian-style architecture, but it was unable to replicate the academic atmosphere that encouraged people to think for themselves.

Just so he could escape the mind-numbing mediocrity at his university, the young journalist frequented online forums, especially the ones organized by dissenting voices. Young people are always looking for ways to assert their identity. Typically they use their education, their job, their branded clothing, games, or even girlfriends. But he was identifying himself with two labels: democracy and freedom.

He loved participating in heated debates online, and he would work around firewalls to read content that was blocked by the government. He looked for information on the Tiananmen Square protest (also known as 6/4 online, for the date of the protest) and on Liu Xiaobo. He tried to find like-minded friends, to whom he would assert his bold opinions. The Internet equipped his generation with power and new ways of getting things done.

His dissertation, entitled 'Symbols of Totalitarianism in Films and Literature', surprised and perplexed the teacher who reviewed it, not to mention his classmates. The word 'totalitarian' was taboo and completely unfamiliar. Every aspect of people's lives was controlled – they didn't have an opportunity, much less the ability, to contemplate these kinds of concepts. He quoted not just Orwell's *Nineteen Eighty-Four* but also a recent German film called *The Wave*, in which a paranoid teacher shows his small class that within seven days he can turn them into a group of fascists. His dissertation was filled with oblique references, each one pointing to China's reality. The crux of his paper was that people should not be afraid of the government; the government should be afraid of the people.

Luckily, he graduated even though he was given no assessment credits for his dissertation. One of the more curious teachers even asked him where he found all the books and films he referenced.

Working as a reporter in China wasn't enough for him. He found he couldn't release his creative energies because of the endless censorship and bans. He remained engrossed by the Internet, participating in forums and making many online friends. The advent of Weibo (China's Twitter) increased the pace of his activities and widened his circle of friends. He and his friends would start exchanging views, immediately supporting each other in their causes, and going on digital crusades whenever they found something they did not agree with.

They never ran out of material – the uncountable conflicts, tragedies and preposterous events in Chinese society gave them plenty to be angry about. The Internet had created a separate society and a separate culture in China, which was easy for the young journalist to navigate. He quickly developed an excited, rushed, and muddled way of expression. He primarily craved excitement, focusing on the effect of information dissemination as opposed to its actual content.

I remember during that night's conversation that they couldn't stop talking about the news stories that were most popular on the Internet, including a rape in Luoyang, Henan province; and a man named Qian Mingqi who had on the same day bombed three government buildings in Fuzhou, Jiangxi province. The young journalist kept repeating his strongly held belief that China had become a state of magical realism and that even the greatest writers could not imagine the absurdities happening every day.

Listening to his words, I felt excited and exhausted at the same time. Compared to many people his age, who are obsessed with material possessions and entertainment, he not only cares about real social issues, but is trying to find answers to difficult questions. Compared to his elders, he has greatly benefited from the open resources of the Internet, and is working hard to become enlightened. He can also look for different friends to overcome the isolation of being a thinker. He is part of a new generation of people who have become very popular because of the Internet. Though he forms part of a minority, the Internet has given people like him a platform on which to speak – and others listen. In many cities, especially second-tier cities like Nanchang, Changsha, and Ningbo, there are a number of people just like him. They are unable to enjoy the cultural resources that cities like Beijing and Shanghai offer, but that doesn't seem to lessen their ambition. They form a distinct group, the Youths of the Outer Provinces, and they use are using various methods to move from the fringes of society to the centre of attention.

Surely this makes the young journalist worthy of admiration. Yet, sitting there, I felt a little uneasy. Did he really believe everything he said? Or was he just speaking before thinking, like many young people? By acting like a bit of a heretic and dramatizing himself, all he seemed to be doing was getting everyone's attention, which is not such an awful thing on the whole. What was really worrying was that he never mentioned literature, poetry, or history while he was speaking. He was fixated on the concept of symbolism and absurd news stories. And in all of these conversations, he never asked questions of anyone else, revealing that he was uninterested in other's opinions. Sometimes I thought he had no heart, and all of his ideas and desires rested outside of his body. There was no part of him that was hidden, ambiguous, or elusive. He constantly talked about the crude and preposterous, but had no understanding of beauty or life. He consciously formed political opinions but he did not know how to think about the meaning of life.

Could this group of youths lead China into a new era? I doubt it.

HU JINTAO'S EXHAUSTING ROLE

13 April 2013

Hu is still unskilled at using body language. When he shakes hands with others, he never thinks to slap them on the shoulder to show his sincerity. His smile is slightly unnatural and he cannot give an impassioned speech. Perhaps he dislikes round-table discussions because the levels of hierarchy are indistinguishable. During his political career, which has spanned over thirty years, he has followed a particular kind of political philosophy. Its basic tenets are speaking and acting prudently and hiding one's true thoughts as far as possible – being a cutting-edge politician might be impressive for a brief moment, but in the long run it would make Hu enemies and cut his career short.

Investigation, debate, persuasion and conciliation are not key elements of Hu's philosophy. The spatial layout of the Great Hall of the People says it all. The high and mighty declarations issuing from the presidium are not just to be followed but admired by the lower levels. Opposing or even questioning a policy is impossible in this forum. That can only be done in private, if at all. All the other meeting rooms he has been in, at his university, the factory, the local government, are miniatures of the Great Hall.

He is fully aware that whenever he speaks, the world listens carefully, because he is the leader of its most populous country, one which seems to have unlimited potential. Many joked that there was a G2 being held at the G20 London Summit, because the only important actors were President Hu Jintao and the recently elected President Obama (the latter being nearly twenty years his junior). China's manufacturing and America's consumption drive the world economy, to the point where one historian coined the word 'Chinamerica' to describe the interdependence of the two countries and the reliance of the world on their economies.

The economic crisis has weakened everyone's trust in the US. It is still the world's only superpower, and is governed by a charming new president, but his ambitious rescue plan was snubbed at the summit. More importantly, people have noticed that cracks are beginning to show in the American system. Karl Marx's bearded portrait had been thrown into the dustbin of history along with his curses against capitalism. Today, he is once again being revered as a prophet. In contrast, capitalism seems endlessly to produce scoundrels like Bernard L. Madoff.

It looks like China represents a new hope. Granted, most observers remain mystified both by the country's long history and by the astounding events of its more recent past. In the 1950s, many believed China to be a utopian society animated by revolutionary fervour, and felt a pure idealism towards it. At one time, just hearing the phrase 'the Great Proletarian Cultural Revolution' stirred the hearts of the bored bourgeoisie in the West. When the truth was exposed, people suddenly understood the country's capacity for tragedy and cruelty. Behind the strongly held beliefs and the simple way of life, China was surprisingly irrational and culturally and morally deficient.

Before outsiders could digest their shock, there was a further surprising development. While paying lip service to Marxism–Leninism, China plunged headlong into a market economy. Just yesterday, it had been purging all remnants of capitalism. Now, it was embracing the ideology of the US, Japan, Europe, Hong Kong and Taiwan, like a fanatical new student of the capitalist world frantically completing assignments that it had previously neglected. The rest of the world thought China had truly changed to be more like it. If the country was accepting a market economy, it would surely accept a democratic government and freedom of the press, too.

But then the Tiananmen Square protests of 1989 proved that assumption wrong. China was still as stubborn and cruel as it had been in the Middle Ages. It had returned to an era of closed doors and oppression. Then it changed again, accelerating plans to join the global market at a pace that overwhelmed the rest of the world. A rookie student before, now it was the outstanding student. When Asia faced a financial crisis, China played the saviour. Its enthusiasm was astonishing, as if it could overcome any obstacle in a single step.

Western evangelists of capitalism had pronounced that a centrally controlled market economy would not work. When they saw it did, they ate their words. They thought they could act as the perfect examples of capability and morality. But while they faced a series of obstacles at home, the Chinese miracle showed no signs of slowing. It brimmed with confidence and promised economic growth at eight per cent. China's confidence both encouraged and shocked the world. As it began expanding internationally on an immense scale, buying up mineral and oil firms, the governor of the People's Bank of China proposed that a new currency should replace the US dollar as the world's reserve currency.

On the international stage, China would rarely make such a high-profile statement. When the Chinese leaders arrived in London in March 2009, it was like a rehearsal for the new world order. According to one seasoned observer, 'China has traditionally been passive on the international stage, being a listener rather than an opinion leader, but this time it's different. China wants to make sure [its] voice is being heard.'

Is China actually as strong as everyone says? Or is this just another instance of hyperbolic language? Many things have been talked up in a similar way: Japan, the Internet boom, or the insufferably arrogant investment banking industry, for example. While the bubble is still growing, people see wealth and strength, and all the internal problems are either hidden or ignored. But at the critical juncture, everything changes and the hopeful optimism turns into agony.

Mr Hu must feel some anxiety when the international community focuses its attention on him. Still, he has always been aware of his distinct advantage. Whenever he makes a decision, he does not have to consider the reaction of Chinese rivals – the opposition parties would never dream of kicking up a fuss, media outlets hungry for incident and scandal don't exist, and the public is easily manipulated.

He is also keenly aware of the other side of China, having worked in Guizhou, its poorest province. He knows that some of the stories from Guizhou clash with the 'China miracle' that everyone is so familiar with. He knows from reading internal reports that tens of thousands of mass protests erupt all over China each year. He is also aware of the extent of the festering problems within the government, where each individual acts for personal gain only, and that his party and government have lost the vitality and idealism it once had. Even policies that are compassionate and courageous on paper get distorted and subsumed by the mammoth bureaucratic system until they ultimately vanish.

In the final analysis, Mr Hu understands that China's exterior splendour will only temporarily hide the gaping holes within. It is as if China is hosting a race to see which will win: its rate of growth or its rate of internal decay. Perhaps oscillating between glory and darkness makes Hu feel helpless. Such a feeling is observable in his familiar gestures and expressions: the way he shakes hands coldly, without tapping anyone on the shoulder. His smile is not natural enough, and his speeches never seem to catch fire.

THINGS SEEN AND
THINGS THOUGHT

A TYPICAL DAY

15 April 2007

I was squashed into the back of the lift, then surrounded by a group of people who were all singing too loudly. They sang the part that went, 'Let's spend the money together!' at an extra high pitch. I had seen them in the hotel lobby just minutes earlier, hugging and slapping each other on the back. They were probably from the same company. After their lively meal, they were getting ready to go to a karaoke bar to sing at the top of their lungs.

It took some effort to push my way out of the lift. The Yinghao Business Hotel in Xi'an where I was staying was a short distance from a metro station. Looking out the window at night showed me an unending stream of car headlights. Next to the road, colourful neon signs twinkled. They hinted that the city was still desperate to modernize; people believed that noise and a nightlife fitting for a 'city that never sleeps' indicated progress. For a long time, the enormous and dazzling signs that made up the skyline along Victoria Harbour in Hong Kong were the envy of every Chinese city. Unfortunately, few cities had a beautiful waterfront like the harbours in Hong Kong or the Huangpu River in Shanghai, and even fewer cities were home to the offices of international corporations, which meant that their neon landscapes were dominated by a different kind of sign.

From Beijing to Changchun to Xi'an, cities and even towns had something in common. If you looked closely, you noticed that most of the attention-grabbing neon signs were for restaurants, spas and karaoke bars. They stood proudly in every corner of the city, and sometimes they clustered together. Just outside of Tsinghua Pioneer Park in Beijing, the sign for a restaurant offering Hunan cuisine stole the thunder from one that said 'Tsinghua University'. In Changchun, I saw an enormous sign for a five-storey spa called Sheraton Spa City, a popular hangout for locals. On the way from Xianyang International Airport to Xi'an city centre I saw a similar enormous sign, this time for a towering establishment called Victoria Spa. And finally, a short distance from the hotel I was staying at was Teal Dream, a karaoke bar and club. The names of these entertainment destinations are just as lousy as many of the consumer goods brands in China. An English word is plucked out of the air and clumsily translated into Chinese characters.

Sometimes I get the panicked feeling that satisfying our taste buds, singing ourselves hoarse into microphones, and having hot soaks followed by massages have become national sports in China. Relaxing our bodies is more important than anything else. I remember when the richest, most admired young entrepreneur was interviewed by the media, he said that his main hobby was getting foot massages. Many Chinese say that they like to talk business at spas.

My encounter in the lift was just one of a series of interesting experiences that happened on the same day. Five hours earlier, I had been sitting in a taxi on the Fourth Ring Road in Beijing. A light rain had brought the afternoon traffic to a standstill. Even though I had left early, I still missed my flight. I waited in a snaking line to reschedule my flight and the young person standing behind me complained that the woman speaking Cantonese-accented Mandarin behind the counter was working incredibly slowly. The noise and chaos of Beijing Capital International Airport reminded me of the railway stations of olden days.

The desire to be mobile motivates China to change, and also demonstrates how China is changing. People used to be confined to their hometowns for long periods of time, but today they can go wherever they like. Even though many desperately want to be swiftly transported into a more advanced era, they often discover that old habits are hard to break. No matter how many reminders staff members give to air travellers, they end up not checking their bags in. The overhead lockers are stuffed to the gills, and spaces under the seats and even in the lavatory are filled too. Travellers are curiously insouciant about the security risks posed by unchecked bags on a flight. They often argue with flight attendants, saying, 'Everyone else's luggage is overweight and still here, why should I have to check mine in?'

The minute the plane touches the ground, people spring up. The flight attendants act like teachers at a crèche, asking everyone to sit back down because the fasten seatbelt sign is still turned on. Some people manage to avoid being told off and successfully take their bags from the overhead locker, which makes them extremely excited. Even though everyone has to slowly make their way through the same tiny door at the front of the cabin, people make an inordinate effort to be first. If you get ahead of just one person, you win; or so it seems.

Finally, in the evening, I reached the bar under the Xi'an city walls where my friend and I had arranged to meet. He had been working for a local television station for ten years. Ten years ago he was a literature buff but today he is mainly focused on ratings. The most important programmes for every television station are the talent shows, and his is no different. It's as if overnight, all the young people in China agreed that singing and dancing are the only things worth doing in life. It might not be possible to become famous in one spectacular performance like Li Yuchun, but at least they could get their fifteen minutes of fame and enjoy the stage for a brief moment. There are myriad television channels in China, but the shows are more or less the same. If it isn't a talent show, then it's a variety show. As my friend put it, 'They're supposed to be entertaining.'

Everything I saw and heard that day epitomized a typical day in Chinese society. For a long time, whenever I talked about these phenomena, I thought they were completely trivial, because they represented daily life becoming more and more vulgar. Now I finally understand that these phenomena are all the result of an enduring problem that the Chinese people are still grappling with. The country is overpopulated, which has led to resource scarcity. The hardest part is that these resources are principally allocated by people in power.

Our character, our words, and our actions are all dictated by this scarcity. The panic has only increased after years of social unrest. From our birth, we are all warned that everything in life is hard-won. There are a limited number of places at the schools, there are a limited number of seats on the bus – even housing is limited. Everything lacks consistent rules and expectations. As a result, you can only depend on the resources that are already in your possession. The only things that allow you to live a decent life are money and power. Time and time again, our society is guided by the desire to increase power, which results in the loss of human dignity. People carry their anxiety with them everywhere.

Traditional morals had at one point provided a delicate veil for Chinese society, hiding its lust and greed for power. When the Communists took power in 1949, a number of movements were forced on the people, and the veil was ripped to shreds. The Chinese economy opened up, forming the characteristics of today's people: they fought each other and they always felt uneasy; they were proud of themselves but also anxious. They were losing their self-control, or perhaps one should say, they were giving up their self-control.

THE EXCITEMENT IN BEIJING

14 December 2007

For some reason, Beijing is bursting with excitement. But, as we babble on happily about nationalism, we have forgotten how to be modest and we have forgotten to reflect on what our desires and capabilities are.

Nationalist sentiment in China is still expressed in ways that companies can easily exploit, even though people no longer say it as blatantly as they did in the past. People used to claim that if you loved your country you had to buy goods made in China; now the tactics are more subtle. After the first Chinese citizen – Yang Liwei – entered Space, I saw ads for milk with his picture and the phrase, 'Strong Chinese people'. Next to the new skyscrapers on the Second Ring Road in Beijing there are towering signs that say 'China flourishes'. A tiny electronics company specializing in voice recorders is called Aiguozhe ('Patriot'), as if to say that it supports both China's former glory and its future accomplishments.

If you live in Beijing today, you can easily tell that there is something in the air. Besides car exhaust fumes and dense clouds of dust, there is an unstoppable aura of self-importance and haughtiness. For some reason, Beijing is bursting with excitement. People talk about past Chinese empires – the Qin, Han, Tang and Qing dynasties – as passionately as if they were talking about house prices. We invited the leaders of forty-eight different African countries to Beijing, and will host the biggest sporting event in history: the 2008 Olympics. Opinion pieces about how to move from an economic powerhouse to a major political and cultural force are constantly being published in the media. *The Analects*, *I Ching* and even the histories of

73

monarchs in *The Three Kingdoms* have become examples of ancient Chinese wisdom. These historical works are not just important to China, but to the whole world. Chinese tourists, running in stampedes to cities around the world, make interesting comments on their foreign destinations. The houses in London are all old and decrepit, and Buckingham Palace is a cute cottage compared to the Forbidden City. The skyline in Manhattan is nothing compared to the skyline of the Lujiazui peninsula in Shanghai. Americans are stupid for not knowing where Tianjin, our fourth largest city, is located. The shopping centres in Berlin are not nearly big enough and their opening hours are depressingly short. Any more complaints and they would sound just like the emperor Qianlong, who ruled China over 200 years ago and refused to open trade between China and the West, 'Such has been the procedure for many years, although Our Celestial Empire possesses all things in prolific abundance and lacks no product within its borders. There is therefore no need to import the manufactures of outside barbarians in exchange for our own produce.'

The sentiment has changed so much. Twenty or so years ago, Chinese people were still wringing their hands nervously about the future. After being closed for so many years, China finally opened its doors. People discovered that not only were the outsiders perfectly happy and not 'needing to be rescued' as had been claimed, but they ate better food and wore nicer clothes than most Chinese people. Our buildings were falling apart, our lights were dimmer than theirs, and people did not live as happily in China as they did elsewhere. Even our own culture came under scrutiny. We used to laugh at the other countries for having short histories and no roots; in comparison, our country revered its traditions and boasted a long and glorious history, a vast territory and plentiful resources. We suddenly realized that things were not as they seemed. We started to bicker about whether we had been excluded from the group and whether island civilizations were going to become more important than civilizations based on continents.

The nihilism in our culture ended when the political chaos did. Then, the entire country from government bodies to individuals – including unemployed vagabonds and philosophical types – started working like crazy to earn money. Our ideals were destroyed and any previous hopes of implementing political change began to fade. As a result, money became not only our collective goal in life but also the thing that brought security.

We should say that we are lucky. We have benefited from the division of labour implemented in the rest of the world and the unhindered transfer of technology and products. China's endless supply of labour helped us easily copy modern technologies from others. We were not hampered by environmental protection activists or labour unions; in reality, as long as companies received a tacit agreement from the local authorities, they could start a business without listing costs like land. We were incredibly hardworking, we were hungry for change and we were willing to be flexible. Just think of all the people with Chinese heritage who were living all over the world; even though they were outnumbered by people living in China, they generated business assets disproportionate to their size. We didn't care about values such as the happiness of our lives or whether our rights were protected. Many civil society movements quickly changed into national movements as soon as the government took control. When the global industrial revolution hit, they seemed to be as impassive as the shareholders investing in stock. They bet on the country's future market, not caring whether or not it would make money in the present.

In short, a lot of factors affected China simultaneously. One day we looked up and realized that we had completed half of the dream proclaimed by the government fifty years ago: surpass the UK and catch up with the US. We overtook the

UK to become the fourth largest economy in the world, and we were overjoyed. We overlooked the fact that the population of the UK is approximately sixty million and its territory is smaller than Henan province in central China, whereas we have 1.3 billion people. We paid no attention to the fact that the Oxbridge universities were light years ahead of Peking University and Tsinghua University. We carefully ignored that they developed their worldview by reading the *Economist* while we read *Global Times*, a tabloid with an obvious pro-government slant.

Thinking critically is not in our blood, and we often neglect to consider the real situation. As long as a statement is worded nicely, we will be convinced that it is true. We think emotionally and not rationally and are obsessed with words. In the past we were immersed in science, or democracy, or republicanism, or socialism. We believed that these abstract concepts could solve all our problems. Now we keep repeating two phrases: 'major power' and 'rise'. It has seemed that as long as we stayed on this track, we would overtake Germany, Japan and the US. In the next fifty years, or perhaps sooner, we could return to the brilliance of the Tang dynasty. We have been too impatient to bother analyzing how we got to where we are, how much of our success has been determined by luck or other uncontrollable factors, or how many risks we are facing.

As we talked about 'major powers', 'China's rise', and 'an age of prosperity', we failed to heed political scientist Hans Morgenthau's warnings. He said the power of a nation depends on a number of factors including geography, natural resources, industrial capacity, military preparedness, national character, population, diplomacy and quality of government. When determining the power of any nation, it is important not to give undue weight to any particular factor.

Is the definition of a major power really just the country that produces the most refrigerators, hats and toys? Surely a major power would not be so uninspired as to copy the *Idols* reality TV shows on all of its television channels? It seems that on the one hand we are justifying our peaceful rise to others, and on the other we are the first ones to exaggerate our own power. A country like ours can very easily be muddled by pride and biases simply because it does not take a realistic approach. There are plenty of examples of this happening in the past. Still, for some reason, Beijing is bursting with excitement.

BEHIND THE THREE GORGES DAM

7 February 2008

Eighteen smooth concrete pillars stood ramrod straight in the river, an immense body of clear water. The sun was still shining brilliantly at three in the afternoon. Flecks of golden light were sparkling on the water's surface and the peaks on the opposite riverbank were just discernible. In the mist, a thick cluster of tall buildings stood like a mirage in front of a mountain background.

I was standing in a square in Taipingxi town on the northern banks of the Yangtze River. A gigantic piece of granite called Taiping Rock stood behind me. It was placed there to commemorate the monolithic dam that would cross the entire expanse of the Yangtze River. A poem written by a local literary talent was carved directly into the rock. It referenced Pangu, Nüwa and Yu the Great. The mythical origin of Chinese history was closely tied to water and rocks.

I saw the Three Gorges Dam for the first time on 7 February 2008, while standing in Taipingxi town, Yichang, Hubei province. The top of the dam was like an endless cement corridor. Still, I thought, it might make for a nice walk at twilight. The river water, held back by this great cement ribbon, had gradually turned into a calm lake. Even people who usually hated flowery expressions would feel compelled to quote a line of verse from Chairman Mao when they came here, 'A placid lake emerging amid high gorges.'

My excursion was planned at the last minute. I didn't know exactly where the Three Gorges Dam was until I arrived at the Yichang Sanxia Airport. It is the largest hydro-electric dam in the world in terms of electricity, and it took fifteen years to complete. It seemed like it had become a part of my life. I never actively followed the issues surrounding the dam but news about it was on my radar. At first I remember approximately one-third of the representatives in the National People's Congress abstained from voting on the Three Gorges Project, suggesting that they were doubtful as to whether it would be a success. That was in the spring of 1992. Chinese society was still reeling from the bloody event that had happened three years earlier (Tiananmen), and Deng Xiaoping's 'Southern Tour' failed to drum up public support for the project. The start of a project that had been repeatedly shelved for almost a century was a sign that the Chinese government, previously mired in intractable problems, was feeling confident again. Yet, despite a government atmosphere that strongly discouraged disagreement, there were a significant number of deputies who did not vote for the project: 177 deputies voted against it, 664 deputies abstained from voting, and twenty-five deputies claimed they forgot to press the button to indicate their vote.

The Yangtze River was successfully dammed in November 1997. Just four months earlier Hong Kong had been returned to China, ending 150 years of humiliation at the hands of foreign powers. Back in 1989, the Chinese government had been beset by crises. It was diplomatically isolated, it was dealing with an internal power transfer, the economy was overheating, and the country as a whole was ideologically bankrupt. Somehow in 1997 all these problems were more or less resolved. Deng's death in February did not cause social chaos, and the potential power vacuum had already been filled. At the 15th Congress held in September, the new generation of leaders had solidified their power. None of the 2,000 delegates had participated in the Long March, signifying the end of a revolutionary era which had shaken the country to its foundations in the twentieth century.

Post-1997 China was like an industrial washing machine. It kept adding people, resources and capital to the mix, as if nothing could slow it down. Anything that wasn't seen as helping the country gain speed was ruthlessly cast off. Population displacement caused by the dam had become a prominent issue, championed by a small group of reporters, environmentalists and human rights activists. Sadly, no matter how sharp their voices were, they were quickly drowned out by the cacophony surrounding China's economic miracle. It gave me a feeling of helplessness: the fate of one million people forced to leave their native place and the historical sites engulfed by the flood waters were unimportant compared to the electrical energy and economic benefit that the dam would provide.

Over the past ten years, the lack of serious public debate has become a clear issue. Every day, new websites, television channels, newspapers and magazines give the false impression of information abundance. In reality, people's minds face the pressure of exhaustion and being closed off from the outside world. Entertainment seems to be the only choice for stimulation. The most authoritative activists casting doubt on the dam have been the journalists Dai Qing and Lu Yuegang, whose attitude and approach is reminiscent of 1980s China. Rational, critical and independent voices are not present in any of the debates about any aspect of public life. A few young journalists have recorded the things happening at Three Gorges Dam using words and photographs, but they have not generated a big enough response.

The only person to have had a real impact is the director Jia Zhangke. His 2006 film, *Still Life*, is the most interesting contemporary Chinese take on the enormous engineering project. The film received widespread international attention, but only briefly stirred debate within China. Ironically, despite being extremely interested to hear outsiders critique our country, we showed no enthusiasm for discussing our own fate. People showed some interest in the film only after it won the Golden Lion for Best Film at the Venice Film Festival.

Standing on the top of the dam, I felt like a tourist. The calm and clear water reflected the afternoon sunlight. Boats passed every so often, against the backdrop of the smooth grey dam and the peaks at the river's edge. Taken together it looked like a surrealist painted scroll. But I could tell that there were many other emotions hidden beneath the calm. This was just the beginning of a long journey.

AN AFTERNOON IN ZHONGGUANCUN

13 July 2008

Zhongguancun is an area crammed between Peking University and Tsinghua University. It has been given the epithet 'China's Silicon Valley'. It might have some clout owing to its size, but no substantial technological revolutions are taking place there. In fact, it is a victim of its own success and is in danger of collapsing under its own weight.

had nothing to do on a lazy afternoon, so I walked from Haidian Book City to the East Gate of Tsinghua University. The trees along Baiyi Road had been chopped down long ago.

Not a single patch of grass broke up the long line of buildings made of steel, concrete and glass. There were still plenty of young people sweating as they carried heavy computer screens on their shoulders, but the middle-aged women selling pirated CDs had gone. It was easy to get pornographic films online, so who would want to buy one off the street? Walking into one of the many electronics markets, your eyes started watering just looking at all the products and eager salespeople. 'China is very homogenous and ruled by excessive competition,' you might say to yourself.

A huge construction site next to Peking University's East Gate never seemed to reach completion. The newer buildings stood proudly, bereft of the restrained elegance of a place like old Yan Yuan Subdistrict. Passing the old physics building of Peking University, I remembered how ten years ago I had taken mechanics classes there. I studied the laws of thermo-dynamics and spent a lot of time daydreaming in the lab at the basement level. The building was still grey, but a bright red real estate ad was now plastered on it, with the words 'Peking University's First Humanities Building'.

The southern wall of Peking University was demolished in 1992, in a move signifying a frantic reaction from China's most prestigious university to a surge of interest from businesses. The pride and joy of the institution had become a conglomeration near the university called Founder Group. Just outside the South Gate of the university's Resource Building was a cluster of small companies which attracted business by borrowing Peking University's name. With the commercialization in the district, the university's reputation, which had been painstakingly built by successive presidents Cai Yuanpei, Hu Shi, Chen Duxiu and Fu Sinian, was reduced to a mere branding tool.

I walked along Chengfu Road perpendicular to Baiyi Road and finally arrived at Tsinghua. For the past twenty years, it has been more prestigious to study at Tsinghua than at Peking. The latter specializes in engineering, making Tsinghua more prominent during an era that puts economics at the centre of everything. More importantly, Tsinghua has produced more politicians over the years. About ten years ago, many business elites wanted to study at Tsinghua just so that they could relish name-dropping the likes of Zhu Rongji.*

A row of brand new, tall buildings stands just outside Tsinghua's South Gate. At night, all the signs of technology giants flash before your eyes: Google, Microsoft, Sohu. It almost seems like they are dancing in the darkness. Inside, the offices of tech and capital investment companies sit next to expensive restaurants. The coffee shops buzz with words like IPO and Web 2.0 and figures in the tens of millions, uttered by young men who are just starting to grow hair on their upper lips.

Ten years ago, this whole area was residential. I lived on Chengfu Road then, a narrow little road that still exists today. When I was a student, I rented a flat for 500 yuan (£37) a month with a couple of friends, which gave me more space and freedom than dorm life would have. In the afternoons in summer, I would play 'Hotel California' by the Eagles on my old computer without even thinking about it. Then I would go up and down the aisles of All Sages Bookstore, and force myself to buy a copy of Arthur Schopenhauer's essays even though I didn't want to spend so much money at once. On some rare occasions, I might convince a girl that I liked to spend the night with me, which meant that I had to convince my mates to sleep somewhere else for the night.

Young people today have much clearer goals than I had.

* Zhu Rongji (b. 1928) was mayor and Party Chief of Shanghai (1987–91). As premier of the People's Republic of China (1998–2003) he was an enthusiastic economic reformer and modernizer.

They are definitely not as lost as I used to be. Google is the flagship company of the era, right? If you can land a job there, you can compete in the global arena, eat at the best restaurants, go to America for job training, and buy a house in one of the nicer areas of Beijing. Everyone would think you were awfully clever, because obviously Google is the coolest company in the world. Even though I was impressed by the dreams of people who knew just what they wanted, I still hoped to run into a young poet who was a bit lost. I never saw one in the Starbucks in the Sohu building.

I don't know what to make of Zhongguancun. With its location, crammed between Peking, Tsinghua and the Chinese Academy of Sciences, it had once generated a lot of excitement. Just a few years ago, it represented knowledge and the productivity of the twenty-first century. China, a country bent on winning the respect of the world once more, had been trying to learn everything it could from the West. That meant we needed our own Wall Street, our own Hollywood, our own Harvards and MITs. By that logic, Zhongguancun had to become China's Silicon Valley.

No one doubts the role that Zhongguancun played when China first opened its doors to the world. Back then people didn't know about the latest scientific advancements, and Zhongguancun popularized information about computers, software, the Internet and venture capital. It was the port through which technology and capital came into China. But now, just like in many other areas of China, it represents successful imitation not innovation.

REMNANTS OF GLORY

October 2008

The British writer Rudyard Kipling said of Hong Kong in the 1890s, 'How is it that everyone smells of money?' By the late twentieth century, the city had developed into a global hub for trade and a major financial centre. After 1997, when the territory was transferred back to China, the territory's exotic identity and hence its mythical power gradually faded. Over the next ten years, the relative strengths of Hong Kong and the Mainland experienced a dramatic change as China's economic growth spiralled beyond everyone's wildest dreams.

During my latest visit to Hong Kong, I spent the night I arrived watching videos on YouTube. The Nobel Peace Prize award ceremony, a documentary on artist and activist Ai Weiwei, a slideshow of images from the Cultural Revolution, and a crowd of people surrounded by a sea of Mao's 'Little Red Books'. Would any of these preposterous moments ever play out again?

It has been eleven years since Hong Kong's return to China in 1997, and nobody seems to remember the gloomy predictions that it would lead to Hong Kong's demise. In Hong Kong, the dancers are still dancing, the horses are still running, and the number of shiny skyscrapers on either side of the harbour keeps increasing. At least on the face of it, it is still a city of magic and modernity.

But Hong Kong's boom has already lost some of its allure. In the second half of the twentieth century, it had more or less become 'the capital of Asia'. It produced dazzling economic growth, a stable social environment, and an endless stream of film stars and martial arts novels. Most people living in Southeast Asia, ravaged as they were by political unrest, poverty and disease, viewed it as a paradise. Chinese people had an especially strong feeling towards Hong Kong. Ever since it was ceded to the British in 1842, it had been a port of refuge. Peasant revolts, battles between warlords, plagues of famine and sickness, and political persecution compelled people to move there. During Mao's reign, China closed its doors, and the fact that Hong Kong was forbidden only made it more tempting. The Great Exodus to Hong Kong occurred at that time – while Red China produced death, hunger, oppression and persecution, Hong Kong became a paradise within reach.

The myth of Hong Kong reached its peak in the 1980s. China opened its doors, but it knew nothing about the outside world. In response, Hong Kong once again took up the task that it was best at: as a role model and reference point for Chinese modernization. From Kang Youwei to Sun Yat-sen to Deng Xiaoping, Hong Kong provided China with a path to the world market, using knowledge, technology, capital and management experience. Two successive generations of Mainland youths were ardent followers of the Hong Kong lifestyle. They desperately wanted to express their passions, ask Hong Kong celebrities for autographs, and learn the secrets to the success of Hong Kong's rich and famous.

The myth lasted all the way until 1997. The gunfire in Tiananmen had only added to Hong Kong's allure. Besides providing opportunities for consumerism and pleasure, Hong Kong repeatedly showed it was willing to make sacrifices to uphold moral principles. In 1898, the Big Sword Wang Wu, a renowed martial artist, prepared to storm the execution ground in order to save the Six Gentlemen Martyrs of a failed political movement known as the Hundred Days' Reform. The rescue attempt failed and the six gentlemen were ultimately executed. Years later, some Hongkongers started a group known as

'Operation Yellowbird', which also tried to rescue political dissidents. Its mission was to smuggle intellectuals and dissident students across the border into Hong Kong so they could go on and gain asylum abroad.

China formally opened its doors again in 1992, and even though the scope of the opening was narrow it was actually quite deep. It seemed as if China wanted to completely abandon the planned economy and embrace capitalism. China was no longer talking about sclerotic ideology; its focus was on markets, money and consumption. China's new orientation matched perfectly with an aspect of Hong Kong. Less than one hundred years after Kipling's observation on the conspicuous wealth of Hong Kong, China decided to jump headlong into the capitalist muck. Hong Kong was famous for having the highest density of billionaire residents in the world and its shopping centres were known for stocking all the famous brands from around the world.

Once Hong Kong returned to the People's Republic of China on 1 July 1997, the relative economic strengths of the Special Administrative Region and the Mainland experienced a dramatic change as China's economic growth went into overdrive. Although poverty and general malaise were still prevalent in villages and smaller cities, bigger cities like Beijing, Shanghai and Guangzhou were producing an enormous middle class as well as a super-rich class. More importantly, China's government had become stronger, richer and more closed than ever before. It was not as desperate for Hong Kong's capital and experience as it once had been. Meanwhile, Hong Kong had discovered that without the Mainland companies' hunger for a market to make an initial public offering, Mainland tourists with extraordinary purchasing power, and real estate brokers with bulging wallets, its economy would not continue to grow. People looked expectantly to Beijing's policies to support the economy. Hong Kong was no longer a signpost for China's future. It had become a decoration.

Yet Hong Kong's magnetic allure endures. Pregnant women from the Mainland come to its hospitals in droves, and young parents empty Hong Kong supermarkets of their supply of baby formula. Mainlanders who finish secondary school sincerely hope that they can enter a Hong Kong university, while tourists at the airport buy books and magazines predicting what will happen at the next National Party Congress, and describing Xi Jinping's background. You can still do many things in Hong Kong that are forbidden in China, like watch protests held by Falun Gong at Tsim Sha Tsui Pier, read opinion pieces denouncing Beijing in newspapers like *Apple Daily*, see statues erected in the squares of Hong Kong university memorializing the Tiananmen Square protests, or use YouTube, Facebook and Twitter to your heart's content.

This allure reflects a new reality in China. Hong Kong does not represent legendary materialism anymore, but rather reliable public systems and freedom of speech. It also helps to show what else was happening while China basked in its upturn. While its economy was rising, its politics and public life were becoming more and more closed, and the social morals and systems of trust had already collapsed. China's political problems could only be given free expression in Hong Kong.

Perhaps Hong Kong is no longer a mythical land, but it is still a reminder to China; an alternative way of living, a different point of reference. But is Hong Kong even aware of its strength? If so, can it hold onto it? This is the first time in 170 years that it has had to face such a powerful China.

DONGGUAN IN NOVEMBER

14 December 2008

Humen village in Dongguan was the place where Lin Zexu burned opium more than 150 years ago. The village also marked the beginning of China's thirty years of opening up to foreign investment. Now it is home to a large number of bankrupt manufacturing plants. Dongguan is synonymous with 'Made in China'. Some say as a result that its transformations, rise and fall have symbolic significance.

An empty piece of land was surrounded by a white wall and a locked iron gate. It was overrun with weeds. On the other side of the empty lot was a row of two-storey shacks, the red paint all but faded from the cracked planks. It looked like a relic from the Republic of China. I did not know the history of these old buildings, but now they are humble shops selling fruit, flowers and other miscellaneous items.

'Yes, it was right there,' the boss of Auntie Fang's Fruit Shop said, pointing at the white wall. 'The factory was demolished just last year.' It was an afternoon in early winter, the nicest time of year in southern China (after the brutal summer heat and humidity have finally left, leaving the air warm and refreshing).

I wandered around Humen, standing on Weiyuan Battery and listening to the distant sound of the Pearl River lapping against the shore. Looking at the cannons, I imagined British warships arriving here in 1839 in response to imperial commissioner Lin Zexu's destruction of a large amount of illegal opium seized from British traders. The supposedly impenetrable Battery had, ultimately, been unable to withstand the firepower of the Royal Navy. At the Lin Zexu Memorial Museum I saw two ponds filled with green algae: in 1839, on Lin Zexu's orders, half-naked workers had dug pits into which they poured the seized opium, along with lime and salt to render it unusable. Lin Zexu's attempt to abolish the trade in opium triggered what the British call the First Opium War, which would lead to the first of the 'unequal treaties' between China and the Western powers, and the cession of Hong Kong Island to Britain.

But the bit of abandoned land that I was looking for was the beginning of a different chapter in China's history. On 30 July 1978, a nearly bankrupt Hong Kong businessman named Zhang Zimi brought a few handbags and some scraps to the Dongguan government, hoping to build a factory in Humen. Zhang finally reached an agreement where he provided all the raw materials and equipment and the government built the factory and provided the workers. The handbags cost 20 yuan (£2) on average to make and the factory charged an extra 12 yuan (£1.20) as a processing fee. Every month twenty per cent of that fee was given to Zhang in return for providing the equipment.

This partnership not only established the Taiping Handbag Factory, it marked the beginning of a new era. The handbag factory's registration number was Guangdong 001, and its business model involved processing supplied materials, according to supplied samples, and assembling supplied parts.

The Chinese miracle happened right on the heels of the handbag factory's success. Within three years, the company had completely paid off the 2 million yuan (£200,000) loan for the equipment, and the size of the factory had increased from 200 square metres to over 10,000. The monthly salary of the workers had also increased to 200 yuan (£20) a month, making the factory so popular that people brought gifts of chickens and ducks in hopes of getting a job.

Taiping Handbag Factory, Humen, Dongguan. Today there are not many people who can make a connection between these three things. In the past ten years, Dongguan has come to seem like an abstract concept. It represents one enormous factory, countless young workers, global brands, and the place where the consumer goods of the world have converged.

The factory was the beginning of it all – its model was copied not only in the other thirty-one towns in Dongguan, but in different provinces across China.

Capital became more diverse, and the production lines became more modern, while the products became more plentiful, and the market kept growing. Swarms of workers from other provinces replaced the locals. Eventually this approach became known as the Dongguan Model. All the philosophies behind 'Made in China' were there – cheap labour, cheap land, a lack of environmental protection; coupled with foreign capital, technology, management and markets. A surging, merciless power was formed.

Very few people note the historical irony here. One hundred years ago, foreign influence was thought to be the source of China's fall, and as such it needed to be eliminated; one hundred years later, we are trying our hardest to get the attention of the outside world. More than 150 years ago, China's doors were wrested open by a triumphant Union Jack, sowing the seeds of humiliation; one hundred years later, Hong Kong, still flying the Union Jack, became the prologue to the next chapter of China's story. Tiny Humen has captured the many moods of history.

Taiping Handbag Factory went bust in 1996 because it was unable to handle stiff competition from rivals. In May 2007, the old factory was razed to the ground, and the roar of the massive diggers signalled the end of an era, as well as a new hope. The Dongguan Model was moving away from low-tech and was entering an age of value-added manufacturing.

When I visited in November 2008, discussions of Dongguan's transformation dominated not only newspaper headlines but local gossip too. In September, a financial crisis had started on Wall Street and quickly spread around the world; everyone turned their attention to Dongguan and 'Made in China'. Its transformation, success and eventual decline were all part of its symbolism.

People have contradictory views about it. Many of the factories had already closed, and large numbers of workers were leaving anyway before they were laid off; the streets were emptier than before, and the taxi drivers and restaurant managers all complained that the good old days had gone. But there are others who say that this was a painful period that Dongguan needed to go through. The factories that closed were using poor technology or were mismanaged, while the ones that survived were much stronger. The most pessimistic believe that the Dongguan Model couldn't be sustained, and that the foreign capital was like a cloud of locusts that swarmed in and flew right out again, leaving only ravaged crops behind. As for the silent majority of Dongguan's population, the workers forced to return to their villages, I can't hear their voices.

The site of the Taiping Handbag Factory, which has been razed, is still an empty lot. It is neither a memorial to the past nor a sign of the future.

WANDERING THOUGHTS IN JINGZHOU

7 June 2009

It was Jorge Luis Borges, the Argentinian writer who went blind in later life, who constantly reminded me of Jingzhou. In Buenos Aires, he filled libraries with works on the East and the West, the changes between historical eras, and the rise and fall of rulers. Living in an endless night, he imagined sunsets over the Pampas, scar-faced gauchos and young fighters, drunk and carrying knives.

There are so many notable people from Jingzhou that listing them all is equivalent to telling a brief history of China. The city is particularly famous for having produced three figures from the Three Kingdoms period (AD 220–80): warlord Liu Bei, who became the first ruler of the state of Shu Han, and generals Guan Yu and Zhang Fei. Their era of history included scheming, betrayal and mass bloodshed. Still, the friendship between the three of them and the intelligence of their military advisor Zhuge Liang – known for always waving a feather fan – created a brief bond of stability and trust in a time of confusion, helping the people to temporarily forget about the inevitability of death.

I was sitting just inside the city walls, trying to read some of Borges's poetry and finding myself rereading the same verses. The poems all had a similar flavour but at the same time were totally different. Borges would never forget the gauchos – the way they were not afraid of death and how they yearned for glory and true love. He transformed their fights and nocturnal meetings with lovers into precipitously short phrases.

Chinese legends always revolve around men, their camaraderie and their aspirations to take over all of China. Love does not play a major role in history, and women are treated like beautiful clothes which can be abandoned at any time. Legends like these are part of Jingzhou's oral history. People used to take a sip of hot tea, slap the wooden table for effect, and open their fan deliberately before mentioning the Ganlu Temple. Even when people lived fast, flashing swords and knives, relationships and social networks rarely disappeared.

Perhaps the old city wall, which has miraculously avoided demolition all this time, shields us from the hubbub of the modern era. The wall lets the people of Jingzhou's old town feel relaxed and unconstrained. Unfortunately, their leisure time has not increased their knowledge of Jingzhou's history. 'It's from the Han dynasty.' 'It's from the Three Kingdoms Period.' 'It was built a long long time ago, long before I was born.' When I asked people on the street about the history of the city wall, they were hazy about the details. And how can I blame them? I could see overlapping pieces of history right in front of me, making it difficult to distinguish each bit and take it all in.

A statue of the poet Qu Yuan stands on the shore of the Yangtze River, looking arrogant. Qu lived in this area about 2,500 years ago during the Warring States period (475–221 BC). According to legend, the literary talent Song Yu, who lived during the same period of ancient Chinese history, wrote *Master Teng-t'u* here, which includes the line, '[She] would be too tall if an inch were added to her height and too short if an inch were taken away. Another grain of powder would make her face too pale; another touch of rouge would make her too red.' The Three Kingdoms period, which witnessed a series of power struggles between the states of Wei, Shu and Wu – resulting in an enormous amount of bloodshed – is just one of many chapters in the city's long history that frequently appears in films, plays and books. The celebrated poet Li Bai (AD 701–62) mentions Jiangling, a county in Jingzhou, in one of his best-known poems: 'And crossing a thousand *li* I returned to Jiangling in a single day.'

The statesman and reformer Zhang Juzheng, who was born in Jingzhou in the 1520s, served as grand secretary during the late Ming dynasty in the sixteenth century. Before Zhang was born, the country had been torn apart by war again and again, and rebuilt during peacetime. Two hundred years before he was born, Jingzhou was put back together by a brave but cruel man called Zhu Yuanzhang, who was the first Ming dynasty emperor. When Zhang became grand secretary he assumed responsibility for managing a vast nation with a population of sixty million, for which he had to design a taxation policy. His endless tasks of organizing a monstrous army, selecting the talent for administrating the empire, and rejuvenating the sluggish bureaucratic system kept him extremely busy. When he was not working, he led the life that he enjoyed the most, spending much of his time drinking, reciting poetry, and commenting on the fickleness of life and history with his cultured friends.

However, as with many ancient cities in China, these historical events have only survived in legend and in old books. In Jingzhou it is hard to bring together the real life traces of history into a meaningful narrative. Occasionally, archaeologists have found stone and jade objects, which make their way into the Jingzhou Museum. All the other buildings of historical significance, from the prominent Guandi Temple to the home of Zhang Juzheng have been rebuilt many times. Jingzhou's city wall is often praised for its significance, but the wall has nothing to do with the Three Kingdoms period. It was actually built in 1861 – the same year that the emperor Xianfeng of the Qing Dynasty died.

Even though most of the city wall is unremarkable, at the wall's East Gate there are a number of interesting marks on the specially constructed grey brick road. There are diamond shapes from the Han dynasty, dragon designs from the Three Kingdoms period and the Jin dynasty, a brick signed in the Song dynasty by a worker named Gao Yu, and a collection of markings from the reign of Zhu Yuanzhang of the Ming dynasty. Carved neatly on the side of each brick are the names of the craftsman, foreman and registrar. One brick, dated 1771, has markings indicating that it was one of 1,000 bricks donated by the offspring of a distinguished family. They were not for use in the main construction; their value was purely symbolic.

It is very difficult to keep all this straight in your mind. I often find that Borges's tales make me envious. Europeans did not reach the strange land of China until 1527, when Zhang Juzheng was only three years old. Borges probably understood better than most that remembering too much can be a burden. The titular character in his short story *Funes the Memorious* (1942) fell off his horse and knocked his head. As a result of his injuries he remembered every leaf on every tree of every forest he had ever visited, noticed the quiet progress of corruption, decay and fatigue, and could see the passage of dampness and death.

Without any effort, Funes learned English, French, Portuguese and Latin, but during long nights in bed, he could not sleep. In the day time, every trivial detail stubbornly floated in his head, making him feel unsettled. His ability to think was hampered by his powerful ability to remember. With too many precise details, he could not make abstractions or generalize. Perhaps one should say he could not expand his imagination, because imagination needs a blank space, and his brain did not have any blank spaces.

But what if someone's memory is too incomplete and too hazy, like Funes' before he fell off his horse? What if we look without seeing and listen without hearing? In that case, life is like a single unbroken dream.

At the foot of the city mountain near the North Gate of Jingzhou, a young woman exchanged her jeans for a loose gown made of pink, turquoise and yellow fabric. She was dressing up as a princess or a lady-in-waiting from an unknown dynasty, and her partner was also wearing a costume and holding a sword, as if he were a hero returning from battle.

The young couple smiled sweetly at each other, waiting for the camera to click. They were not interested in examining the grass growing between the cracks of grey brick on the North Gate of the city wall, nor did they want to watch the two ponies grazing leisurely nearby. If only the ponies were photographed, it might look like a scene from 300 years ago, or 1,000 years ago – the ponies enjoying a few brief moments of tranquillity before the fighting begins again.

COLLECTIVE AMNESIA

12 June 2010

Twenty years ago, while hiding in the American embassy following the events in Tiananmen Square of 4 June 1989, Fang Lizhi remembered the lasting impact that the Anti-Rightist Movement had on him in 1957. Back then he was a university student in New China and still a believer in Marxism. He even thought that some of the Party's criticisms of free thought were not without reason.

What he couldn't understand was why the Communists would use such cruel tactics against intellectuals. His confusion caused friends of his to laugh, partly because they wanted to lighten up his mood, and partly because there was nothing better that they could do. They were a bit older than he was and they were surprised at how little he knew about history. He was unaware, for instance, that back in 1942 there had been a 'rectification' movement in Yan'an, in which the Communist Party had used the same methods as they would in 1957. Fang's friends were forced to engage in self-criticism and in 'struggle sessions'. The ideas that they expressed led to their being humiliated and in some cases even beheaded.

By the 1970s, Fang had become a physics professor with enough understanding to be able to laugh at the younger generation for not knowing anything. His students showed endless loyalty to the Party at the beginning of the Cultural Revolution, and then were the targets for criticism, denunciation and purging. They were sent to villages and mines, where many died. The younger generation seemed to know absolutely nothing about the Anti-Rightist Movement.[*]

While the next generation was maturing, the passion and courage of the young intellectuals who participated in the Tiananmen Square protests attracted the attention of the world and earned the sympathy of many. Even though that generation was enthusiastic about its cause, few knew who Wei Jingsheng[**] was or that the generation of the Xidan Democracy Wall (see note on page 22) had espoused the same views just ten years earlier.

'The technique of forgetting history has been an important device of rule by the Chinese Communists,' wrote Fang Lizhi in his essay 'The Chinese Amnesia'. At that moment, in June 1989, the whole world was shivering in alarm at the cruelty exhibited by the Chinese Communist regime, while Chinese society experienced widespread fear and desperation.

But unlike all the previous tragedies, this one was recorded by countless cameras and witnesses. Fang was even asked to write the calligraphy for the titles of two books while he was staying at the American embassy. The fact that so many people had recorded the facts of Tiananmen comforted him, because it would make the truth of that historic event difficult to hide. As a result, the tragedy would be difficult to forget, and a complete memory of these kinds of events was exactly what China needed if it wanted to move forward.

---

[*] A campaign (1957–59) instigated by Mao Zedong to purge supposed 'rightists' from the Chinese Communist Party.

[**] Wei Jingsheng (b. 1950) is a human rights activist who placed a poster calling for greater democratization on the Democracy Wall in Beijing in December 1978.

Ultimately history has mocked Fang once again; his optimism of twenty years ago has turned out to be premature. Not only has the collective amnesia which worried him continued to affect people, it has presented itself in a new form. Within China, the work of deleting memories continues to press forward, so that it is difficult for people to find any record of the Tiananmen protests in any public space. Furthermore, in an era of data overload, even a sober recollection of the events may be quickly swallowed by an ocean of information.

Today, Fang himself is being forgotten in a wave of amnesia. When his death was reported in the news, the younger generation knew almost nothing about him. People who lived through the 1980s, or who were particularly interested in the period, only had the sketchiest impression of him. He was a famous dissident who lived in exile; he was a physicist who spoke out about democracy and human rights. People had a hard time remembering that he also represented emotionally stirring ideas and philosophical thought. In the raucous, jumbled and high-spirited Eighties, he was called 'China's Sakharov'. His own training and behaviour seemed to represent the fundamental goal for Chinese intellectuals in the twentieth century: science and democracy.

Patterns of repression and reform repeat themselves in Chinese history. After Emperor Guangxu's Hundred Days' Reform (1898) failed in the last years of the Qing dynasty, the reforming ministers Kang Youwei and Liang Qichao were lucky to escape with their lives, having to rely on foreign powers for protection. Some ninety years later, when Communist Party liberals lost power, Fang Lizhi had to hide in the American embassy in Beijing. And yet, three years after the failure of the Hundred Days' Reform, in 1901, Empress Dowager Cixi enacted new policies in order to change the old dynastic system. Similarly, three years after the Tiananmen Square incident of 1989, Deng Xiaoping went on his 'Southern

Tour' so that he could reassert his economic ideas and restart market reforms.

People are hoping that they can use science and democracy to break the vicious circle of history, but the slogans supporting these ideas have never taken root in China, even after being shouted for a century. There are many reasons for this, but people often forget the most important one: the advocates and practitioners of these ideas, the intellectual elite in China, have been eradicated in body and in spirit, one generation after another.

The Chinese people are living in a state of anti-intellectualism. Consequently, they have nearly forgotten that every moment in the twentieth century when China was free and showed promise was connected to the educated elites. Whenever the latter were at the centre of public opinion and social forces, they were able to create new possibilities, whether during the May Fourth movement* in the 1910s or during the 1980s.

There have been very few passages in the history of humanity comparable to the past sixty years in China, in which the most intelligent, idealistic thinkers have been systematically and regularly eradicated or expelled from society. As a direct result of these decades of intellectual eradication, China has become the country we know today: one which has lost its moral and aesthetic standards. Young people are not given an opportunity to stand on the shoulders of those who came before, forcing each generation to fumble along, starting from scratch. If you observe carefully the depth and breadth of public opinion and investigation in China, and compare it with the China of the 1980s, you will discover that this country has not only failed to progress, but is actually going backwards.

* The May Fourth (or New Culture) movement (1915–21) was critical of traditional Chinese culture in the aftermath of the failure of the Chinese republic.

CHONGQING'S COLOURS

12 June 2011

'Chongqing is blue!' he blurted out. The car was driving along the Jialing River, and from the window we could see tiny white lights and pitch-black river water. The city was filled with highrises, the rooftops going higher and higher. The roads curved this way and that while the light rail passed overhead. I noticed a stiff pair of jeans drying on a line strung from a sixteen-storey residential building.

We all got drunk together that night. I was with a group of people who grew up during the founding of the People's Republic of China, aged around sixty. They were the salt of the earth, tough and romantic. We recited the verses of anonymous poets including one called 'Empire', talked about the rise and fall of Russia and the Prague Spring. Of course we also talked about Chongqing's eight years of war and the savage bombing it suffered because it represented a bastion of freedom and resistance. Chongqing locals said that more bombs were dropped on Chongqing than on London, and that it is the only theatre of the Second World War whose role remains underappreciated. The city rose to fame precisely because it was not deterred by the bombing, otherwise who would care about a city in the mountains on the banks of the Yangtze River? Thousands of people came from all over China seeking asylum in the capital of free China.

The men I was drinking with were outsiders in this city. Perhaps they felt that when Chongqing was underestimated, they were underestimated as well. But the thing that really made them angry now was not being underrated, but a different and new insult. The city flew red flags, sang red songs, and organized campaigns against crime and corruption. The higher-ups promoted all this as the 'Chongqing model', and the outsiders found it repulsive.

Everyone there had lived through the period when red ideology permeated every aspect of life. Two of them had fathers who were secondary school teachers. They had watched their fathers being humiliated, walked through the streets, publicly denounced and beaten. Excitable young people had shouted impassioned slogans that disturbed the peace of the night. Not only did they want to destroy the bodies of their elders, but they wanted to humiliate their spirits. Some tyrannical governments use race to distinguish between groups or people; others use colours. The sons and daughters of officials and the working class were 'reds'. Secondary school teachers were 'blacks' and bore the brunt of constant discrimination.

Red represented many things in China, including violence. In Shaping Park, not far from the place where we were talking, several hundred bodies lay buried. They died young, expressing their passionate anger and their ideals. They eagerly waved the 'Little Red Book' and shouted that they would defend Chairman Mao to the death. That park became their final resting place. They were somewhat lucky, because only two of all the Red Guard cemeteries in China survived – the others were demolished. I examined a tall and imposing tombstone reminiscent of a Soviet tombstone; it was engraved with the numbers '8' and '15'. '8.15' and 'Crusher' were the two largest factions fighting in Chongqing during the Cultural Revolution. They drove tanks in village streets and refitted boats on the Yangtze to become military vessels. Less than fifty years ago, this city was the site of a civil war. At that time, red songs echoed through the city. Today the iron gate to the cemetery remains locked, and grey concrete walls surround all four of its sides. Weeds grow unchecked.

Not even family members were allowed to enter the cemetery to pay their respects or offer sacrifices – the only possible way in was to climb over the high walls. A bottle of alcohol had been placed on the outside of the wall, never having reached its intended tombstone.

The inflammatory colours have returned. A red implying extreme violence, humiliation and ignorance was once the symbol of progress, and it is still possible that it represents China's future. People are unable to imagine what horrible things would happen if the world's biggest economy were to once again be guided by red ideology. Nevertheless, red is once again sexy and fashionable: young women dress up as the revolutionary hero 'Sister Jiang'* and perform outside Zhazidong Prison. The prison has become a patriotic Communist heritage site because Communist supporters were once held there, and the women try to profit from this by acting like steadfast revolutionaries and being flirtatious at the same time. In this instance, red is once again harmless. It is used in a short performance by a group of people who believe in nothing, not even the content of their performance.

Red groups started to lead campaigns against 'black groups'. Over time, the definition of 'black' had changed from the persecuted members of the Five Black Categories,** to members of organized crime rings. But the campaign methods were the same. Society was constantly shaken up by movements and

---

* Sister Jiang is the main character in a novel called *Red Crag* (1961) and is based on a real person named Jiang Zhuyun. Jiang was characterized as a female revolutionary who was imprisoned by the Kuomintang (KMT) in Zhazidong Prison and ultimately sacrificed her life for the Communist cause. She was considered a Communist role model.
** The Five Black Categories denote five groups that Chairman Mao regarded as enemies of the revolution during the era of the Cultural Revolution (1965–75): landlords; rich farmers; anti-revolutionists; bad-influencers; and rightists.

initiatives. Individuals had no recourse to rules or procedures that would protect them.

After the party, one of the outsiders drove me back to my hotel. He once again mentioned Zhang Xun and Yuan Shikai,* two men who had hoped to bring back an era that had already ceased to exist and who had, as a result, both faced inevitable, disgraceful defeat. He was the most debonair one in his group. If you put him in one of the black-and-white photographs of Zhou Enlai's former residence that we had looked at that afternoon, he would fit in rather well. Perhaps the outsiders think that everything in China is in decline – politics, society, culture, even the average person's facial features. The only thing that is on the up is the quantity of material goods – and unbridled greed.

In his mind, blue, the blue of a fine day and of the Kuomintang, turned into a colour wherein he could entrust his spirit, a romantic delusion. 'Yes, Mr Chiang [Kai-shek]** was a gentleman,' he told me. The dictator of days past was once ignored by young people, but lately he has become a symbol of democracy, freedom and modesty.

We listened to music, from Tchaikovsky to Teresa Teng to a song which was used as the national anthem over seventy years ago. Each verse was arranged in an elegant and refined four-character phrase. At that time, political China was facing serious crises, while cultural China was still breathtaking. '*This* is my country,' he said.

---

* Zhang Xun (1854–1923) was a general who attempted to restore the abdicated Qing emperor Puyi in 1917. Yuan Shikai (1859–1916) became first President of the Republic of China (1912–15) after the fall of the Qing dynasty, and later briefly restored the Chinese monarchy, with himself as emperor (1916).

** Chiang Kai-shek (1887–1975) was leader of the Chinese Nationalist Party (Kuomintang or KMT) from 1925 and was China's wartime leader. After losing the civil war to Mao Zedong's Communists, he retreated to Taiwan in 1949, and was President of the Republic of China until his death in 1975.

The car drove towards the People's Liberation Monument.* So many words need to be redefined; does the word liberation here really mean liberation?

SHANGHAI IN JUNE

25 June 2011

In Shanghai in June, the Party is everywhere, coexisting with glass buildings that pierce the skies, beautiful women wearing Chanel, noise echoing in the alleyways, brand new sports cars in motion, stock market trends updating on computer screens, and the continuous downpour of the monsoon. The city is a great place to earn some money, but it is unsuitable for breathing, living, raising children – or keeping calm.

The Party is everywhere. The flowerbeds at the end of the street have been formed into a hammer and sickle, and the university walls are painted with the slogan 'Wholeheartedly following the Party'. Meanwhile, red songs float from the community centres in alleyways and the ads on bus stops promote a film called *The Founding of a Party*.

Ninety years ago, the Party was born in this city. That was when Shanghai was the most fashionable and ambitious city in China, bursting with adventurers and people who wanted to change their fortune. They opened factories, tried their luck in stock exchanges, watched films, drank

---

* In 1946, the 'Monument of Victory' in the War of Resistance was erected in Chongqing – which had served as wartime capital of the KMT government – to mark victory in the Second Sino-Japanese War. In 1949, following their victory in the Civil War, the Communist Party of China rebuilt it and called it the 'People's Liberation Monument', also known as the 'Jiefang Monument'.

coffee, experienced life in the big city, founded magazines and publishing houses, joined gangs, and even started a political party. People wanted to try everything and they weren't afraid to pursue incredible ideas.

To some extent, the Communist Party of China is a product of the diversity present in Shanghai at that time. The collapse of central authority in China provided greater possibilities for individuals. The tiny political party which started in the Chinese settlement within Shanghai ultimately gained enough strength to rule all of China. At first, many people put their hopes in the Party. China was weak, and the Party promised to make it strong. In contrast, the Kuomintang (KMT) was a corrupt dictatorship promoting democracy and trying to come across as honest. Old society was evil, and the Communist Party wanted to make it clean and healthy again.

In the end the Party behaved extremely differently from how people expected it to, and Shanghai changed drastically as a result. The foreigners were chased out, private enterprises were swallowed by the state, and dancehalls, racecourses and stock exchanges were all closed. Successful businessmen, intellectuals, artists, and people living privileged lives were imprisoned, exiled or even killed. Their way of living represented the first thing that the new regime wanted to destroy. From that point on, there was no more Mozart, no more blue and white porcelain, no more English breakfast tea, no more thread-bound books. Shanghai's diversity, globalization and hedonism disappeared; the multitude of channels to richness dried up. The Bund, which had been the pride of Shanghai, became spookily quiet; meanwhile, PRC flags were stuck into every corner and crevice of ancient buildings. Crazed youths rushed into museums, private residences, temples and churches, claiming that only by destroying all old objects and removing all foreign influences could a new China be established. Endless campaigns almost destroyed the entire country. Generations of people faced difficult times, and Shanghai lost all of its charm.

Sitting in the Peace Hotel, all of this history seemed so far away as to be irrelevant. This old hotel was recently restored in order to make it the pride of Shanghai again. The swankiest parties, the most wanted luxury products and the most beautiful people can all be found here. History, which had been disdained and even buried, has become glorious again. People are amazed by the beauty and the lasting charm of the legacies brought over by foreigners that have been pushing Shanghai into a second golden era. The tall, dazzling buildings on the other side of the murky Huangpu River suggest that Shanghai is already there. The city is the symbol of China's rise, and it has never stopped accumulating wealth and power. Observers marvel at the ability of Shanghai people to bounce back, to forget the past and happily embrace the new era.

The city is famous for its political apathy. The diversity of ninety years ago has changed, leaving only hedonism. If you enjoy being a party animal, then why would you care about what the self-important Party is doing? The best way to deal with it is to ignore it, be subservient to it, pretend it does not exist, or look at it as a source of funding. But is that really what people are doing?

'They really want me to emigrate,' J said. She was a refined lady of around forty, who worked for a fashion company. We were drinking coffee together on the eighth floor of the Peace Hotel. Her parents are both engineers and had emigrated to Australia five years ago. Not only were they insisting that their daughter leave China, they were also nagging her to pay the Party membership fees. During the Cultural Revolution, her father's education in Great Britain had become a liability and he had been sent to live in the countryside, where he was tortured. He now lived in a foreign country and, at seventy-five, he had no plans to return to his home country to live out the remainder of his days. Even though he was no longer afraid of persecution himself, he still felt that paying the Party membership fees might help his daughter and his grandson in some way, especially while they still lived in China.

I felt a chill go up my spine. J did not understand why her father worried so much, but it was possible that he understood China better than she did. He understood how the Party could be cruel and unpredictable, how it could do unthinkable things. It could use all kinds of techniques to charge you for a crime. It is impossible to tell if not paying the Party membership fee could become one of the reasons for your arrest. Her father's generation knew that they had to act extremely carefully in order to survive.

H was younger than J. One year ago, she transferred from working at a magazine to start working for the system. 'The longer I work here, the stranger I think it is that this country can last for such a long time. Eventually, something bad is bound to happen.' She is an absolutely typical girl for Shanghai: pretty, smart and immersed in the trivial pleasures that make up her daily life. She had not become a Party member because of zeal for the cause. She thought that membership of the Party and following its beliefs were completely unrelated. Her main considerations were convenience and safety – if a similar power struggle were to happen, perhaps being a Party member would give her some advantage or extra protection.

She isn't trying to curry favour with anyone; she is just used to thinking this way. Everyone thinks this way. They do not fear for their safety, but they do feel a little insecure. The whole country is run according to a set of rules that defy common sense. China is a great place to earn some money, but it is unsuitable for breathing, living, raising children – or keeping calm. The government ministry for which she works operates like an organized crime syndicate, and everyone knows how to use threats and bribery to make profit. More than anything, people working in business are afraid of new government policies. But she knows that this way of life can not go on. Her parents had already travelled to Australia and Canada to search out a place where they could emigrate.

H and J's stories are typical of Shanghai. A flourishing China has been built on a foundation of widespread fear. Even while singing happy songs, everyone wants to escape.

A NIGHT AT ORANGE ISLE

10 July 2011

I have never been to Orange Isle. When I visited Changsha the island was closed for a performance of red songs. I was hoping to see the former British consulate and the bust of Mao. The British consulate building is a memory of old Changsha. It was built in 1904, the year that Changsha opened its ports to foreign trade. It escaped a huge fire in 1938 and avoided the chaos of the Cultural Revolution. Even the past twenty years of renovation have not affected the consulate because it is safely tucked away on the island.

There are few cities like Changsha, which are extremely famous but do not have any sense of history. On the west bank of the Xiangjiang River, the old Yuelu Academy still stands. There are also a few buildings with 1950s architecture belonging to Hunan University. But they are the exception – everything else is a jumble of new buildings, making Changsha look like a chaotic and new city. When I was there, construction workers were labouring throughout the night. Clusters of mediocre buildings were squeezed in on either side of the roads while neon signs flashed annoyingly. It is nearly impossible to find a quiet and dark street or alleyway, or even a café or bookstore where you can sit and relax. Everywhere you turn you see karaoke bars, spas and snack stalls open late. Changsha is a city of sensuality and hedonism. Completely ignoring the history of the heroic Xiang Army under Zeng Guofan,* and the lofty sentiments of a young Mao Zedong, the city has attracted most attention in the past ten years for creating fabulous variety shows. Television programmes like *Happy Camp* and *Super Girl* reveal a spirit that demands non-stop entertainment.

In some respects, the Young Mao Zedong Statue is just an extension of the city's 'entertainment forever' spirit. Built in 2009, it is very different from the typical Mao statue. Rather than the old statesman standing and waving at the viewer, it captures a youthful, handsome Mao, his hair parted and flowing to one side. He looks like the Beethoven of the East. The bust stands on a giant granite base, its outline resembling the sphinxes of Egypt. It is so unexpected and bizarre that instead of calling it a unique expression of art, it makes more sense to call it a preposterous fantasy resulting from arrogance and stupidity.

I tried to imagine a group of people singing 'The East is Red' in front of the statue. Standing at the edge of Orange Isle, the young Mao had gazed at the Xiangjiang River flowing northward. He remembered his classmates from his youth, and thought, 'I ask on this vast land, who rules over destiny?' He probably could not have imagined that he would become a god.

People used to worship Mao, but today they display a false affection for him and use him for their own devices. He deserves this. The Chinese have faced drastic changes over the centuries, and perhaps this is the first time in their history that they can be cynical and profligate. They respect nothing, they

---

* Zeng Guofan (1811–72) was a Qing dynasty official who raised the Xiang Army to counter the Taiping Rebellion in the 1860s.

revere nothing, they do not consider the past or the future, and they are willing to abandon everything for either temporary safety or instant gratification. Mao's behaviour, his supposed superhuman ability, is a key factor behind the tragic situation we have in China today.

Even today, people are still living in his shadow. Those in power thank him not for his incredible political wisdom, but because the system he created was so cruel that several generations have lived in fear of it. People are silent and do not criticize politics; they are exceptionally submissive. The system has erased the people's memory, razed city histories to the ground, and burned written records. It has got to the point where there is no place for a person to rest peacefully. The best that anyone can do is live parasitically off the revolutionary leaders and be fanatical about an ideology.

No matter what happens, people need a place to exert their energy and creativity, so they produce and consume feverishly. Political fear is the twin brother of either utilitarianism or hedonism. If you have no way of expressing yourself or participating in public life, then you'll move all your attention to private spaces; if your spiritual space is hampered, then you'll bury yourself in a world of materialism and sensuality. So people are disconnected, and some aspects of their lives are compressed while others are magnified. The people in the audience of *Super Girl* who wave light sticks and the people who were Red Guards and waved Mao's 'Little Red Book' are actually much more similar than one might expect.

I was unable to see the statue of Mao Zedong in his youth, but standing on the top of Mount Yuelu in the dark night, I could see its outline. On a thin strip of island, one thing was shining through the gloom – the spotlights onto Mao's bust. Even though the rest of Changsha was in complete darkness, the bust stubbornly proclaimed its existence. All leaders have to radiate in all directions; they are not allowed to stop and rest. Unfortunately, the air was too dirty and thick, so the rays of light were indistinct.

A pleasant breeze blew on the mountain top. Endless groups of hikers kept arriving because this was one of the best places to escape the summer heat in Changsha. People were talking, playing card games, and microblogging with their iPhones. I had never seen so many shirtless men, letting their bellies hang out without becoming self-conscious.

I have heard that if you belittle Mao in front of a person from Changsha, you'll find yourself in a very heated argument. Even though daily life may be happy for people focusing on worldly things, sometimes deceased leaders are their only source of meaning. When people revere nothing, what they really want is an idol to cling on to.

ON THE BANKS OF XUANWU LAKE

7 August 2011

A few tanned men dived headfirst into the water, thrusting lotus roots into the mud so that flowers would grow there. They were fit, had big smiles on their faces and were speaking to me in Nanjing dialect, which I did not fully understand. The teahouse near Xuanwu Lake where I was sitting was empty. I was daydreaming and for some odd reason I suddenly thought of *The Travels of Lao Can*, perhaps because the novel begins at Daming Lake in Jinan – a lake also filled with lotus.

The events of *The Travels of Lao Can* take place in 1903, on the cusp of the collapse of the old system. After a war against Japan in 1895, an attempt at reform that was aborted prematurely in 1898, and the Boxer Rebellion in 1900, the Manchurian Qing regime had lost its legitimacy and was imperilled. As well as the political crisis, the country faced cultural, social and psychological traumas. China's spirit had been crushed. Not only did it believe that it had suffered military and political failure, it started to worship everything that came from the West. China was a huge, sinking ship and nobody knew how to save it. This was Lao Can's favourite metaphor. His mission was to observe and record the lives of the people before the ship sank completely.

Have we reached another watershed moment like the one recorded in *The Travels of Lao Can*? Will this moment give birth to insightful novelists of the calibre of Wu Woyao (1866–1910) and Li Baojia (1867–1906)? The past ten years have given us unjust imprisonment, families self-immolating, corrupt officials having love affairs, ostentatious mistresses, murderous piano teachers, bloodthirsty Internet users, a rail collision, peculiar books and a host of other strange things. It has become hard to distinguish right from wrong and black from white.

I sat at a table in a restaurant in Nanjing, where the usual topics were politics, dirty jokes and a long list of complaints. We talked about the moment when we thought the Chinese economy would go bust, the latest episode in an entertainment show called *If You Are the One*, the popularity of 'red songs' in Chongqing, and the bombing in Jiangxi. We even tried to predict who would become the next members of the Politburo Standing Committee. The conversation went better with the alcohol than it did with the Nanjing salted duck. We vented our anger, expressed dissatisfaction, and tried to console ourselves. The more powerless we felt, the more we said things we probably shouldn't have.

How were we supposed to understand all of this? Was our situation utterly hopeless? For a start, China is not the same as it was in the early years of the twentieth century, because it is not facing a crisis of national identity and it is stronger than ever before. At that time, the Imperial Palace received petitions from gentry in every province, but was unable to do anything about them. Today, no one would challenge the government's China South Sea policies. Still, there are many similarities between modern and early twentieth-century China: meaningful thought and values have crumbled; morals are bankrupt. This has caused a number of outrageous things to happen.

Three years after the fanfare for the Beijing Olympics has died down, you can tell that the national mood has changed dramatically. The sense of unthinking pride and confidence has vanished; replaced by discontent and restlessness. Recently, this discontent has transformed into anger and violence. It seems like the people have finally realized that the regime that advertised itself as being the one that would make the Chinese proud again to be Chinese is more a regime of exploitation. In the past, people deliberately avoided talking about politics; now they have no choice but to talk about it.

People feel like they are simultaneously stuck in a mire and restive. Some believe that the current situation will be interminably long, while others think that the future will arrive quickly. China might face a collapse or it might be reborn – either way, the current situation is not sustainable. If you lived in China in 1910, what would you imagine the future to look like? When the future finally arrived, then what? Wouldn't it just be old wine in new bottles? The serious crisis had not let up in the slightest; instead it has intensified.

The more confused and powerless people become, the more China appears a mystery. It seems like it was always this way and it will always be this way. A sinking ship, a rotting jar of sauce, or perhaps an iron cage. In Nanjing, I heard the latest metaphors about China's situation, 'China is a bus driving straight towards a cliff. Nobody knows how to stop the bus, and anyone with the ability to do something is jumping pell-mell off it,' a historian told me. Another person said that China is like a camel on the brink of collapse, bearing an ever-increasing burden of straw, and nobody knew which strand would finish it off.

These metaphors are comforting, because they simplify complex problems and make it possible to avoid taking personal responsibility for things. We are not willing to face our own problems and are afraid to take responsibility, so all we can do is constantly reiterate our collective problems. A hundred years ago people would have started a magazine or a newspaper, or given a speech expressing their anxieties. Today people post on Weibo to exchange their views on recent tragedies, their reactions to incredible events, or entertaining stories; the only difference is that they do it in a fraction of the time.

These jokes, complaints and worries are just another form of self-indulgence or another way to affirm one's identity. We are so self-obsessed and self-satisfied that we are incapable of turning trivial thoughts into profound insights or more targeted action.

In 1957, during his travels in the Soviet Union, the British historian of ideas Isaiah Berlin described the people who lived there while the totalitarian system was relaxing its policies. They talked about politics very excitedly, he wrote, but 'they [spoke] with the gaiety, curiosity. . . of schoolboys discussing serious public issues outside their ken, more or less for fun, not expecting to be taken too seriously, and with a pleasing sense of saying something daring, near the edge of forbidden territory.'*

Maybe when we talk about China, this is the level of realism we reach.

---

* *The Soviet Mind: Russian Culture under Communism*

A NOSTALGIC NIGHT IN HONG KONG

30 October 2011

I arrived at the club in eastern Beijing in the middle of the night, as promised. We had not seen each other for a long time. We used to be colleagues many years ago, and when we were younger we used to mess around in bars late at night. My friend is working in middle management now, but he has had a hard time changing his *fenqing* (angry youth) attitude. Yesterday he told me on the phone that he had a surprise for me.

When we entered the room, several young women wearing short skirts came in and sat next to us, as per usual. We drank Chivas whisky cut with lemonade, played drinking games with cards, and exchanged the latest news. Having no self-control, we kept refreshing our phone screens to check for updates on our favourite microblogs.

'So, are you a revolutionist or a communist?' he asked, teasingly. We hadn't seen each other for ages, and we had never talked about politics before.

'I'm not sure if I'm a revolutionist, but I'm definitely not a member of the Communist Party,' I laughed.

After we had been drinking for a while, he stood up suddenly, and a hush went over the room. He pulled out a cloth from his backpack and at first all I could see was red, then some blue. When he began to open it I realized that this was the 'Blue Sky, White Sun, and a Wholly Red Earth' flag, the national flag of the Republic of China.

'Tonight let us celebrate! It's the 100-year anniversary of the Republic of China,' he said excitedly. He had bought the flag a few months ago during a visit to Taiwan. I had nearly forgotten that it was 10 October.

The girls were startled; they did not know what this was all about. He explained the story of Lu Hao-tung and Sun Yat-sen,* and then for dramatic effect went tangentially into the story of General Cai E and Lady Balsam. According to folklore, while he was protecting the Republic of China, General Cai had a love affair with the young prostitute known as Lady Balsam. Amazingly, one of the girls had heard of the story, and she made sympathetic noises.

He hung the flag on the cabinet near the television and started to sing the national anthem of the Republic of China. The lyrics are composed of beautiful four-character phrases, much more elegant than phrases like 'Arise, ye prisoners of want.'** It also has a more authentic Chinese flavour than the national anthem of the People's Republic. When he had finished, we could not come up with other songs to sing that would be appropriate for the Republic of China. The best we could do was Teresa Teng,*** who was from Taiwan and therefore reminiscent of the Republic. Plus the girls could sing along. After singing those lovely songs, we reached a climax of excitement singing 'Song of the Guerrillas', 'Sending Off the Red Army', and 'The Internationale'. For us, they represent the romanticism of revolution while we were growing up. A whole generation of young people sang these songs as they fought for the end of the Republic of China.

So, was this a scene of pure absurdity? No, just a snapshot of the growing passion people have for the Republic of China.

---

* Lu Hao-tung (1868–95) and Sun Yat-sen were classmates at school. Lu designed the 'Blue Sky, White Sun' emblem that came to be used as the flag of the Kuomintang (KMT); while Sun (1866–1925) was the Provisional President of the Republic of China (1912) and co-founder of the KMT.
** These words come from 'The Internationale', and were originally written (in French) by Eugène Pottier in 1871.
*** Teresa Teng (1953–99) was a hugely popular Taiwanese singer of romantic ballads and folk songs.

It started as a fad at the end of the 1990s within a small group of intellectuals who were nostalgic for the character of universities during the era of the Republic of China. Even though the atmosphere could be very turbulent, the principles of scholarly independence, the rule of universities by professors, and the tolerance of diversity all took root.

After Lien Chan, former vice president of the Republic of China, visited in 2005, and especially after the KMT politician Ma Ying-jeou was elected president of the Republic of China and visited the People's Republic in 2008, the wave of excitement started to spread. In the name of reunification with Taiwan, the Chinese Communist regime relaxed its harsh evaluation of the history of the KMT, causing a more widespread re-assessment of history. Not only did this involve the role of the KMT army in the Second Sino-Japanese War, but it extended to a renewed understanding of the political, academic and social environment of the Republic of China. Like the protagonist in *Nineteen Eighty-Four*, people realized that the Communist Party had fabricated an entire history. Not only was the past less tragic than people expected, but it contained many shameful episodes that took the splendour away from modern China.

A few years later, as the quality of politics, society and education rapidly deteriorated on the Mainland, positive sentiments towards the Republic of China continued to grow. Bookshops were stocked full of biographies of Chiang Kai-shek, people were less critical of the era of the northern warlords in the 1910s and 1920s, and floods of media reports discussed the Republican trend (*min guo fan*). People were disappointed that society was unable to produce more great minds like Lu Xun, Hu Shi and Chen Yinke.* Visitors from Taiwan are extremely

* Lu Xun (1881–1936) was a novelist and poet; Hu Shi (1891–1962) a philosopher and diplomat; and Chen Yinke (1890–1969) a historian.

surprised to discover how highly we regard Chiang Kai-shek and his son Chiang Ching-kuo.

Compared to an omnipresent and predatory regime, the fragility of the power of the Republic of China's regime is attractive and has even become a symbol of freedom. Compared to the powerlessness of living under a mighty regime, the Republic of China means limitless possibilities for individuals (at least for the elites). In terms of aesthetics and dignity, the Republic of China glitters with charm unaffected by the numerous movements spearheaded by Communism and with its integrity intact, its ethics and aesthetic unblemished. The desire to revive the old ways seems to be matched in strength by the desire to reject reality.

A popular wave of nostalgia is often the precursor to social change. Before the Soviet Union collapsed, memories of the Tsarist period became very popular. Everyone believed that the glory of traditional Russia had been destroyed by communism. Similarly, when I visited Egypt in 2011, portraits of King Farouk were hanging everywhere. He had been overthrown by Major Gamal Abdel Nasser in 1952, and people used that fact to call the current regime illegitimate.

Unfortunately, nostalgia is often accompanied by wishful thinking, which is an extension of black and white thinking. Imagining the world in absolutes nearly always signals the beginning of a tragedy in history.

THE SECRET KEEPERS

17 November 2011

The Wenzhou rail crash happened three months ago, but the death toll is still a mystery. This accident and the way it has been handled are a metaphor for China's development: although China has achieved technological marvels, it has shown a frightening indifference towards the value of individual life and human dignity.

The car's headlights were shining on the bamboo fence, making the immediate area look like a discrete island. The fence was over 3 feet (1 m) high, surrounding an area approximately 30 feet (10 m) in diameter. Small white signs were hanging on the fence, each one with the word DANGER painted in red. Only a deep pit filled with water was visible from the outside of the fence. The water was probably an accumulation of rain. It looked calm and dark, but no one could fathom how deep it was.

I wanted to drive around the circumference of the fence. It was surrounded by a flat plain of yellow dirt. House lights twinkled in the distance. Every so often, I heard a rumbling sound overhead, which reminded me what had happened here. Although I could not see the carriage itself, it probably belonged to a high-speed train. An enormous cement bridge stretched above me, like a python extending its body towards darkness.

Three months ago, more or less right above my head, one train had smashed into the rear of another. The collision derailed one of the trains, causing its four carriages to fall off the bridge and thrust themselves straight into the ground. Public outrage at the crash and the way in which the Railways Ministry handled the matter spread across the country.

New technology has given the public new powers. By leveraging Weibo, hundreds of fragments of information can be pieced together to put pressure on officials. It doesn't matter if you are from Haikou on the coast, Xining in the west, or Tengchong in the south; it doesn't matter if you are a businessman, a professor, or a worker in a shoe factory, you still have a platform on which to express your views. The platform is not designed for discussing philosophical thoughts, but it nevertheless encourages you to state your position on certain issues. If you do not have your own opinions to articulate, you can forward someone else's with just one click. You can vent your frustrations about the daily annoyances in your life through discussing current events. The tensions in modern China are those between the overbearing, constantly greedy, and abnormally detached bureaucratic system and the common people. The bureaucracy is like a monster that does not know when it's full, eating up the wealth and creative resources of the entire country.

The bureaucratic system has become more and more adept at coexisting with pressure from the public. Some opinions are held by so many people that one would conclude they had a tremendous influence; however, since they do not have any internal logic or organizational support, they are held together merely by ephemeral emotions. The pressure from public opinion looks staggering, but it is temporary and spontaneous; like an information dust storm, it arrives suddenly and leaves just as quickly. As long as the government can hold out for ten days, even if it makes no substantial changes, the people will become fatigued and public opinion will move onto the next hot topic. It doesn't matter if the Chinese authorities' words and deeds are filled with loopholes, stupidity or arrogance; the method is still highly effective. It undermines and destroys all political and civil organizations, and without the power of an organization to provide sustained pressure, no substantial change occurs.

After walking around half of the fence, I heard the police siren go off. I looked up and I could see red police lights flashing on the uneven ground. They were getting closer and closer.

Instinctively I was afraid, even though rationally I understood that there was nothing to be worried about.

As a citizen of this country, I could come and look at the scene of an accident in the middle of the night; there was no regulation forbidding that. Still, my fear did not abate, and as uniformed policemen stepped out of the vehicle, it only intensified. One was bald; the other two had crew cuts. Using the light from the flashing car, I tried to make out their faces. They looked like they were weary but still had the capacity to be violent. 'What are you doing here?' the baldy asked.

'We were just looking,' my colleague said, then switched into Wenzhou dialect.

I couldn't understand what they were saying, and then I was asked to show my identification. I wanted to argue with them, but reflexively I reached into my wallet and pulled out my ID. As I handed it over, I asked, 'What happened, why can't we come here?'

'There have been a lot of robberies in this area. We were worried that you would get robbed; it's very dangerous.' Even though I was prepared to hear a lie, his answer was beyond my wildest imagination.

Who would try to rob someone in this deserted open space? Many people know that in the busiest city districts, the police always arrive a long time after someone has been robbed. Out here, they had arrived in less than ten minutes, and there was nothing even threatening us. What's more, if they were here to protect us, why did they need to see our IDs?

In today's China, these kinds of questions are silly and superfluous; the fear, on the other hand, is real. Their badges and uniforms were really terrifying. The police never seek to protect, only to investigate 'misdeeds'.

So we gave up and retreated to a restaurant in Wenzhou city centre where we could drink tea and talk about what had just happened. We were angry but helpless at the same time. We were definitely suspicious about the police arriving so quickly. We also wondered what would have happened if we were friends or family of the victims? Would they have prevented us from visiting the crash site to pay our respects?

Were the police feeling at all uneasy carrying out these tasks? They were guarding a black pit filled with rainwater, not letting members of the public approach. The remains of bodies were still buried within it. Perhaps their spirits lingered still. The crash had occurred three months ago, but the death toll was still a mystery. A figure should have been easier to obtain because a system had been implemented whereby anyone who wanted to buy a rail ticket had to use their real name. People found it hard to believe that even though four carriages full of people had plummeted off the bridge, only about forty people had died. The country had achieved 'management by numbers', as anticipated by historian Ray Huang, and this particular number was going to remain unclear forever.

At that moment, Yiyi appeared on the television screen on the wall of the restaurant. As the last survivor to be rescued from the disaster, 'Yiyi the miracle girl' had stolen the hearts of millions around the country. She was only two and had an adorable face. Her image of innocence was so different from the dark reality of the accident that it seemed almost like she was playing a part written in a play. She survived, but that night she had lost both of her parents.

It happens in politics everywhere: children always become tools when public relations teams want to manage a crisis. The premier went to visit Yiyi while the Ministry of Health sent the best experts in the country to diagnose and treat her. Little Yiyi was shown on television, walking and revealing a cute smile. I don't know if that image shows the pride of our country or consumes us with grief.

THE SHADOW OF LINCHUAN

4 December 2011

'Super middle schools' such as Linchuan No. 1 were built on an immense scale, even larger than universities, and are famous for their strict discipline and ability to get pupils into top universities. They also reflect the distorted exam-oriented education system that dominates China. Everyone talks about the universities that their children could get into. No one is asking what the children themselves are feeling.

The rules cover everything. Boys are not allowed to wear their hair long and girls are not allowed to wear high heels. Girls and boys are not allowed to show affection in public. They aren't allowed to leave handprints, footprints, or the print of a playground ball on the spotless white walls. They aren't allowed to walk on the grass, climb over fences, smoke or gamble. Above all, they are not allowed to visit Internet cafés.

There are a wide variety of punishments for breaking the rules. Anyone who breaks two is disqualified from getting an 'excellent' award, and if three students in one class break the rules then the entire class is disqualified from getting a 'civilized class' award. Many of the punishments involve fines. Anyone who sends a text message or answers their mobile phone in class has it confiscated, and doesn't get it back until their parents have collected it. Anyone using their phone in an examination room is fined 10 yuan (£1). Anyone who is caught playing games in an Internet café is fined 50 yuan (£5), and if they had spent the night there, the fine is doubled. If any pupil is caught more than once in an Internet café, they are expelled.

The ten rules for pupils of Linchuan No. 1 Middle School fit onto a single sheet of A4 paper. Even though the paper is gradually turning yellow, it is still firmly pasted on the wall. There is no indication as to when the list was written. Seventy desks are crammed into a fifty-square-metre classroom. Not including the podium, each student has less than one square metre of space. A formula is written on the board along with the name of the member of staff on duty: Yang Zhibo.

The classroom belongs to the Fuzhou City Linchuan District Library. The library is no longer in use. The reading rooms are permanently locked and you can see thick layers of dust piling up on the books. Even during opening hours, the library employs no staff except security guards – who were sitting and watching the sun set when I visited. The guards said that Linchuan No. 1 borrowed the library classrooms to allow pupils to resit their exams.

Across the narrow, nearly unrecognizable, little road was the school. Behind the large iron gate was an enormous red sign. Both the top scorers for the college entrance examination in Jiangxi province for humanities and sciences in 2011 were pupils of this school. Twenty-seven pupils were admitted to Peking University and Tsinghua University, and a handful of pupils were admitted to the Chinese University of Hong Kong and Nanyang Technological University in Singapore.

None of the other middle schools in Jiangxi province can beat its excellent test scores. In Fuzhou, the school's status is elevated even higher, Linchuan No. 1 is not just a middle school, it is the foundation of the city and carries everyone's hopes. A sign on the school entrance reads 'Jiangxi Fuzhou (Linchuan) Education Corporation' above the school name. This is significant for two reasons: first, it shows that the school ranks higher than the Linchuan District Education Bureau and is directly governed by the city. Second, it demonstrates the industrialization of education. Schools are not just schools now; they are corporations.

Approximately ten years ago, Fuzhou had a public discussion about education. The Fuzhou government hoped that education would become a driver of economic development, so it needed to make its education bigger, better and more outstanding. The city, situated in the northern part of Jiangxi province, lacked resources and proper transportation links. But it had a long and impressive history of education. Wang Anshi, a statesman and government reformer; Zeng Gong, a scholar and historian; and Tang Xianzu, author of the *Peony Pavilion*, were all born here. In the history of the imperial examination process, this area produced a host of scholars. Many people called it 'the home of the talented'.

The talents of today are not expected to write poetry or recommend governing policies as they were during the imperial examination. Today, they are asked to show their knowledge of maths, physics and the formulaic modern Chinese essay. Just as it was in the past, the examinations are an important way of ensuring social mobility. They are the only hope for pupils living in poorer regions.

The city government finally drafted a set of working principles for education and gave it an extravagantly long name. It was written in the typical bureaucratic style, combining the phrasing of an engineer with the passionate ideals of a populist.

At first it looked like the government's expectations had been met. Linchuan depends on education to survive. During term time, the streets are filled with students every evening. Linchuan No. 1 has 14,000 students and Linchuan No. 2 has 7,000. They belong to the 'super middle schools', erected all over China in the past fifteen years. These schools were built on an immense scale, even larger than universities, and they are famous for their strict discipline and their ability to get pupils into top universities. They also reflect the distorted exam-oriented education that dominates China.

There are over 20,000 young people living here, and as many of the students are not locals, they rent rooms while living in Fuzhou and their parents travel long distances to visit them. They all need to eat, sleep and entertain themselves, which has created a huge market for local business. Rows of new residential buildings are under construction with names carefully designed to attract parents: Talented Apartments, Tsinghua Gardens, Nobel, Garden of the Greats. The most popular real estate slogan is 'Less than a minute away from Linchuan No. 1!' Older buildings are filled with ads for student accommodation, and the ads for evening classes brag 'Famous teachers of Linchuan are changing the fate of more and more students!' Red signs sent from famous universities like Peking, Tsinghua and Fudan are clustered along the top of the four-storey teacher's building at Linchuan No. 1, congratulating the top scorers in humanities and sciences. Apart from the name of the university, the wording of the signs is exactly the same. They are arranged so closely together that it is hard to tell where one stops and another begins, reminding me of the banners displayed at the opening events of new shopping centres.

In this gilded education economy, what is the fate of individual students? Rows of bookshops line the entrance to the school, all hawking stacks of revision materials and English-language learning materials. If you are keen to find a book about the two famous people to come out of Linchuan – Wang Anshi or Tang Xianzu – you're out of luck. Exams have been refined to a technical science, and they have nothing to do with cultural heritage. Everyone talks about the universities that their children can get into, but no one is asking what the children themselves are feeling.

I thought of the image of the pupils resitting exams in the library, on red lacquered tables shoved together. Besides the usual scrapes and scuffs, words have been created by tiny knives and an astonishing amount of Tippex. Some are film titles like *Charlie's Angels* and *My Sassy Girl*, but more often it is 'I love _____' or 'F*** your mother, _____'. Of all of the students, the ones required to resit exams are under the most pressure. They have already failed once: can they bear to do so a second time? The air is thick with punishments and pressure; and these tiny desks are the students' only chance to vent their feelings freely.

Those who are interested in understanding how Chinese society is managed could start by visiting Linchuan No. 1 Middle School.

HONG KONG'S POLITICAL DRAMA

25 March 2012

The front page always has the chief executive of Hong Kong, C. Y. Leung, on it, while the last page always has the Mainland Chinese politician Bo Xilai. To some degree their appearance and temperament are similar. They are both remarkably younger and more handsome than their peers, it is hard for them to conceal their immense ambition, and they seem to give off an air of trickery. Yet their fates could not be more different: one is a rising star while the other is sinking fast. But everyone knows that they are being controlled by a strong, mysterious force. One day they might be pushed to the top; the next they could fall into an abyss.

I just so happened to be living in Wan Chai, a district on the northern shore of Hong Kong Island, during the week of Hong Kong's chief executive elections. Every morning I read *Apple Daily*, a tabloid newspaper that has a massive impact on Hong Kong. Reports of murders in Hong Kong, the latest price for prostitutes in Macau, and political commentary by Lee Yee certainly make for a brilliant tabloid. Fearless voices for democracy are naturally important, but if newspapers whip readers up into a frenzy they might destroy some basic and important elements of democracy itself. Democracy is not only the competition between – and rebalancing of – different interest groups, but a way of life and an affirmation of the value and dignity of individuals. Only a society which has a deep sensitivity and a comprehensive understanding of the complexities of life and the world can establish the kind of democratic system that we expect.

The atmosphere of the city was extremely passionate, which must have deeply surprised the outsiders who call Hongkongers 'economic animals', and the scholars who are used to describing them as 'politically apathetic'. Radical members of the Legislative Council publicly voiced their opposition, political posters were hung in the university campuses, and protests and demonstrations had become a daily occurrence. Different media outlets took sides on the issues and argued ferociously.

This former city of fortune has become a city of protest. People are constantly taking to the streets and expressing their views on democracy. This is not only an explosion of pent-up energy following a long period forbidding political expression, but a case of people venting their social and economic frustrations. These frustrations are multifaceted, some more superficial and others with deeper underlying causes. Even though it is one of the richest and most open cities in the world, and it is inhabited by some of the most hardworking and flexible people, Hong Kong has never been able to control its own fate. When it was ruled by Britain, it gave up its political rights for economic success and personal safety. But now, more than fifteen years after returning to Chinese rule, the people of Hong Kong have discovered that every decision depends on Beijing's approval, and that the situation is worsening every day.

The fate of seven million people in Hong Kong is controlled by the 1,200 members making up a Chief Executive Election Committee, but this committee is a huge disappointment to the people of Hong Kong because an overwhelming majority of its members do not even pretend that Hong Kong has an independent will. Beijing's influence is completely undisguised and permeates Hong Kong life. Rumour has it that the capital is backing a candidate widely believed to be a secret member of the Communist Party. Hongkongers use the boiling frog story to describe the way that the city is gradually losing its uniqueness. Clearly, the lukewarm water is getting much hotter. This is the most powerful China has been relative to Hong Kong for 170 years; it is also the first time that China's power has been so unsettling.

Apart from Beijing's blatant political interference and the friction between the Mainland and Hong Kong after the former's economic rise, Hong Kong is facing deeper challenges. Like many areas in the world, it is troubled by a widening gap between rich and poor, decreasing social mobility, and a crisis of identity. This is related to Hong Kong's economic and social structure, but also closely tied to the global economic environment. From the late 1970s to the late 1990s, the city was not impacted by economic globalization. However, owing to issues of political legitimacy, Hong Kong's separate crises have been muddled together. People are uninterested in analyzing and understanding each individual problem, so they have consolidated multiple issues into a feeling of political outrage. As a result, all social and economic problems have morphed into political crises.

Seeking universal suffrage was naturally crucial, and it has been by far the most important goal of the people of Hong Kong. But they have discovered that their fate is more and more tightly linked with that of Mainland China. C. Y. Leung being on the first page and Bo Xilai being on the last page of *Apple Daily* is not irrelevant. Thirty years ago, Deng Xiaoping's promise that

'The horses will keep running, the dancers will keep dancing' boosted the confidence of everyone in Hong Kong. At that time, the living standards on the two sides of the Shenzhen River were completely different. Hongkongers defined their identity by differentiating themselves from Mainland people. Their primary desire was to keep the status quo.

But now, life on Mainland China is more capitalistic than capitalism itself, and Hongkongers have realized that Deng's promise was a gross underestimation of Hong Kong's ability. Hong Kong was and is about more than horseracing and dancing. In the same vein, people need more political rights, a sense of identity, and democracy to consolidate their dignity and self-worth. For the past few years, the discussion of Hong Kong's 'core values' has resurfaced. Hongkongers should not and cannot go back to living 'under Lion Rock'* as they did in the past, and they should not encourage romantic ideas about British rule. The discussion should be about bold plans for Hong Kong autonomy. This kind of autonomy is not closed, and it is inextricably linked with China's reforms.

THE FOG SURROUNDING CHONGQING

27 May 2012

'We support the decisions of the CPC Central Committee,' he said, in slightly accented Mandarin. When he noticed my incredulous expression, he quickly added, 'This time we really support it.' Chongqing

---

* 'Beneath the Lion Rock' (1979) is a popular song, celebrating the spirit of the people of Hong Kong, by Joseph Koo and James Wong, which came to be seen as an unofficial national anthem of Hong Kong. The Lion Rock is a distinctively shaped hill between Kowloon Town and Tai Wai in the New Territories.

was hot, humid and shrouded in a dense fog. Everything was hazy: the buildings, the trees, the bridges, even the Jialing River.

He was a partner in a local law firm, and had worked in the industry for nearly thirty years. After an introduction from a mutual friend, he agreed to meet with me. The only problem was he had decided early on that he was not going to talk about anything.

Chongqing Police Chief Wang Lijun had run away to the United States Consulate in Chengdu three months previously, and then the Communist Party chief of Chongqing, Bo Xilai, had left the public eye for nearly two months; still, Chongqing remained strangely silent.

Of course Chongqing kept buzzing with its daily noises, and at night the streets were filled with stalls selling street food. The scent of spices from hot pots wafted in the air and the club next to the People's Liberation Monument was crowded with sexy girls. If you took a taxi or ate at a local restaurant, the people you came in contact with were very happy to talk about 'Secretary Bo', as they called him. Their outlook was fairly consistent: they all said that Bo was a good official, and that Police Chief Wang Lijun was 'alright'. Their judgments came from direct experience. It was true that the city was cleaner, the traffic was freer, the neighbourhoods were leafier, and people felt safer. Many of the 'Five Chongqing' posters, pledging to make the city liveable, convenient, green, safe and healthy, had been removed. But the lights on top of the police platforms were still flashing, and the police were courteous. The taxi drivers said that police officers did every task you needed them to do, and a woman who worked night shifts said that she was no longer afraid to walk home at night. When asked about the red songs that were no longer popular, people typically said that singing them or not singing them was equally harmless. As for the sex scandals, the rumours of huge sums of money

grafted by the Bo family, Gu Kailai's ambiguous relationship with a British businessman, and a strange trial involving
murder, people barely showed interest let alone moral outrage.

The scandals surrounding officials in Chongqing seem
to occupy a completely different social stratum which has
nothing whatsoever to do with ordinary people. Some people
believe that the crimes were fabricated: clearly, they take
everything printed in the newspaper with a pinch of salt. The
only things they believe in are things that they have experienced for themselves and reports that come directly to them.
Sometimes you believe that what they say is true. After all, if
all the bureaucrats are corrupt, when one of them does something significant for ordinary people, why not cherish that
person? Whether that action was actually due to a bribe can
seem unimportant.

My lawyer friend told me that these people's opinions are
all short-sighted. In the few years after Bo came to office, no
group had felt the pressure more than the lawyers. The government claimed it was actively fighting against crime and
corruption, which no one could find fault with, but those campaigns quickly evolved into them trampling on the rule of law,
before the rule of law had a chance to develop or become independent. As a result, lawyers were treated badly.

Meanwhile, the melodies of red songs brought back
extremely painful memories for the descendants of intellectuals. Even though he said he did not want to talk to me, my
lawyer friend couldn't help but comment on some things. In his
estimation, the Chongqing incident of 2012 is more significant
than the Lin Biao incident of 1971. 'Back then it was just the
higher-ups fighting. This time China might change its course as
a result of the incident,' he said. If the rumours of a conspiracy
to seize power are true, will Bo Xilai copy the 'Chongqing
Model' all over China? Will he put the entire country in a time
machine and send it backwards?

'In about two months I can tell you everything. That's when it would be more convenient to talk,' he said, after sitting uncomfortably for ten minutes. The sweat on his forehead had not dried yet. Compared to the forthright speech of the lower-middle class, the core of the city were all reticent – officials, business people, professors, journalists and lawyers. Many work units have already promoted policies of speaking through spokespersons so that if a journalist from outside Chongqing comes asking questions, everyone can tell them to speak to the spokesperson, who is presumably more enlightened. People seem to tacitly agree on one thing: they do not have their own willpower, and even if they did, it is not enough to affect anything. All anyone can do is rely on higher powers who decide which way the wind blows. If the Party Central Committee decides a direction that fits with your unspoken expectations, you celebrate them for their wise decision. Meanwhile, in these sporadic conversations, you notice that different groups have completely different perceptions of the incident. Bo's behaviour in Chongqing for the past few years has had a Rashomon effect on people.

Everything seems to be hanging in the air. The population is waiting for the People's Congress, which happens in Chongqing only once every five years, and the overall tone of the Congress is decided by Beijing anyway. Everyone is sure that Bo Xilai's fate will be decided by China's leaders in the Zhongnanhai compound, behind closed doors.

In the few days that I spent in Chongqing, I read a book about Chinese politics and culture whenever I had spare time, and one passage struck me as particularly memorable. The former prime minister of North Vietnam, Pham Van Dong, once told a US diplomat not to feel frustrated if he did not understand Vietnamese politics, because in reality even the Vietnamese did not understand it. I think many people in Chongqing would say the same thing to a Beijing native like myself. As a Chinese person, I might say it to a curious European.

THE OTHER SIDE OF WENZHOU

October 2012

I admire the grey-blue bricks, wooden window frames, and grey tiles of the two recently renovated courtyards. They stand on Siyingtang Alley looking lonely, surrounded by tall buildings. From March to October 1923, Zhu Ziqing lived here. He was a Chinese teacher at Zhejiang Middle School No. 10 and quickly became a literary giant. At that time, China's literary tradition was changing drastically, and the challenge for Zhu and his generation was to craft a writing style that was both conversational and elegant.

Zhu Ziqing's former residence has become a museum exhibiting objects from his life, a small number of which elaborate on his connection to Wenzhou. I realized that the poems I had studied at middle school, including 'Green' and 'Moonlight over Lotus Pond' were all written by Zhu while he was in Wenzhou. Rereading the poems displayed on the board, I found their adjectives overwhelming; Zhu's work was too emotional, too syrupy-sweet. Was that because they were the work of a generation that had started a language revolution? Or was it because we have been through decades of revolution, struggle and re-engineering? I lost the ability to enjoy these simplistic feelings a long time ago.

I was the only visitor on that autumn afternoon. Nearby, the museum caretaker was chatting idly with her friends. The middle-aged women were speaking Wenzhou dialect and I could not understand a word of it. The locals liked to say that the dialect was used as a code language in the Vietnam War – the pronunciation was so unique that it was hard to break.

I did not know if they were talking about high interest rates or something else. That was why I had come to Wenzhou.

News about the Wenzhou credit crisis was first reported by newspapers in September 2011 and it spread around the world. Some people disappeared, some committed suicide, but most were just scared out of their wits. One city's credit crisis had the potential to become something much bigger.

For a long time, Wenzhou served as a barometer for China's reforms. It boasted the first private business licence, the first joint-stock enterprise, the first regulation on private enterprises, the first farming city, and the first multinational agricultural company. In 1978, it successfully managed its economic transformation before any other region in China, by using the power of the market to replace the planned economy and by transferring the rural labour force to the city. In the past ten years, Wenzhou has become a microcosm of China's explosive growth. Its streets are filled with expensive cars and French wine flows as if it were water. Everyone is always on the offensive here, buying and selling houses, coal mines, even wine; as long as it has a high profit margin, someone is willing to sell it.

Some people in Wenzhou sell money for a profit, relying on the usury network to become rich. In a short thirty years, they have gone from industrious manufacturers to people living on inheritances. The purpose of any activity is money: eating, sleeping, singing karaoke and meeting others. Money, as Marx once said, flattens out relationships in society which are historically complex.

After I had viewed several factories, met with complacent investors and frustrated businessmen, smelled the stench of the industrial zones, and talked to people thronging the labour market, Zhu Ziqing's former residence had a particular attraction for me. It was peaceful, refined, historic. It reminded me that this city was famous for something besides a shamelessly money-chasing spirit.

After I left the residence I went to the port by the Ou River. It was a pity that the old houses that used to line the river had been demolished. All that is left are wide streets stretching along the river and a line of buildings forming a screen across the river. I boarded a ferry called *Gilda* and in five minutes arrived at Jiangxinyu Island. There were plenty of noisy tourists and some romantic couples on the ferry. The old woman standing next to me was going to the island to pray at Jiangxin Temple.

Jiangxinyu is long and thin. Its key attractions are Jiangxin Temple with its yellow walls, a former British consulate building, and the East Pagoda and West Pagoda. The pagodas were built under the Song dynasty (960–1279) and the West Pagoda has a distinct Chinese style with white walls and numerous tiers of eaves. In contrast, the East Pagoda is bare, like a lighthouse, apart from a tree growing crookedly out of its roof. After the locals burned the churches, the foreigners were so panicked that they fled to the island, bringing their followers with them.

On this particular afternoon, a couple was taking wedding photos in front of the consulate building. 'Tilt your head towards the groom!' 'A little cuter!' 'Pose gracefully!' the photographer called to them. Before the next shot, the bride picked up the hem of her dress and paced back and forth. The groom, looking tired in a tailcoat, waited obediently.

The sky grew dark and rain chased the couple away. The river became turbid again and flowed more swiftly. At high tide, shrill whistles came from some of the passing barges. The temple closed its doors, and the old consulate turned on its lights. It had been reinvented as a posh restaurant called International Mansion. When I asked about prices the maître d' said coldly that the cheapest meal cost 500 yuan (£45).

The tourists took the ferry back across the river, while restaurant enthusiasts kept arriving. They lifted their glasses and sang karaoke.

How should I describe Jiangxinyu at night? The famous poets Li Bai, Du Fu, Xie Lingyun and Wen Tianxiang all visited this place. From the ancient poets up to Zhu Ziqing's generation, Chinese people were intoxicated by the beauty of Jiangxinyu's landscapes and moonlight. They sat in temples after the rain and talked about Zen. We have completely lost the frame of mind and the basic capability to follow in their footsteps. The meaning behind the old trees, flowing water, *jueju* poems, moonlight and temples has all vanished, to be replaced by tall buildings, neon lights, automobiles, glass, metal, cement, profits and earnings, and high interest rates. I do not know how to extract poetic meaning from those things.

EARTHQUAKES AND GRAND OCCASIONS

CHINA IS EAGER AND NERVOUS

7 January 2008

I bought a copy of the *South China Morning Post* in Seven-Eleven and ate a quick meal at Café de Coral. Then I squeezed into the airport train link, and in twenty minutes I had gone from Lantau Island to Hong Kong Island. This is how my trip to Hong Kong always begins. Beijing Capital International Airport is vast and totally disorganized, while Hong Kong International Airport is efficient and clean. I like Hong Kong's airport a lot. It was 7 January. As I was walking in the familiar main terminal I saw something new: a digital countdown clock. According to the digital clock, there were still 214 days until the Beijing Olympic Games.

Even though China is vast, it is definitely unified: I spent three and a half hours travelling from the frigid and dry air of Beijing to the refreshing air of Hong Kong, but on arrival I was immediately enveloped by the same atmosphere of obsession with the coming Olympic Games.

This was the eleventh year since Hong Kong's return to China. I remember a countdown was used for that event as well. On 19 December 1994, a new-fangled clock was installed in Tiananmen Square. The return, on 1 July 1997, was considered a historic moment for the country, something worth waiting for and celebrating every day. This country is obsessed with huge celebrations. In the 1990s, ideology was struck from the list of things people believed in, so politicians looked for alternatives to fill the vacuum of beliefs and values in society. National pride was the safest and most effective option, even though a common side effect of national pride is ego inflation and narrow-minded arrogance.

Even eleven years after returning to China, Hong Kong remains more competitive and more modern than any other city in China. The contrast is palpable when you take the high-speed train from Kowloon to Guangzhou. As soon as you cross the border into Shenzhen, you notice rubbish and plastic bags next to the tracks, ramshackle temporary building structures, bare patches of unused land and gaudy advertisements. Similar scenes can be found all over China. Whereas if you come from the Mainland, as soon as you enter the New Territories your eyes are treated to lush green hillsides and slopes girded by concrete walls. The area next to the tracks is perfectly clean and although the low buildings are far from exquisite, they are still neat and trim. If cleanliness and order are considered core objectives of capitalism, then after copying Hong Kong for thirty years, Shenzhen still has a long way to go.

In Hong Kong, everyone can feel the eagerness and nervousness of the Chinese government in the lead-up to the opening ceremony. There was a similar atmosphere surrounding the Tokyo Olympics in 1964: the Japanese were anxious to prove that they were no longer a country defined by military defeat, destruction and economic decline, but a successful, modern, democratic country. Beijing wanted to celebrate its thirty years of reform and demonstrate that 'the China way' works. More importantly, Beijing wanted to show that this ancient country had undergone a renaissance after its decline under the Qing dynasty (1644–1911) and the political turmoil of much of the twentieth century. Now, in 2008, China was being restored to its former glory under the Communist Party.

China was so desperate to prove itself that any voices that were not celebrating the Olympics were deliberately repressed. I saw how China was willing to make any sacrifice just to prove itself, and thought it was possible that no city had ever spent as much as Beijing on a sporting event in the history of sporting events. But perhaps the deeper meaning for the Chinese people is not the event's unprecedented size or the incredibly smooth way it has been executed, but the opportunity it gives us to reflect on ourselves and our past experiences. It's possible that instead of proceeding without mishap, the most beneficial course for the 2008 Beijing Olympic Games to take would be one that involved mistakes and even failures, because these would truly test Chinese society and so make it stronger.

During the 1964 Tokyo Olympics, the Dutchman Anton Geesink took on Akio Kaminaga, the three-time All Japan Judo champion, at the open class judo finals. At that time, the Japanese believed that judo required subtle technique and patience; in other words, it was not a sport that a tall Westerner could win with pure brawn. But Geesink defeated Kaminaga in front of an audience of 15,000 people at the Nippon Budokan in Tokyo. Japanese people seated in the arena and watching on television fell silent. After Geesink bowed respectfully towards Kaminaga, according to judo tradition, everyone started cheering. To some extent, that was the moment when Japan finally matured. Before that moment, the Japanese were trying hard to show that they were polite, that they were efficient organizers, and that their cities were prosperous. Now they made it clear that they were also tolerant and understanding.

The latest news on the Beijing Olympics is that Switzerland has withdrawn from the equestrian dressage event. One of the riders from Switzerland has cited concerns that the extreme Hong Kong August heat will cause her horse to suffer. This is the first blow China has had in its preparation for the Olympics. Just two weeks ago, the wife of a news anchor interrupted a press conference to expose her husband's infidelity, causing such a scene that the conference was not aired on the CCTV Olympics Channel. It is clear that in the next seven months, similar things could happen, both inside and outside of the arena. China needs to deal openly with these mishaps. When underlying problems are revealed, China should see them as opportunities for reflection instead of trying to deny or hide their existence. If it can do so, then 2008 will be an even more significant year in China's history.

PORTILLO'S ANALOGY

1 April 2008

Even though I had heard about columnist Michael Portillo's comparison, in the *Sunday Times*, between the 2008 Beijing Olympics and the 1936 Berlin Olympics, when I finally read the entire article online I was shocked to read its first two sentences: 'Adolf Hitler's glee at exploiting the 1936 Berlin Olympics as a showcase for Nazism turned to fury when the black American athlete Jesse Owens won four gold medals. The Chinese leadership must by now be wondering whether staging the Games in Beijing will bring the regime more accolades than brickbats.'*

Comparing Beijing to Berlin showed that the West was very anxious about China. At the same time, Portillo's comment caused me to worry less that the West had been ignoring ethics in favour of pursuing economic opportunities. Nevertheless, his Berlin analogy was inappropriate.

Portillo, a former Conservative cabinet minister with a long political career and now a hardworking broadcaster, must have known that there would be a clamorous response to his article, especially after choosing such an unsubtle headline: 'Tibet: the West can use the Olympics as a weapon against Beijing.'

* 'Tibet: the West can use the Olympics as a weapon against Beijing' by Michael Portillo. *Sunday Times*, 23 March 2008.

The intertwined events of the Tibet protest and the Olympic torch relay have become more and more dramatic one month ahead of the Olympics. More and more public personalities and politicians are becoming involved. British Prime Minister Gordon Brown has been dogged by questions after he announced that he would not be attending the Olympic opening ceremony. President of the International Olympic Committee (IOC) Jacques Rogge has refused to make a positive response towards China and has joined others in criticizing China's record on human rights issues.

But even in an environment where criticism has continually been voiced as events have unfolded, Portillo's words stand out. I don't know how the Olympics will unfold at the end of August, and I cannot predict whether China will act differently in the future, but Portillo's analogy suggests that in the next ten years the West's attitudes towards China are going to be dominated by deep anxiety, jealous suspicion and even hostility.

People love imagination much more than reality and they prefer making comparisons to conducting proper analysis. When the 'Four Asian Tigers' started their swift economic upturn, people said they were like Japan but on a smaller scale. In 2003 when the US invaded Iraq, people were constantly debating whether that would turn into an unwinnable war, like Vietnam. When Dubai built a number of striking skyscrapers, people said it was turning into the Hong Kong of the Middle East. When Putin moulded Russia using an iron fist, people said he was emulating Peter the Great and Catherine the Great. When people link events of the present with happenings from the past, or link two simultaneous events, they are looking at the whole picture for continuities, and are able to achieve a form of understanding by doing so. However, people are often fooled by appearances. They ignore intrinsic complexities and, having made their neat comparison between present and past, or found a satisfying descriptive label, they sit back smugly to enjoy their understanding of things.

China has had many labels attached to it over the years. But its history is too long, its territory too vast, and its population too enormous to comprehend fully. Its past and present and many complicated problems are all mixed together. What's worse, China's strengths and flaws are magnified because of its population of 1.3 billion people. China is like a sun, but also like a black hole. This is exactly why it excites the complicated emotions of so many observers. They marvel at it and are frightened by it; they try to approach it and are afraid of being changed by it.

And no matter what kind of radical changes the West's image of China has undergone over the last 500 years, it has changed even more dramatically in the past twenty. Up until 1979, China had been a socialist country with the label 'market' affixed to it. It represented something different from the Soviet Union, a potential ally to the Western world. When the Tiananmen Square massacre ruined this image, China became a typical tyrannical country moulded by the two traditions of communism and dynasticism. An American journalist claimed that even after market reforms, China had not changed in essence, and coined the term Market-Leninist to describe its political system.

Another popular analogy was that the China of the 1990s was like Germany at the turn of the twentieth century. But the numbers game was what mattered most. In 1993, when the World Bank re-evaluated the economic size of all the countries in the world, China suddenly became the second largest economy, which shocked and frightened people around the world. People began to see China not as a poor and backward country but as an emerging superpower. The Cold War was finally over and China was no longer being placed in an ideological camp. Instead it was put in its historical context, as a great country experiencing rises and falls. China's rise was again compared to the rise of Germany or Japan in the twentieth century. It was seen as a growing power that was going to overturn the existing world order and possibly cause serious conflict.

At the same time, China entered a new round of economic growth, and the country best known as 'the world's largest market' quickly matured. Thus, the West has had two approaches towards China in the past fifteen years: on the one hand, it has been enticed by China's enormous market, as if China was once again the Land of Gold mentioned in Marco Polo's diary; on the other, the West has felt nagging suspicion and anxiety. The West has never tried to really understand the complexities of this country, which is why it constantly swings from one extreme to the other in its treatment of China. Most of the time, the desire to do business outweighs other emotions, which is why reports of China's economic miracle and of China being the world's factory are the most popular in the mainstream media. But an underlying fear and anxiousness continues to accumulate: Westerners feel bad for abandoning the ethics that they claim to support, in the name of making a profit. These two conflicting forces torment the Western world.

Tibet and the Olympics will never be intertwined in this way again, which is why the West has jumped at the opportunity to release pent-up anxiety about China. Comparing Beijing to Berlin expresses a worry about China's rise, and at the same time it releases pressure that Western interest groups have exerted; groups that claim that Western countries put themselves in an ethical quagmire by pursuing 'appeasement policies'.

Still, it remains a very unsuitable analogy. China is facing all kinds of challenges, and has many skeletons in the closet. But to a large extent, China is following its own course. In the next few decades, China will be caught up in its own contradictions. The most important difference between contemporary China and the Nazi state is that the latter sought to increase its power through territorial expansion abroad; whereas China seeks to expand its strength by oppressing its own people.

A DANGEROUS TREND

8 June 2008

No one talked about Tibetan independence or the confrontation between China and the West after the Beijing Olympic torch relay on 31 March. In private, people might have cursed the government for being corrupt and deceptive, but as soon as the topic related to 'the nation and its people' they became uniformly supportive. Then the Sichuan earthquake came out of nowhere, bringing with it tears, sympathy, and heart-rending stories. Such caring emotions have been largely neglected in an overly utilitarian era.

The earthquake brought an end to an isolationist atmosphere that hung like a cloud around China's borders. The Western world's sympathy towards the disaster victims overcame previous distrust towards China, and the Chinese government's prompt and large-scale response to the disaster earned it widespread praise. It was as if the aggressive China had vanished and been replaced by a grieving China.

After the earthquake, a trend became clear within Chinese society: unrestrained government power and uncontrollable public sentiment were converging. Both opposed any independent or dissenting opinions and powers, and both claimed to be patriotic. Their actions, however, are liable to turn China into an unproductive desert.

Since March 2008, this trend has grabbed my attention. First came the riots in Lhasa, then the torch relay, and each time the propaganda apparatus used monotonous words laced with a violent tone to communicate a one-sided, highly filtered message. I did not think it would still be effective because people are by now accustomed to treating any official propaganda as lies worthy of ridicule. Society is only interested in sneering at everything, because apart from their own interests, people do not believe in anything. But this time the public was both angry and approving. In private, people might curse the government for being corrupt and deceptive, but as soon as the topic relates to 'the nation and its people' they become uniformly supportive.

I have not determined a clear reason as to why this trend is happening. Perhaps it has to do with people's recognition of a common identity. Belonging to a specific group has been a human need since the beginning of mankind, whether that group be a family, clan, tribe, socio-economic class, religious organization, political party or nation state. In the past, Chinese people found a sense of belonging from their clan, their geographical region and their religion. By the twentieth century, the nation state provided a different and potentially powerful sense of belonging. Chinese people realized that their country was different from others and felt humiliated. After 1949, the sense of belonging derived from the nation state became stronger. Once it melded with feelings for the CCP – the Chinese Communist Party – and Mao's personality cult, they were completely inseparable. At the same time, all other sources of belonging were obliterated. Ancestral halls and cultural traditions were destroyed, religion was deemed an opiate of the masses, and, apart from workers and peasants, people from all other classes had to be re-educated.

China entered a new era in 1978 and people found a new way to affirm their identity through the possession of material things. *You are what you buy.* But there are still ideological remnants left over from the Mao era, meaning people do not get a satisfying feeling of belonging from consumerism. It seems that the only institution capable of satisfying the need for belonging is the nation state. Unfortunately, after so many years of propaganda and education, the Party, the state apparatus and the nation state have been lumped together. The young people in the streets who were protesting against CNN and the French supermarket chain Carrefour,* were not only snatching a rare opportunity to express their views in public, they were enjoying a strong sense of belonging. Their actions said, 'Look, I'm shouting slogans in the name of a higher purpose and not just for my own benefit.'

After the Sichuan earthquake and the reporting of the developments that followed, people wanted to know the truth. When the complexity of the disaster became clear, the government was unwilling to admit that it was having difficulties. It stubbornly repeated stories of pathos and the selfless courage of the army to avoid answering the public's questions about the facts. The public did not complain about this, indeed they themselves praised the sanctity of life and spouted patriotic sentiments. The public was unwilling to consider that individuals have different ways of expressing grief, and thought that anyone who was suspicious of the government had ulterior motives. After pressing for conformity, they felt like they were no longer isolated. Instead, they had moral superiority.

So in this new version of public opinion, the government's power continued to grow unchecked. We saw it happen during the Olympics and during major disasters: whatever action the regime took was granted a new legitimacy. Reform in China used to mean the government stepping out of social matters, because an almighty government causes disasters. But now, it

---

* In May 2008 there were calls, disseminated via text messaging and the Internet, to boycott the French hypermarket Carrefour because of claims that its major shareholder was donating funds to the Dalai Lama. CNN was accused of biased coverage of the riots in Lhasa.

seems clear that only the government and the military can solve problems. In other words, people should revere its power rather than be vigilant towards it. At the same time, in the name of patriotism, the public is rewarded for its ignorance with a sense of power. Independent and clear-headed thinkers in society, or any other force that might balance out the government's power, are challenged by the people.

There are plenty of examples of this happening in the world throughout history. Perhaps the trend makes people feel strong in the short term, but over the long term it kills creativity and limits opportunities, with ultimately dire consequences.

TIANANMEN AND THE SICHUAN EARTHQUAKE

15 June 2008

While the fate of the barrier lake in Tangjiashan was still hanging over everyone's heads, a thunderstorm hit southern China, and over nine million people across twenty provinces and municipalities were deluged by rainwater. Roads, houses and bridges were destroyed. On 31 May, ninety-three deaths were reported.

On 1 June in the afternoon, I was reading *Ming Pao** and I saw a China that was constantly facing disaster. The front page was a report on the pressure group Tiananmen Mothers. It included a photo of the grey-haired, seventy-two-year-old Ding Zilin, arms folded across her chest. Her gaze was soft but determined, and a quote written by Hu Shi hung on the white wall behind her: 'I would rather die than live in silence.' After her seventeen-year-old son was

---

* A Chinese-language newspaper published in Hong Kong since 1959, with a commitment to bias-free coverage.

killed next to a flowerbed on 3 June 1989 in Fuxingmen district, Beijing, the resolute Ding Zilin became a symbol of the search for truth and justice. She now collaborates with other mothers who lost their children in the national tragedy and constantly relates her sad memories in the hopes that the deaths of those young people can be understood in a new light. However, after nineteen years of hard work, her dreams have not been realized. The government still refuses to comment on the deaths. The younger generation have already grown up and because they have no memory of the event, they have no sympathy for her cause. *Ming Pao* published a message left on the Tiananmen Mothers website, which was created by international students. It was written by 'a person younger than your children'. He or she believed that the Tiananmen deaths were necessary because they prevented China from dissolving and declining in the manner of the old Soviet Union. The message also claimed that the mothers were refusing to come to their senses, and were probably corresponding illicitly with foreign countries.

The title of the essay was 'The Soviet Union never had a Tiananmen Square Incident'. I was already used to angry youths on the Internet who were narrow-minded, bad-tempered, illogical and unwilling to take responsibility for their words, but reading this kind of response in print shocked me. The arrogant writer had no concept of history and refused to understand the truth.

It is easy to guess what the fate of Ding Zilin will be. She never changes her demands, but Chinese society changes without her. A strong but unthinking wave of nationalism has swept across the country, reaching a new zenith thanks to friction with the West and domestic disasters. When people are worried about their own identity or feel vulnerable in the face of a disaster, making an agreement with a strong force is a convenient choice. If that force claims to represent the name of 'the nation' or the 'nation's people,' the choice feels legitimate as well as convenient.

Yet even strong forces are vulnerable. Using lies to cover up other lies has long been the grease that helps the state to operate. But not recognizing those lies and mistakes does not mean that they will automatically disappear; wounds left untreated will fester and endanger other healthy organisms in the body.

I can't forget the picture of the parents standing in front of Fuxin No. 2 Primary School in Mianzhu City, each one holding a photograph of their child. On a sign placed in the centre is the slogan 'Natural disasters cannot be controlled, but man-made disasters are the most shameful of all.' When a disaster strikes, people are shocked by the menacing strength of nature. Everyone's attention is focused on individual tales of tragedy and on the saving of lives. When these emotions subside, other problems revealed by the disaster appear as clear as day.

When people are vulnerable, they are more likely to be attracted to superficial things. That's because they want to console themselves and make themselves believe that things aren't as bad as they seem; that they are starting to gradually improve. I worry that the Chinese government's response to the Sichuan earthquake is not that of a government that truly wishes to change things for the better. An authoritative government can easily deploy people and supplies to take action in the face of a disaster but in a society like China where the media has such a dominant role, as long as the government can employ propaganda, it can easily make people feel grateful and trusting. Ultimately, people innately want to support the government because they know that they themselves are weak compared to the forces of nature; the government automatically benefits from this way of thinking.

But the real challenge for this country is just coming now. Five million people need to be resettled, houses and buildings need to be rebuilt, commerce needs to recover, schools need to start teaching again, a large amount of resources needs to be allocated, and communities need to be reorganized. The work will be slow and difficult, requiring support from experienced managers and NGOs. It cannot be accomplished by relying on the direction of a single authority.

Every person, every regime and every nation lives in the context of history. When faced with a challenge, they react to the situation at hand in a manner that reflects their accumulated experience. It is not surprising that the administration's responses to such disasters as the Sichuan earthquake have exposed a lot of problems in China: the arrogance and corruption of the bureaucratic system in China; the absence of civil society; the paucity of experienced experts capable of handling the disaster; and the people's lack of resilience which arises from their flawed education, the pressures they face in daily life, and their moral confusion. All these factors will create major obstacles to the rebuilding process.

Doesn't every aspect of this situation relate back to the incident in 1989? After Ding Zilin and other mothers experienced a tragedy they could never forget, Chinese society became debased and obsessed with materialism, the educated elites abandoned their ideals and principles, and the government and the Party devolved into nothing more than a series of interest groups. Everything in this country can be traded, including the children who represent our future. School buildings can be jerry-built; it doesn't matter. Education is not designed to nurture people but rather to push them towards specializations. People don't respect anything unless it can provide short-term benefits.

BEIJING ON THE EVE OF THE OLYMPICS

26 June 2008

The taxi was taking us from Anzhen Bridge to the Olympic Village. 'Even after all these years, I'm a little wary of big-nosed foreigners,' the driver said. He was over fifty, had a strong Beijing accent, and I could see the mirth shining from his small eyes.

I admired the flower pots installed on either side of the road. They had been carefully designed, and spruced up with large plastic leaves in an attempt to make several small pots look like one huge bouquet. But the plastic additions only served to make the real flowers look unnatural. The forty million flower planters did not add a touch of beauty as expected by the planners; instead their work looked like a tacky decoration.

We began by talking about the Olympics. It was the end of June and, after a brief lull, Beijing was back in the swing of Olympic preparations. Our taxi driver clearly did not like the flowers; in fact he felt slightly worried about the whole Olympics, which were scheduled to start on 8 August. 'I have to stay outside of the Fourth Ring Road during the Olympics,' he complained. 'If I try to pick up any fares in the city centre and get reported, I'll be in a lot of trouble.'

I could understand what he was going through. He had been required to learn English, follow a strict set of rules, and keep the interior of his car permanently spotless, all for a sporting event. If a 'foreign guest' complained about anything, he would be in big trouble. In short, he didn't feel like the Games were something to celebrate, because they meant a slew of impositions on him.

He scorned the event, asking why we all had to change the way we lived just because a bunch of foreigners were coming to visit. Apparently, even foreigners were running into obstacles, because, he said, 'My Italian friend in the garment business did not get a visa to stay here.'

This conversation was just a taste of the general mood in Beijing. From the perspective of outsiders (especially white people) it must look like we are completely at a loss. That is because we still have pride deep in our bones and we think that people should respect us by default. But we lack the confidence to face the new realities, so we try our best to please others. As a result, whenever someone ignores us we are furious, and whenever someone praises us we are pleased and proud, but not an ounce more confident than before.

Margaret Thatcher once described the Chinese mentality as convinced of its own superiority, vulnerable and ashamed. Our sense of superiority comes mainly from our unique and long-standing traditions – we have always believed that we are at the centre of the civilized world. The reason for our vulnerability is hidden in the depths of history. No matter how brilliant Chinese civilization became, it had a difficult time withstanding attacks from barbaric foreign peoples. The Han dynasty entered into a humiliating peace settlement with the Xiongnu, the Song dynasty was ultimately conquered by the Mongols, and even the prosperous Ming dynasty was defeated by the Manchus (a group of tribes from north of the Great Wall). Our shame has more recent origins, mostly belonging to the second half of the twentieth century. At least the civilizations from beyond the Great Wall eventually assimilated into the great Chinese civilization they had inflicted pain on. In contrast, when Westerners arrived on the scene, they completely changed the rules of the game. They refused to assimilate; what's more, they were unimpressed by our form of prosperity and modern technology.

At this moment, China is beset by problems. Our memories and customs keep troubling us. Our hope that the Beijing Olympics will become a grand sporting event and our

invitations to heads of state from around the world is reminiscent of the era from the Tang to the Qing dynasty when
we invited outsiders to marvel at our splendour. We displayed
extra attentiveness towards them, but wasn't that another way
of appeasing them from afar? Fundamentally, this appeasement
was an expression of a deep distrust. The message was, I have
never actually trusted you and in the future I will never treat
you as an equal. A century ago, outsiders had to live in concessions, which on the surface looked like a privilege. However,
from the perspective of the Chinese rulers it was a measure to
prevent them from entering. Even twenty years ago, foreigners
coming to China were put in 'diplomatic residences' and were
only allowed to buy things at the Friendship Hotels, which were
really an extension of the concession system. Today, outsiders
can be seen in all parts of China, and especially Beijing, but
they are still treated differently. No matter what their nationality, they are all called foreigners (*laowai*). Instinctively, we
do not trust them. At critical moments, we hope to hear their
praise and also hope that we can either avoid or control them,
so that we don't have to cause any discord.

The Beijing Olympics of 2008 might produce a similar result:
China is desperate to present itself as a prosperous, powerful
and constantly improving country. But after careful examination, people may find that our most prominent characteristic is
our propensity towards outdated thinking and customs.

FLAWS IN INDIVIDUALS

4 September 2008

Song Binbin was carrying the hopes of the members of the Red Guard
throughout China. It was 1966, and she was standing on Tiananmen
Gate next to Mao Zedong. She was a student with a bob haircut, who

went to the Experimental High School of Beijing Normal University. She took Mao Zedong's arm and pinned a red band onto it.

Mao was seventy-seven years old. He asked her what her name was, and after receiving her reply, continued, 'Binbin, as in "educated and refined"?' When she said 'Yes', he advised her to change it to something more aligned with his views, 'How about Yaowu ('Wants Violence')?'

The next day, the *People's Daily* published an article with the headline 'I pinned a red band on Chairman Mao', which had the by-line Song Yaowu, though someone else had written it. Song Binbin discovered that she was no longer able to control her image or even her own name. She had never liked violence, and yet she had been transformed into a proponent of violent measures. When Red Guard members flocked to her high school, they were disappointed to find that Song Yaowu was not nearly as revolutionary as they had imagined. Nevertheless, when she was sent to work in the countryside, rumours spread throughout the village that Song Yaowu had beaten and killed countless people.

I watched a documentary called *Morning Sun* (2003) in which Song Binbin was always in shadow when she was interviewed. It was as if her real face and expressions had been swallowed up by the clamour of that era. Today, few people remember the episode on Tiananmen Square. Those who actually lived through it have seen too many inflaming and absurd things in real life to be affected by watching a documentary about it. Yet the episode perfectly demonstrates the characteristics of that era and that system: the value of the individual and even individual characteristics became insignificant. They could be modified or substituted at any time. The reasons for a substitution usually related to some higher purpose, such as the national interest, or the needs of the revolution, or someone just claimed it was part of the regular pattern of history. In the name of these higher purposes, individuals were diminished and made abstract. What came afterwards was, not surprisingly, an abandonment of principles which valued the individual and individual courage. The youths who tortured their own teachers, betrayed those closest to them and mercilessly beat strangers have all been mischaracterized. Rather than saying their hearts held evil and ugly thoughts, it would be better to say that they were completely unable to think for themselves. But according to the rest of the world, they had lost even the most basic ability to understand and make judgments. At the behest of the revolution and the collective, they rejected individual responsibility, and promptly felt immensely free and unrestrained. However, some of the more sensitive souls discovered this way of life to be insufferable. Their lives were completely out of their control and lacked meaning.

We have been forced to forget our historical tragedies, but we are also actively working to forget them. After hurriedly finding our scapegoat, we give up the right to get to the bottom of things. (Moreover, we have lost the courage to ask the difficult questions we would need to in order to get the bottom of anything.) Then we repeat 'Look to the future' to comfort ourselves, as if the mantra can make the ghosts who are torturing and hurting us disappear.

When I heard the reports about nine-year-old Lin Miaoke 'cooperating' with Yang Peiyi by lip-syncing her pre-recorded voice during the Olympic opening ceremony, I thought of Song Binbin's story. On 8 August 2008, a little girl stood in the spotlight pretending to sing while a different little girl sang for her. The one on stage was considered the cutest, while the one backstage was considered the better singer.

'In a live broadcast, the girl on stage needed to be flawless in terms of facial expressions and the feeling that she gave to the audience,' said Chen Qigang, the chief music director of an opening ceremony so lavish that money seemed to be no object.

'We did this because we needed to make the country's national interests our top priority.'

Was this a trivial incident, or does it have some deeper meaning? In some ways, Lin Miaoke and Yang Peiyi's fates are an extension of Song Binbin's.

Granted, the China of 2008 is entirely different from the China of 1966; not only in terms of material possessions, but because people now have more freedom of choice in their lives. A country that had once thought the world was its enemy and had desperately wanted to export revolution, had now opened its arms, hoping to please outsiders and introduce them to its splendid culture.

But if you go below the surface you might discover that the essence of things has not changed at all. In Lin Miaoke and Yang Peiyi, you can see the substitutability of individuals; they are just tools used by a greater force. In the breathtaking group performances directed by Zhang Yimou, individual faces were indistinct. They were replaceable elements that formed a bigger picture. Nobody can deny that the group performance was spectacular, but people often forget the sacrifices made to produce such a performance. Were we looking at a twenty-first century version of the sea of identical red uniforms that used to so fascinate foreign observers of China? Although the splendour of the Olympic ceremony revived memories of the glories of Chinese civilization, it caused me to think about the way history oppresses individuals too.

Perhaps I am making a mountain out of a molehill with all these associations. But China is rife with lies, and its people are already used to the arrogance and hypocrisy of those who govern them. They have trained themselves in the skills of adapting to circumstance and of closing their eyes to the truth. But I believe that until the power of the individual is given room to grow, and individual values are respected, the strength of a country is completely meaningless.

THE OTHER SIDE OF VICTORY

7 September 2008

About two and a half years ago I asked the academic Steve Tsang how the Olympics would change China. We were speaking in a staff room in Oxford University, where an Indian woman served coffee and a snowy-haired man was leafing through the *Sunday Times*. I have to admit that the room left a deep impression on me. Tsang said, 'It will not change much. The government will spare no expense to make the event a success, and this success will continue to increase the government's legitimacy.' I gave a noncommittal reply.

C omparing the Beijing 2008 with previous Olympics is very popular. The most common analogies are with Tokyo 1964 and Seoul 1988 – not only did they represent the emerging success of those countries, but also the West's more general acknowledgement of Asia's importance. Sometimes Seoul 1988 and Mexico City 1968 are lumped together with Beijing, because hosting the Olympics helped the first two countries to become more democratic. Finally, some people have compared Beijing to Berlin 1936 and Moscow 1980, because those two totalitarian states used their Games to try to show the superiority of their systems of government. Ironically, the Moscow Olympics ended up being the last hurrah for the Soviet empire.

People love making comparisons, partly because it is interesting, and partly because they need a simplified way to understand new things. China has been so hard to understand that in the past several decades, nearly every attempt to pin it down has proved fruitless. The country is adaptable, which makes it difficult for analysts to comprehend.

In the early 1980s, outsiders were surprised to find that the people who had previously repeated political quotations were now diving headlong into capitalism. Those who had said that capitalists were a disgrace now hoped to get rich. Back then having 10,000 yuan (£800) was enough to be considered a rich person. In the early 1990s, observers believed that China was doomed to collapse because all the other socialist countries had. The bloodied bodies of Tiananmen were so numerous it seemed like they might cause a collapse on their own. But in the ensuing years, China embarked on its jaw-dropping path of economic growth. At the end of the 1990s, many believed that free trade, a market economy, the power of the Internet, and open communication between China and the outside world would eliminate the Party, which would make way for an open and democratic society. But again, they were wrong: in the early 2000s Beijing became stronger and stronger. Economic growth did not bring democracy or social diversity, and the whole world started talking about the 'Beijing consensus'. In other words, it had been proved that a political dictatorship and economic freedom could coexist, and that combining them meant greater efficiency. The governments of other developing countries found this model inspirational.

These dizzying changes make it difficult for people to draw conclusions about China. Each new label applied to the country quickly becomes irrelevant.

Both foreign observers and the Chinese people are at a loss to describe China. The former are sometimes duped by superficial change while the latter perhaps lack keen powers of observation after having lived in the country for so long, or otherwise are unable to really judge the situation after receiving filtered and distorted information over such a lengthy period.

The Beijing Olympics has only added another layer of fog for people trying to understand China. The country has built unique new sporting facilities, used technology to prevent rainfall at certain events, designed and performed a fantastical opening ceremony, deployed tens of thousands of volunteers, and won a total of fifty-one gold medals.

Some would argue that only a totalitarian government would be able to deploy human and physical resources on such a massive scale. Yet Beijing looks like a glittering host city, filled with fashionable architecture and clubs. It has nothing like the harshness found in Moscow in 1980. Even people who use labels like 'China is a threat' and 'China has a totalitarian government' admit that the country has never shown aggressive expansionism in the way that Germany did in the 1930s and the Soviet Union did in the 1980s. People can't help but compare today's China with Maoist China. They conclude that Chinese people have much more personal freedom than they did under Mao. Some Western commentators are even prepared to believe once more that China's view on human rights is different, and therefore it is inappropriate to evaluate its situation based on Western values.

It is easy to perceive the pride that Chinese people feel towards their country and the regime. They believe that the China of today is richer and more powerful than it has been at any moment in the past 200 years. They find it remarkable that about 100 years ago China was dubbed 'the sick man of Asia', and at Beijing 2008 it ended up top of the gold medal table. They get a tremendous sense of satisfaction from these national achievements.

To some extent, Tsang's prediction was correct: the Beijing Olympics were a smashing success and the CCP's legitimacy did increase. Yet that was not the success of the Chinese people, but of the country's historical characteristics and its system.

In China's long history, the value and uniqueness of individuals has frequently been overlooked. The passion and creativity of generations of people has been deemed unimportant, and power and tradition have controlled every aspect of life. During Mao's rule, China was at the mercy of a clearly totalitarian government. State authority seeped into every corner of society and destroyed individual thought and moral values. Even though these forces are on the retreat now, they have not disappeared. They are frequently disguised in a fashionable coat of modernity, but are still at work. Wasn't that principle embodied in the performances of the opening ceremony? The show on the whole was modern and high tech, but the thousands of performers were all wearing traditional Chinese clothing, and their individual identities were wholly subsumed by the collective identity of the group. China won fifty-one golds, and yet none of us can remember even a handful of the unique characteristics and stories of the Chinese athletes who won them. The way they carried themselves and their achievements has been downplayed because the power of the state always surpasses individual glory.

The China of today is showing people around the world the success of a new form of statism. The surface brilliance of the Games reflects a collective triumph of the Chinese state. But it conceals a shocking waste of the talents, principles and beliefs of individuals, which are brutally disregarded in the state's relentless pursuit of its own ends.

But in the heady optimism following China's victory, people have temporarily forgotten all that.

FROM INSTANT GRATIFICATION TO INSTANT FORGETFULNESS

19 October 2008

The sound of sheet metal falling onto the concrete road assaulted my ears. Three workers held onto the scaffolding and kicked against the sheet metal a few times until it came crashing down to the ground. Then they moved on to the next section. The metal originally formed an enormous billboard that constituted one of the exterior walls of an unfinished building. Over the past four months, many billboards have sported the same slogan in bright primary colours: 'One world, one dream.'

During the run-up to the Olympics, Beijing looked like it was wrapped in colourful gift paper. Positive messages about the Olympics appeared on street signs, at bus stations, and on the perimeters of construction sites. Pictures of ceremonial marble pillars, the Great Wall, the Bird's Nest and the Water Cube commonly featured next to those messages, to represent a harmony between the traditional and the modern in Beijing. But now the stylish and colourful sheet-metal billboards have been partially folded away; they look like the empty shells of molluscs.

Now, all anyone is talking about is baby formula tainted with melamine and the financial crisis. In just two months, the Olympics have been relegated to the dustbin of history. When a news piece reviewing the Sichuan earthquake of May 2008 was aired on television, it felt like the disaster took place ages ago. The Tibet riots in March and the torch relay incidents in April captured the attention of the entire country, but they have already disappeared from our group consciousness without a trace.

People have probably already mentioned how this era seemed to be the beginning of a long period of decline, but it has never seemed as obvious as it did in 2008. One story after another grabbed people's attention but was then swiftly forgotten. And the stories that were forgotten the quickest were the ones that had been most influential when they first broke. That seems to be the norm in this age of information overload. A story needs to be influential to capture people's attention when it is already spread so thin. But that same story must then be quickly forgotten so that people's brains are empty enough to absorb the next information storm.

People have lost their sense of continuity. It is as if each section of time has become isolated and self-sufficient. The river of time is now a stagnant pond. If you close your eyes and think about what has happened in the past few months, you might only remember fragments unconnected by logic. You would also have a hard time coming up with a deeper significance for any individual event. It is as if our psychological fatigue and inability to have strong emotional reactions has become an infectious disease.

For years, Chinese society has suffered from a lack of information. The authorities have controlled it all and ordinary people have felt totally helpless. If they could only receive a constant flow of information, the public would become stronger and Chinese society would become more vibrant. But it is no longer as simple as that. New trends are becoming clear. For example, access to more information can make people isolated instead of more open. The public opinion that has gathered steam on the Internet has never translated into real social progress; it is only done for the spectacle. The participants may be briefly satisfied, but this kind of improvised intervention is not enough to build a social movement. It is too fragmented and oversimplified. People allow themselves to express deeply personal emotions, which turn a public space into a forum for private thoughts, so that a private argument or personal emotion can quickly blow up into an Internet-wide issue. Everyone has entered a collective game of ignorance: they allow themselves to abandon reason and to think about things only in the shallowest sense; meanwhile they become captive to all kinds of emotions.

These new factors make it even more difficult to draw conclusions about modern China and how it will develop. But in the past ten months, our ability to remember things has certainly deteriorated. We go from instant gratification to instant amnesia. How then can we characterize the era in which we live with any degree of precision?

A GRIEF MONOPOLIZED BY THE STATE

24 May 2009

It was clear that many thousands of people had died, but detailed casualty figures were not forthcoming. People were especially angry about not being told exactly how many schoolchildren had been killed. Figures for the number of dead and missing were not finally made available until 7 May 2009, nearly a year after the earthquakes.

One year ago, everyone thought that the earthquakes would be an opportunity for China to reform; that the harsh reality of the enormous disaster and its accompanying death toll would force the entire country to take a step back and re-evaluate. For example, the vast piles of rubble from schools that had been built out of cheap materials demonstrated how people were willing to jeopardize the future for immediate personal gain. Some change has occurred, and the government's reaction has been effective. The television reports have shown our country's politicians grieving deeply and full of righteous indignation. The mania of the people subsided as the disaster prompted widespread sympathy, selflessness and the desire to help.

But the changes haven't lasted. News reports that had become open and representative of different opinions suddenly started toeing the Party line. All the eager volunteers who wanted to help the victims discovered that they had to be invited by the state in order to do so. No one was allowed to get to the bottom of the various questions that had been unearthed as a result of the disaster. Parents and family members who had lost children were threatened and illegally detained. People were forbidden from talking about their suffering, their outrage or their suspicions. Even the death toll became a forbidden topic.

The number of deaths seems to have left the enormous and terrifying bureaucracy unperturbed. The bureaucracy has shown itself ready to swallow everyone's kindness and generosity at a moment's notice, replacing it with apathy and timidity. A year after the disaster, we have no choice but to admit that the bureaucracy has been the greatest beneficiary of this tragedy. Before 20 May, it was mired in political crises from the riots in Tibet to the Olympic torch relays around the world. The government did not know how to respond to these issues, but once disaster had struck, it no longer faced condemnation. It didn't have to defend itself or change its ways.

Now things are clearer: 68,712 people died and 1,800 people are still missing. Among the dead and missing 5,335 are students.

When those numbers were finally announced at an official press conference, they felt like an arrogant and impatient response to long-term public allegations. *You want numbers? Fine. Have some numbers!* The subtext was clear: only the authorities could provide these numbers; individuals or community organizations had no right to meddle in these affairs. The government did not provide the names of the dead. Abstract numbers were all that was left of these individual peoples.

The whole process has highlighted the biggest challenge China faces: the bureaucratic regime's monopolization of everything. Not only is it monopolizing state power and key economic interests, it has the audacity to monopolize the deaths of people too. Even though the monopoly is not as pervasive as it was during the Mao era, it is still incredibly prevalent.

Twenty years ago, the world was still talking about the ugly consequences of dictatorships: economic stagnation, moral decline, disregard for the value of individuals, and loss of creativity. But then the Berlin Wall fell and the Soviet Union collapsed, and dictatorships became a less important topic. Soon a mutation of dictatorship arrived, with a fresh face.

This dictatorship appeared to be close to the people, always wore Armani suits, and was adept at turning new communications technologies into propaganda tools. Most importantly, the mutated dictatorship provided a space for society to participate in the economy.

Even though it has a new exterior, the substance of the dictatorship has not changed. According to its system of values, people are just instruments for achieving a goal or for displaying strength – individuals have no intrinsic value. It is impossible for the bureaucratic authority and the public to have an equal relationship. The former gives and the latter passively accepts. The former possesses all the country's key political and economic resources and creates a master–servant relationship through the liberal use of bribes. The clever people quickly notice that once you have stepped onto a high enough rung on the ladder of privilege – and as long as you can stay within the rules of the game – you will have vast riches and freedom. If we assume that absolute dictatorships instil fear, obedience, apathy and a feeling of insignificance in society, we can say that this new dictatorship has brought about a new distortion of society. On the one hand, people still feel as afraid, obedient, numb and insignificant as they did before; on the other, they are allowed to be indulgent, presumptuous, loud and obnoxious.

The announcement of the number of pupils who died in Sichuan underlines these Chinese characteristics. The public are allowed to express empathy, righteousness and a will to participate, but only within the boundaries set by the government. If people want to go outside those boundaries, they face many obstacles. As a result many have lost their initial eagerness and become disheartened as they try to ascertain exactly where the boundaries are. They have become cynical. And the small proportion of people who persist have become embittered.

I am not discussing this issue to make us feel more pessimistic, but rather in the hope that if we can recognize the slow pace of change we might be able to pull off the mask of deception worn by bureaucracy. That way all our efforts will have a more lasting impact.

THE POST-TOTALITARIAN WEATHER

2 May 2010

It was April and spring still hadn't arrived in Beijing. 'We're wearing our winter clothes all the time,' said my friend on the phone. 'If it's not a sandstorm, then it's low clouds and freezing temperatures, as if someone has put a lid on the whole city – I would call this post-totalitarian weather.'

After living in Cambridge for eight months, I felt like I understood why British people always talk about the weather. Blustery winds, rain storms, hail and sunshine could all make an appearance in the course of an hour. Everything in their lives is meticulously planned: when they start work, receive pension payments, go on holiday. They even buy rail tickets to go to Paris a month in advance. Weather, being the one thing that is uncertain, makes for a great topic of conversation. A heavy snowfall is enough to cover the front pages of all the newspapers in Britain. I even remember an article published in *The Times* that used the phrase 'cold war' in reference to the weather. It included a photo of people shovelling snow.

In the United Kingdom, more young people watch *The X-Factor* than participate in general elections, and the worst crime that politicians commit is getting their licence fees paid for as expenses. If you watched the first debate between the three candidates for prime minister in 2010, you would surely have concluded that the British Empire has gone and that the UK is no longer chained to its imperial history. It was also clear that there are no major differences between the Conservatives, Labour and the Liberal Democrats. As a result, the candidates competed on personality, appearance and speaking style. They looked like a group of American MBA graduates competing to become senior vice president of a company. Each candidate tried to seem clever, clean, decisive, aggressive and polite – as a result, they were all tedious. The framework of this country was established long ago, and the reforms which the politicians were proposing were so minor as to not warrant anyone's attention. Some might even say they were less interesting than the changes in the weather.

If the UK's weather represents the end of history, then is the weather in China a sign of future historical unrest? There are dust storms in Beijing, April snow storms in Harbin, droughts in south western China, and an earthquake in Qinghai. But China has always been like this. Its territory is so vast that it is bound to have multiple natural disasters at any given time. Yet if we consider the political defeats and the social dissatisfaction that have also occurred during this period, it does begin to seem like these natural disasters are an omen. The heavens were angry and wanted to punish the people. This was their condemnation of the rulers of China.

If you have lived in Beijing in the past few years, you will probably have experienced 'post-totalitarian weather'. Pollution and dust hang in the air like a giant cover blocking out sunlight and clean air. When the sandstorms come, the weather is truly suffocating and oppressive.

Yet the thing that really makes Beijing locals feel oppressed is not the weather but the house prices. 'No matter who it is or what the occasion, everyone is talking about houses,' a friend said to me. In less than a year, the price of housing has doubled (even tripled in some places). Few people would bat an eyelid at prices as high as 30,000 yuan (£2,800) per square metre. People are generally more irritable as a result of the surging prices. All over Beijing, people have an obsession with houses, just like they do in Hong Kong and Shanghai. Houses have become the exclusive source of happiness, tragedy, security and meaning in life. But beneath the obsession is a deep sense of despair. A person's future prospects have already diminished and dangers are lurking everywhere. We only believe in tangible material things. All we can do is hide in our houses and briefly enjoy a feeling of safety and contentment. It is all part of a tacit agreement made twenty years ago between society and the government. Society gave up its desires for political reform and the government provided an opportunity to live a life, especially in the material sense. This agreement has already provided twenty years of stability, especially for middle-class families living in major cities. They have felt their options in life to be rapidly expanding. They have pretended not to see the other inequalities in society; as long as it did not affect them personally, it did not matter.

But now the temporary feeling of comfort is falling apart. First they discovered that the stock market had made life difficult for them. They had to face a harsh new reality: not only were house prices high enough to wipe out their pathetic savings, but they would continue to drain their future earnings for thirty-odd years. Some were not even given the opportunity to wipe out their many years' worth of savings because they did not have enough for a deposit on a house, even with help from their parents.

In stark contrast to this is the fact that China's economy is growing at a rate of twelve per cent a year. Yet apart from the bureaucracy, no one is able to benefit from this growth. The sixty years of growth in China has not been shared with the people. By robbing the peasants, China developed its heavy industry. By robbing the migrant workers, China became the world's biggest factory and was able to build new skyscrapers. By robbing the middle class, China was able to hasten the formation of a real estate industry. By selling poisonous baby formula and harmful vaccines, China was robbing future generations. Many people are entering a new kind of poverty, and it seems that only the government can preserve its wealth forever.

A dense fog of repression and hopelessness has covered Beijing, making a stark contrast to the jubilant city of two years ago. People are slowly beginning to realize that the glory of a rising power has nothing to do with them as individuals. China has been rising in the international ranks, while its people suffer intense pressure and anxiety. History is repeating itself and freedom is once again being swallowed up by the powers of authoritarianism. There are no changes to the political system, which means that all prosperity is temporary.

THE ELEPHANT IN THE COURTROOM

30 August 2013

In August 2013, as Bo Xilai waited for his trial to begin at the Jinan Intermediate People's Court, I was reminded of another courtroom scene, from almost ninety years ago. Then a politician and his accomplices had been arrested after botching a coup attempt modelled on Mussolini's 'March on Rome'. They were charged with high treason. Much to the surprise of the judge, the defendant had wholeheartedly agreed with the charges against him, except that he saw his failed putsch in the Munich beer hall not as a crime, but as a heroic attempt to save Germany. The man claimed he was not a criminal because he was trying to give Germans a better life. That man was Adolf Hitler.

The public trial rescued him from despair. He knew that he was a gifted speaker and he could influence audiences like a magician. He was in touch with the mood of the nation. He knew that the people were frustrated with a number of problems in their country – humiliating military defeat, enormous war reparations, unbearable hyperinflation, a nominally democratic but ineffective government. He also knew that they wanted to fight back.

His speeches in the People's Court in Munich enchanted Germany and left the rest of the world in awe: crowds of people had to be turned away from the courtroom; women offered him flowers; the newspapers published his story, catapulting him to fame. On 1 April 1924, Hitler was sentenced to five years in prison, but he would be released in December of that year after being pardoned by the Bavarian Supreme Court.

This 'traitor' would singlehandedly change the course of history. A debilitating economic depression and the structure of German society at the time would help him become Führer of an expansionist Reich.

Over ninety years later, a sixty-four-year-old Politburo member faced his own trial in China. Although his was very different from that of the thirty-five-year-old frustrated war veteran, there were some key similarities between the two cases.

When Bo Xilai introduced his political and social agenda in Chongqing, he was undoubtedly the most charismatic politician in China. Looking at his relaxed demeanour, his broad smile, and his decisive way of handling matters, you felt a sense of surprise: in the CCP system, the best are weeded out and the mediocre rise through the ranks; yet somehow this fine character had survived.

In reality, Bo is as dangerous as he is charismatic. In the past four years, he has turned Chongqing into a theme park revolving around the themes of ideology and violence. In his attempt to create a highly effective dictatorial system, he has achieved great efficiencies but at the expense of personal liberty and morality. He has deftly covered up the enormous economic and social cost of his projects, and the people have no idea that his projects are unsustainable in the long term. At the same time he briefly experimented with a personality cult. He was not trying to imitate Mao Zedong so much as imitate the way Hitler operated in the early part of his career. This was most evident in the way Bo exercised totalitarian control in certain areas, while making a series of wonderful promises to the people.

His experiment actually won the hearts of a large number of people. In Chongqing, people noticed that the streets were safer, transportation more convenient, trees planted and civil servants intimidated; the government cracked down on corrupt bureaucrats and organized crime; and built affordable housing. Bo was directly addressing the problems that vexed Chinese society. Perhaps some of his campaigns were a bit dreary, like the red song contests, the publication of revolutionary stories and of stodgy old television programmes. But wasn't it a worthy attempt at redressing the failings of Chinese society, which is becoming more chaotic every day?

His work in Chongqing might be a sign of how China will develop in the future. China and its government is at a crossroads and does not know which route to take. The markets are ruthless and society has lost all sense of order. It is desperate for a powerful leader who can come along and show the way. In other words, China's political situation and society make it a breeding ground for dictators.

Standing in court, Bo was still able to stir up the emotions of the people. When pitting himself against a system that blocks the expression of public opinion – and has a ludicrous judicial arm to boot – he could easily take the moral high ground. Ironically, Bo was both the main target and the elephant in the room. He and the judges both carefully avoided appearing overly earnest, to the point where it became clear that the trial was unimportant.

The exciting days of Chongqing's transformation have already come and gone. In a trial lasting five days, Bo managed to once again sway the people with his scrupulous adherence to form. People praised his grace, his logic and his propriety. He seemed to be acting in the interests of the people. But, when you consider how much damage he has done to individual people and to the system as a whole, that cannot be the case. Bo himself has shown no remorse for the harm he has inflicted on others. On the contrary, in his closing statement he proclaimed his innocence. Ultimately, he came across as very idealistic and supportive of the Party, and he made it clear that he was willing to support Party objectives by any means.

Hitler's rise in 1924 had its roots in a deteriorating economic and social climate, which made him seem like Germany's only saviour. Bo's fate could also change drastically depending on external factors.* If he avoids a heavy sentence, it is even possible that the next time society faces a major crisis he will be seen as a saviour, opening a new set of possibilities for him.

INSUBSTANTIAL REFORMS

21 November 2013

China analyst Simon Leys previously said that 'reading Communist literature is akin to. . . swallowing sawdust by the bucketful'. He pointed out that reports are filled with clichés and slogans, and

---

* On 22 September 2013 Bo Xilai was found guilty of corruption and sentenced to life imprisonment, having earlier been expelled from the Party.

analysts not only have to sift through pages of text to discover subtle differences, they also have to determine the true significance of those subtle differences.

The report on the Third Plenum of the 18th National Party Congress, which took place in November 2013, is no exception. During the Central Committee Plenary Meeting, which is held every five years, President Xi Jinping, who had taken office eight months previously, outlined a series of reforms. Some believed that the ensuing report on the Third Plenum would be as significant as the one that followed the Third Plenum of the 11th Party Congress 1978, in which Deng Xiaoping announced the opening up of the economy.

The only problem is, after seeing the word 'reform' hundreds of times readers are still unsure what it means. At first blush, some minor changes seem to be in store, but in terms of China's way of thinking it remains conservative, perhaps more so than before. The secret location and tightly closed doors of the plenum make it clear that citizen participation has been firmly rejected. Those in power decide about reform and China's future course; having made the decision, they announce it to society without any opportunity for negotiation. The authorities are so absorbed with China's rise that they have forgotten that reform is supposed to be a bottom-up phenomenon. Even at the Third Plenum of 1978 – a meeting the current crop of Party leaders wished to emulate – reform had come from the people. Before that plenum, two dozen villagers of Xiaogang, Anhui province, had signed a pact promising to divide their communal land into individual farms. The Politburo merely approved that decision. The Central Committee in power has forgotten that the thrust of Deng Xiaoping's reform was experimenting with ideas and then replicating them nationwide, not designing schemes and forcing them onto the people.

Simon Leys was an excellent sinologist, but not all of his contemporaries were as gifted. After swallowing so much sawdust, they repeatedly misinterpret China's future direction. In the past, China watchers praised Chairman Mao's revolutionary spirit without understanding that he was the most terrifying dictator in history. They believed that the Cultural Revolution would liberate the people, and failed to grasp the catastrophic reality. They even believed that the CCP would create a just and honest society and found it difficult to believe that it was actually ridden with oppression and deficiencies.

This is how totalitarians rule a country: they manipulate and obscure the meaning of words until everything is ambiguous, putting people into a permanent state of confusion, a state in which the only way they feel they can protect themselves is by following the instructions given to them by the authorities. This of course gives the authorities plenty of room to manoeuvre: they can manipulate meanings and change their course without fear of reproach.

Reading the communiqué and the report on the Third Plenum of the 18th National Party Congress still feels like eating sawdust to me. Yet I have heard puzzling cheers and expressions of approval. It seems that the people who approve of the report have eaten sawdust for so long that they have started to believe they are tasting something with substance. Should I congratulate them for their keen perception, or dismiss them as poor analysts?

True, China has improved significantly since the Mao era, but in terms of its isolation and its manipulation of language, the Party has improved shockingly little. The regime has the entire country in its control; it loves to talk of 'democracy' and 'the people', but in reality it is anti-democratic and constantly thwarts its people. 'Reform' has been bandied about so often that in most cases it has come to mean absolutely nothing. The reforms lack substance, like the emperor's new clothes.

When the leaders of the current administration were first announced, Chinese society was filled with hope. The previous decade of economic development had been commendable and China's status had risen just as quickly as the economy, but people still thought that the Hu Jintao administration amounted to a wasted decade.* Groups representing vested interests had been on the rise and they quickly grabbed the main sources of wealth. Meanwhile, political reform ground to a halt and innovation was restricted. While it looked like everything was growing in the 1990s, in reality substantial reforms were being curtailed. Someone needed to come in and restart reforms, and the new leaders held promise.

Xi Jinping's** authority is automatically increased by his revolutionary pedigree. His father, Xi Zhongxun, was part of the generation that built the People's Republic of China. Xi senior was known for implementing reforms and being relatively open-minded. He was persecuted by the government several times during his life, and suffered personally as a result of internal power struggles. He spent many years working at the lowest levels of government, and then experienced the climax of his political career under Deng.

By contrast, Premier Li Keqiang came to political maturity during an era of enlightenment which began in the late 1970s. He is friends with pro-democracy advocates and his mentor is one of the founders of the modern Chinese market economy.

They may not have the gumption that Gorbachev and Chiang Ching-kuo*** showed, but they do have the potential to give Chinese society a breath of fresh air, as well as to curb

---

* Hu Jintao was the General Secretary of the Communist Party between 2002 and 2012.

** Xi Jinping became General Secretary of the Communist Party of China in November 2012.

*** Chiang Ching-kuo was the son of Chiang Kai-shek, and served as president of the Republic of China (Taiwan) from 1978 until 1988.

the growth of bureaucracy and vested interests. They might relax restrictions on the market economy and civil society, they might ultimately become more open-minded rulers. They are more likely than Hu Jintao and Wen Jiabao* to be at the helm when China faces a difficult international situation, because China's rise has increased international frictions. At least they seem to have more influence than the previous generation.

But over the past year, despite some noteworthy achievements and a few calls for reform, their way of thinking has seemed terribly outdated. They are not moving towards a new era but stubbornly looking backwards. China faces many complex challenges today. Unfortunately, Xi and Li have decided to use heavy-handed measures borrowed from the Mao era to break up the bureaucracy. They have used campaigns to deal with corruption, and outmoded ideology to fill the moral vacuum. They believe that diversity in society will inevitably create conflict and chaos, and are under the illusion that China will become a great power only once all of its citizens believe the same thing. On the international stage, they are making use of nationalism (a blunt and inappropriate tool) and are seen by others as overly aggressive. They continue to believe that China will overtake America and soon rule the world. It is impossible for them to revive the China of the past, but they can create a new China, one ruled by secular nationalism.

For many years, China's problem is that its power has been too consolidated, stifling other voices and making checks on that power unfeasible. China needs community organizations to grow and different voices to express themselves. It does not need a powerful voice telling everyone what to do next.

The determination shown by China's new leaders makes me think of the last German Emperor, Wilhelm II. A historian

---

* Wen Jiabao was premier of the People's Republic of China from 2003 to 2013.

once said that Wilhelm wanted fundamental change and the status quo all at once. He saw Germany as a modernized industrial giant and he established a new agenda for diplomacy. Under his reign, Germany became a formidable naval power for the first time. But at the same time, he held on tightly to old customs and institutions, believing his own power to stem from a pre-modern Prussian dictatorial philosophy.

Historical analogies such as this are, of course, dodgy ground, but everyone knows how the story ended for Wilhelm. Such an ending might not be possible in China today, but it reminds us that even while China celebrates, history may take an unexpected turn.

CHINA: THE INSENSITIVE GIANT

22 May 2014

I.

When I travelled to Vietnam nine years ago, it felt a little like I had travelled back in time. Hanoi reminded me of Beijing in a 1980s summer – slow-paced, simple and insatiably curious. You could see China's influence everywhere you looked. A Confucius Statue stood in the Temple of Literature, a testament to the long-lasting influence that Han literature has had on Vietnam. The only thing was that Confucius did not look like the man the Chinese would recognize; he looked more like a local Vietnamese.

The two countries also share memories of grand twentieth-century revolutions, which have resulted in plenty of patriotically named streets, statues and red flags. Vietnam's revolution was heavily influenced by China. Vietnam's former president, Ho Chi Minh, not only received training and refuge in Guangzhou, in Guangdong province, he even wrote humorous poetry in Chinese.

The mark that China had on Vietnam's politics and economy is undeniable. Three examples will suffice. First of all, beginning in 1991, Vietnam copied most of the ideas Deng Xiaoping had promoted, implementing economic reforms, relaxing government control and encouraging the growth of markets. Secondly, as an economist at the University of Social Sciences and Humanities in Ho Chi Minh City told me it was tremendously difficult for Vietnam to break with Marxist doctrines and establish a market economy. Thirdly, market stalls in alleys sell cheap goods made in China as well as pirated Chinese television dramas.

Some Chinese might get a swelling feeling of superiority after hearing all this. Their country has had a similar influence in other poor communist countries across Asia, including Myanmar, Cambodia and Laos. It has dominated in terms of historical influence, geographical resources, population size, economic output and soft power. A famous writer once said that watching someone else suffer on a road that you have already walked is a pleasure. That is why power is so seductive.

The most memorable moment of my trip was a conversation I had in a café on Ngo Quyen Street. A pleasant Vietnamese writer told me that popular novels by Vietnamese authors tend to feature tall men who are always Chinese. She said Vietnam was usually personified as a subservient woman who is frequently assaulted and needs protection. My café companion had been compared to Zhou Weihui, author of *Shanghai Baby*, and she admitted that Zhou's descriptions of taboo topics had encouraged her to write. I was surprised by what she said, because in the Chinese consciousness, the stronger person in the relationship described in the novel is a white man, and the weak and gentle one is a Chinese woman. In *The Lover* by Marguerite Duras, a Chinese businessman is supposed to be imperious in his affair with a fifteen-year-old French girl, but I found him to be moody and vulnerable, reaffirming the literary stereotype that white people are stronger in any relationship.

The Sofitel Legend Metropole Hotel is only a short walk from the café. That's where novelist Graham Greene wrote *The Quiet American*. The main character, Alden Pyle, is an idealist, fresh out of university and serving as an officer in the US army. Pyle ardently wishes to marry a young Vietnamese woman who lives with a world-weary and cynical British journalist. Later Pyle's ambition grows as he fantasizes about rebuilding Vietnam. *The Quiet American* managed to capture a mood during a historic transition in international affairs. As the US celebrated its rise, Europe felt helpless. Its only options were to ridicule the Americans, accuse them of wrongdoing, or write fiction in which they repeatedly failed.

In reality, America did fail, but never permanently; it always made a spectacular comeback. I travelled through the bamboo-pole-shaped country by minibus, and when I finally arrived in Ho Chi Minh City I could see that many Vietnamese missed the America that they had chased out of the country years ago. Pirated English biographies of Bill Clinton and Hillary Clinton, and memoirs of US soldiers who had served in the Vietnam War, were being hawked all over the city centre. Many locals still called the city Saigon. Their nostalgia was incredibly familiar to me; it made me think of locals in Shanghai wishing they could return to the time when their city was called 'The Paris of the Orient'.

Very few people talked about the Sino-Vietnamese War of 1979. Perhaps they did not want to offend me. I did not ask probing questions because I did not understand much about the war. Thirty years after a war that the Chinese euphemistically called a 'defensive counterattack war', everything appeared to have turned into a mystery.

II.

Nine years have passed since that trip, and many of my memories of it have faded, to be replaced by new ones. But the conversation with the female writer remains as fresh as ever.

A century of Chinese people have grown up believing that, as far as world history is concerned, China is a victim of foreign aggression. Even though the CCP claims that 'the Chinese people finally stood up' in 1949, it never stops emphasizing how it has been invaded by imperialist forces. As the Chinese economy sprinted ahead in the 1990s, nationalistic education was taught to children around the country, and it focused specifically on the 100 years of history in which China was humiliated. That collective sense of humiliation was enough to build a kind of demented national cohesion.

China became strong again, creating a very strange national psychology. Generally we are proud of our long history and our recent rise. But at the same time, we are overly sensitive and angry about the wrongs we have suffered in history. This became apparent during the torch relay in the run-up to the Beijing Olympics. As the whole world watched fashionable and affluent Chinese youths sincerely express their nationalist beliefs, non-Chinese were frustrated by what they saw as mere theatrics.

As well as being oversensitive towards those nations who were once more powerful than us, China also often displays a sluggish response towards those who are more vulnerable. We are so absorbed with our recent history of victimization that we forget that, from the perspective of neighbouring countries, we are in a position of strength, not weakness.

Nine years ago, China's influence was expanding faster than ever before. That expansion has continued and has had a profound impact not just on China but on its neighbours.

Explaining the current situation would require a story much more complicated than the one written by Graham Greene.

China's neighbours are fully aware that China is a dominant power. They also believe that history is repeating itself. Commenters on South East Asian affairs have been making allusions to the tributary system of imperial China for quite some time: if China becomes as powerful as it was in imperial times, it will expect other Asian nations to kowtow to it. Equally important is the fact that until very recently China was a totalitarian state bent on exporting revolution. Such ideology and its political logic has not been completely eradicated. China is still a closed government, which has implications for the rest of the world.

When it comes to reducing these anxieties, Beijing is at a loss. This has always been a thorny issue: at the end of the 1970s, Deng Xiaoping met with then prime minister of Singapore, Lee Kuan Yew. Deng hoped that Lee would join China in the fight against Soviet imperialism. He was taken aback when Lee said that South East Asia's chief worry was in fact the communist ideology exported by China.

No matter whether China calls its changes a 'peaceful rise', or uses a more euphemistic term like 'peaceful development', there is no way to dispel the misgivings that other countries feel. First and foremost, there are very few countries in the history of the world who have had a 'peaceful rise', because a rising country frequently leads to conflict and disorder. In the past two years, China has abandoned this euphemism and acted tough instead.

China is not the same as before; it is no longer exporting revolution or causing humanitarian disasters in the name of ideology. However, it is still willing to preserve its own interests by any means. Granted, every country must do what it can to protect its own interests, and those actions are going to affect others. The problem is that the China of today has immense power and at the same time shocks people with its lack of moral principles. So of course its rise causes unease.

When it comes to ethics, China is obtuse in a way that affects political authority and Chinese society in general. Chinese people are totally unaware of how their country negatively affects the lives of people in other countries. After the death of Kim Jong-il, Chinese people made fun of the images of North Koreans weeping hysterically at the loss of their leader, calling them aliens from another planet. Have they forgotten that only thirty-five years ago Chinese people mourned the death of Mao Zedong in the same way? Wasn't Mao a tyrant just like Kim? More importantly, China's support has been instrumental in creating the situation that prevails in North Korea today. Most of the educated Chinese elite, not to mention average people, do not bother to think about the feelings of people in North Korea, Myanmar, Syria, Sudan, Vietnam or Cambodia.

Is there any way to explain why China is so obtuse when it comes to morals and sympathy for others? A political dictatorship causes the people under it to have a distorted view of the world, so that they do not properly understand events that take place outside of their country. More importantly, people spend their time avoiding conflicts with the government and because the government's mistakes have nothing to do with them, they feel like they do not have any responsibility in the matter. People restrict themselves by only looking out for their self-interests and struggling with their own pain. As a result, they are too busy to pay attention to the pain that others feel. It is possible that most people in China believe in the law of the jungle and nothing else. They believe themselves to be victims while they act like oppressors.

This underlines the biggest flaws in China's rise – lack of wisdom and a broken moral compass. Chinese people have now settled all over the world, but they have no knowledge of the cultures they live in, and no way of understanding the anxiety and sufferings that the locals face. And what's worse, they are not interested in finding out.

If China believes only in pushing development and the ruthless struggle to satisfy self-interest, then it will use those same beliefs when it interacts with the rest of the world. If China is truly interested in winning respect, it must first learn to reflect on its own actions and to understand the anxiety and pain of others. But as long as our warped political system remains in place, these changes are unlikely to occur any time soon.

THE LEGEND OF JACK MA

18 March 2015

'It is true that a man of Napoleon's truth of adaptation to the mind of the masses around him, becomes not merely representative, but actually a monopolizer and usurper of other minds,' Ralph Waldo Emerson once wrote. In his book, *Representative Men*, Emerson considered the French leader to be the psychological representative of nineteenth-century France, and even all of Europe, because he was born into a modest family but had the potential to rise to prominence, and did. The dramatic political and social changes of the French Revolution provided unprecedented opportunities for the youth of France – it even allowed people from remote areas to climb up to the apex of political power.

I thought of Emerson's quote while watching Jack Ma on television. On 22 September 2014, Jack Ma, a former English teacher, broke the record for the largest US-listed initial public offering in history. He established his company, Alibaba, in 1999 and it quickly rose up the ranks of the world's most valuable companies. Countries across the West were obsessed with Ma's story, because it represented the larger story of China's economic and political rise. Ma also represented the way in which China would begin to play a leading role on the international stage in the twenty-first century.

In 1992, the year of Deng Xiaoping's 'Southern Tour', Jack Ma founded a translation agency. In 1994, he was first introduced to the Internet. When he founded an online commerce platform called Alibaba, nobody took him seriously. People joked that he would soon discover that 'open sesame' did not unlock every door.

But Alibaba *did* unlock doors. Its timing was good, and it was one of many Chinese companies which integrated into the world economy. China needed new channels to sell its products if it wanted to become the factory of the world, and Ma provided a platform for small businesses. Then he managed to take advantage of rapidly increasing consumption within China. Companies under Alibaba Group, including Taobao and Lynx, claimed their own sales records. His company handled enormous numbers of transactions and capital flows, compelling him to enter the finance industry. In order to increase access, he made changes in retail, distribution and wholesaling.

Alibaba now has its tentacles in so many different areas it has become like Amazon, eBay and Facebook all rolled into one. It has even announced that it wants to expand its platforms to other countries.

Ma is different from other Chinese entrepreneurs. He speaks fluent English and has a charming personality. He relates his life story clearly and with ease. His words and actions and his obvious ambition frequently remind people of tech titans from Silicon Valley, except that he can also talk about Tai Chi and the philosophy of martial arts. In some ways he reminds people of the businessman Akio Morita, the co-founder of Sony, because both came from the unfamiliar East and have been extremely successful in America. They both have a power and a philosophy that leaves others in awe.

People in China are obsessed by Ma's rags-to-riches story. Besides being a successful business executive, he is a rock star, a life coach and a prophet. He has the ear of government officials, bankers and businessmen; and he gives speeches that leave packed gymnasiums enraptured. He is the idol of countless young people in China. Someone recently drew a cartoon portraying him as the god of fortune. It is as if he has the Midas touch.

People have strong feelings about him not just because of his impressive wealth but because of how he earned it. Alibaba is about more than just commerce. It enabled small- and medium-sized businesses in China to participate in the global market and innumerable individuals to set up new enterprises. He has shaken up the structure of business and employment in China. Alipay, a payment-processing affiliate founded by Ma, has helped rebuild the system of trust in Chinese society. His online platform has let hundreds of millions of Chinese participate in ecommerce, whether as producers or consumers. Bargaining hard and surrounded by products, people feel a sense of belonging and a sense of accomplishment. These simple feelings are lacking in everyday life and are extremely valuable to people. Beautiful cities still basking in their former glory have been transformed into modern centres of production and consumption.

And most of all, Ma is one of them. He was born into an ordinary family, has had an ordinary education and looks ordinary. His first projects were relatively unsuccessful and he was considered a failure. Ultimately he changed himself into a success by his own hard work. He is worthy of the epithet 'the people's tycoon'.

In fact, he is more like the American business tycoons of the Gilded Age – John D. Rockefeller, J. P. Morgan, Leland Stanford and Jay Gould – than the tech titans of today's Silicon Valley. Those men built railways, formed oil trusts, and founded the American stock market. They established business organizations that are still in existence today and they represented a dream held by many Americans that anyone could get rich if they worked hard. To the rest of the world, they represented the rise in America's power. At the end of the nineteenth century, America transformed itself from regional power to world power.

Though they were not politicians, the tycoons' impact included dramatic political and social change. Their extraordinary wealth caused so much controversy that some vilified them as robber barons. A new period, called the Progressive Era, was born out of these frustrations. Politicians, journalists and union leaders all tried to make America a fairer place. Tycoons formerly labelled as robber barons built some of America's greatest universities, museums and libraries, using their wealth to enact social progress.

Modern China is undergoing a transition similar to that of the United States at the end of the nineteenth century. Yet the large amounts of wealth Jack Ma and other tycoons are able to create has not equated to greater political or social influence. The flip side of China's economic miracle is the possibility that, since nothing is protected by the rule of law, any individual or company could be attacked at some point. Not even someone as successful as Jack Ma is immune to this.

China's businesses face two major challenges. The first is ideological: for hundreds of years, merchants were considered members of the lowest class. Society still believes that they lack moral fortitude, and so rarely gives them an opportunity to play leading roles. The other is political. In modern China – as in ancient China – the government does not recognize private property. As a result, business owners are weak in the face of state power. They have to be careful not to disturb the delicate balance between business and bureaucracy. In practice, they frequently have to use bribes and other corrupt measures to continue doing business. The fact that they must submit to state power generally prevents them from acting according to their will. When the state tends to be more open and relaxed, business owners work feverishly during what they know is an indefinite window of opportunity. They are constantly competing to be recognized as capitalists supported by the Party. This explains Ma's inappropriate comments about the Tiananmen incident, in which he implied that Deng's decision was not a perfect one, but the most correct one. Alibaba quickly released a statement after the article had been published, saying, 'Alibaba has inadvertently touched upon some subjects which it does not have experience in handling. . . The company feels powerless.'

Even if the leadership in China centralizes power the way Putin has in Russia, Ma will not become a threat in the way that Mikhail Khodorkovsky, the former oil billionaire, was for Putin. Within the existing political system, there is no possible way for Ma to become a challenger.

I interviewed Ma about fourteen years ago, in a café in Fuxingmen, Beijing. At that time, Alibaba was a small enterprise from southern China tirelessly seeking market visibility and Ma was eager to have a chat with journalists who wanted to know more about him. He left a favourable impression on me. I remember that he was interested in answering the more philosophical questions I put to him, and that he spoke so eloquently that I was reluctant to interrupt him.

Jack Ma is the 'representative man' of this era and many people believe him to be as influential as Napoleon was in his time. He is a combination of the people's best qualities and their most ambitious dreams.

FEAR AND FEARLESSNESS

THE DIFFICULTY OF DEFENDING LEGAL RIGHTS

5 August 2010

The car stopped at Jimen Bridge in Beijing and Xu Zhiyong got out: 'The worst that can happen is that I'm arrested and imprisoned. Nothing too bad.' We didn't take the possibility very seriously. At dinner that evening, he had seemed as confident and optimistic as ever, even though the Open Constitution Initiative (Gongmeng) in defence of human rights that he led had been closed down by the authorities nine days before. The reason given was 'tax evasion', but everyone knew quite well that this was political repression and the tax charge was a pretext.

Since the 2003 Sun Zhigang case, Xu Zhiyong has become one of China's most celebrated human rights lawyers. The traditional way of appealing against local government decisions in China is to go to Beijing to petition for justice. He worked on behalf of these petitioners, claiming damages on behalf of parents whose children were poisoned by melamine-tainted milk, visiting 'black jails' where petitioners are illegally detained, and was beaten up and detained for his pains. All because he sought justice for those who had suffered and could not speak for themselves.

The Gongmeng, which he co-founded, was one of China's most famous NGOs; it mustered scores of lawyers who offered free legal aid for community groups working for various different causes, from the abolition of the enforced removal of people from their homes back to their registered birthplace, to the defence of Deng Yujiao, who stabbed to death a man who was trying to rape her. Gongmeng presented in microcosm a picture of the legal process in China over the last six years, and showed how a group of young people can use the power of the law to help ordinary people obtain their basic legal rights, and respect. They favoured a constructive approach, promoting citizens' rights by means of concrete actions, and offering hope and confidence to those desperate people who face ridicule in the public arena. As Xu Zhiyong himself said in a lecture, he and his fellow lawyers worked towards unity, consensus, participation and dedication. They were making small efforts to change the iniquitous political climate that has prevailed in China for so long. At times they were successful, at other times they failed. Of course, they also fell foul of powerful interest groups, because every time they won justice for those who had suffered, the privileges of the privileged were commensurately reduced.

Behind the unremitting efforts of Gongmeng and Xu Zhiyong lies a country where social tensions are sharpening day by day. Economic progress no longer brings widespread benefits to the whole of society and the gap between rich and poor continues to widen. Politics and business have forged a new alliance, allowing a cartel of dominant interests to emerge. The opportunities available to ordinary people have diminished and the benefits of progress have eroded. Political power has become bloated with money, and that has warped the economy. The distorted economy, in turn, has inflicted damage on the natural environment and trampled morality underfoot, adding to the toll of victims. As the engine of China's gigantic economy rumbles forward, many people are crushed beneath its wheels their cries drowned out and unheard.

These victims have few alternatives: they can go home and lick their wounds, they can pack into petitioners' camps and wait in vain for justice, or they can stand silently outside the law courts, the chief prosecutor's office, or even the China Central TV station, holding up placards demanding redress. Those in the media are unlikely to give them space, not only because they have been brainwashed but also because the media is awash with cheap entertainment. The elite pays little attention to petitioners; they would much prefer to hype up the topic of China's global leadership and economic growth. The weak are simply regarded as unavoidable victims of the process of development. Bureaucracy is even less likely to be interested in their plight since the regime is built on the philosophy of contempt for human dignity. People are no more than tools or materials. After all, if Premier Liu Shaoqi could be beaten to death during the Cultural Revolution, why should these people expect any better? As for the vast masses of the Chinese public, let them better themselves by their own efforts, and gain a modicum of security that way.

A new reality has been created where power and money are all that count, and justice, sympathy and conscience have fallen by the wayside. The strength of the powerful, far from making them feel compassion and responsibility for the vulnerable, simply makes them arrogant and indifferent. The vulnerable feel angry and resentful and, perhaps because they have lost all sense of self-respect, they'll do whatever it takes to get redress. Somewhere between these two extremes is the majority: those who have felt neither the arrogance of power, nor the humiliation of being at the bottom of the heap. They take a generally flippant and scornful attitude to the predicaments of others, but beneath that lies a deep sense of helplessness. Reality is hard to change, so they tacitly accept it.

Xu Zhiyong and his fellow lawyers were a beacon of hope. They refused to follow the traditional trajectory of intellectuals who imagine they can change China by writing manifestos about freedom, democracy and the constitution. They were well aware that freedom, democracy and constitutional government are no more than empty words unless they are given meaning through concrete changes in the law. They never expressed their political opinions by openly challenging government because they favoured a pragmatic approach, and changing the fate of individuals, and because extremism only achieves the personal goals of a minority. They tried to inject order and hope into this chaotic and angry society. They believed construction to be so much more powerful than destruction.

But even this approach got them into trouble. The assets of Gongmeng were seized on 14 July. Then, at dawn on 29 July, thirty-six-year-old Xu Zhiyong was taken away by the police. It is unclear what the reason was or where he was taken to. The prediction he had made to me in a casual conversation on the evening of 23 July had unfortunately come true. I remember that evening he was his usual optimistic self, convinced that Chinese society as a whole was set to progress and develop, and that the public mood, and the spread of information through the Internet, would force the government to abandon its cavalier attitude towards its citizens.

Xu Zhiyong liked to emphasize the importance of acting together. If the core goal of dictatorship is to destroy community organization and turn everyone into individual grains of sand, helpless in their isolation, then uniting, helping and taking responsibility for others is the most effective way of opposing dictatorship. Yes, we should use all possible means to support Xu Zhiyong, and to get Gongmeng working again, so that we can tell them: You are not helpless in your isolation.[*]

ANOTHER TURNING POINT?

24 October 2010

In the three weeks following the award of the Nobel Peace Prize to Liu Xiaobo, anyone with even the slightest interest in politics could sense the mounting tension. Cui Weiping has been arrested, Xu Youyu

---

[*] In January 2014, Xu Zhiyong was sentenced to four years imprisonment for 'gathering crowds to disrupt public order'.

is in detention, Yu Jie is under house arrest, and Liu Suli has been hospitalized after being injured when resisting forcible removal by six officers from the Domestic Security Department (DSD).

As the *People's Daily* newspaper mounted a campaign against Liu, Norway and other Western countries, there has been a new round of political repression. This has clearly showed the increasing powerlessness of the Chinese government. The government did not know how to react to the award, and so it has picked the weapons it is most proficient at using: shameless propaganda and gangster-style violence. The regime seems intent both on showing how anxious the prize has made it, and on pretending that it could not care less. The message is, 'If any of you pay attention to these "Western anti-Chinese powers", we will arrest you.'

These four – Cui Weiping, Xu Youyu, Yu Jie and Liu Suli – are outstanding examples of China's dissident community. Their reputations have caused them a lot of grief, although they have also afforded them some protection. Some less famous people have been arrested and beaten up just for drinking toasts to brave human rights activists who have never won a Nobel Prize, before being summarily 'deported' to wherever their ID card records as their place of birth. This new criminal charge is so preposterous that people have invented a phrase for it: 'drunk and disorderly'.

There are very few people who understand what is going on here. The Internet revolution has not only brought about an opening up and spreading of information, but has contributed to people shutting themselves off and only caring about what is happening in their own small community. When something earth-shattering happens within one group, it can remain completely unknown to another. The joy that Liu Xiaobo's prize brought to some, and the plight of these four intellectuals, are good examples of such isolated events. In the callous, mindless maelstrom that is daily life, they don't stand comparison with the romance between the Taiwanese actress Barbie Hsu and the entrepreneur from Mainland China Wang Xiaofei.

Nevertheless, Liu Xiaobo's Peace Prize came at what one could call a turning point for China, (though the phrase is often misused). No matter how confused society's values are, and how much the interests of different social classes diverge, a consensus has been reached: things must change. And those changes must reach the political system, otherwise the economy will stagnate and there will be an explosion of social tensions.

For a lot of people, Premier Wen Jiabao's bold speeches are far more indicative of change than Liu Xiaobo's Nobel Prize. The former marks a schism within the upper echelons of the Party, with the reformists once again making themselves heard. In the two years since the 18th National Party Congress, the shift in power has brought with it new possibilities. And schisms and changes at the top level of politics will win breathing space for all kinds of social forces. Because of the depth of corruption within the old system and a sharpening of social tensions, it is possible that these changes, rather than merely causing an adjustment within the system, may actually bring about fundamental changes. When people say 'fundamental changes' in China, they mean something like what happened twenty years ago, at the end of the Eighties, in Taiwan, Eastern Europe and the Soviet Union, or the demise of the Qing dynasty in 1911. Imagine you are a user of Weibo, you might feel that China is on the brink of such changes, because of the corruption of officialdom, the collapse of social morality, and increasing tensions between officials and ordinary people. The present situation can only be changed, you might think, by a storm that sweeps away everything in its path.

But this may also be to overstate what's possible. Some people throw themselves into discussions about potential change as if they're rebelling against a long period of repression, when in fact their enthusiastic talk about momentous social change is akin to a youthful sexual fantasy: the less likely it is to come to fruition, the more uninhibited the language used to describe it.

The Communist Party's regime may well be stupider and weaker than people imagine, but its very lack of principles, together with its nihilism, has often given it great strength. Even more importantly, the Party is not an import from outside. It was born in this society and of this people, and is an integral part of every individual's life. Sun Liping, the sociologist, was right: Chinese society is rotten and the reason for this is the dominance of, and corruption in, the Party. And it is very hard for a rotten society to give birth to forces that seriously challenge the status quo.

I may sound defeatist when I say this. I may even – as one friend put it – have 'lost my political imagination'. But in today's China, even if big changes do come about, I suspect they will make sober analysts say, as Lu Xun put it ruefully: This is just old wine in new bottles.

FROM YANG ZHENNING TO LIU XIAOBO

31 October 2010

A number of years ago, I was watching a retrospective on the physicist Yang Zhenning on TV. In his words, the significance of the Nobel Prize for Physics he was awarded in 1957 was that 'It gave the Chinese people confidence internationally.'

The generation that lived through war and invasion will know only too well what he meant. There was a time when the self-confidence of Chinese people had reached rock bottom. They felt inferior in everything – even being a race with yellow skin and black eyes seemed to be a problem.

As a result, the goal of generations of Chinese has been to be a rich and powerful country and to achieve technological progress, a thriving literary scene and success in sports. The question is, however, whether Yang Zhenning's success was because he was Chinese or because he was working within the American research system. The truth is, if he had returned to China, as his friend Deng Jiaxian did, he would certainly never have received the honour.

However, Deng Jiaxian raised Chinese self-confidence by other means. He led the country's pioneering research into the atomic bomb and the hydrogen bomb, and became known as the 'father of China's Nuclear Programme'. The success of this work was a cause for national celebration. China was now one of the few countries in the world with nuclear weapons and need no longer worry about Stalin's point that, 'Those who fall behind get beaten.' Yet this new confidence had been hard won. Life for ordinary Chinese remained miserable and harsh, even for Deng Jiaxin. He did not even have a decent house to welcome Yang Zhenning when he came to visit, and hardly said a word during their conversation.

Since Yang Zhenning and Li Zhengdao, a considerable number of Chinese have won Nobel prizes, mostly in the sciences, but all of them were educated and worked overseas or in Taiwan. It is all very well for us, as Chinese, to bask in their reflected glory, but their success has nothing to do with China, and was only achieved by their leaving the country. Cui Qi, winner of the Nobel Prize for Chemistry in 1998, was born in Hunan and it was only good luck that saved him from dying like his parents during the Great Famine (1959–61).

China may have become richer and more powerful but its 'Nobel Prize complex' is as acute as ever. As far as the regime is concerned, winning a Nobel Prize is up there with making the atomic bomb, exploring space and hosting the Olympic Games, as proof of the superiority of the system, proof that it is capable of intellectual achievements as well as material wealth. So many Chinese intellectuals suffer extreme anxiety about the West. Because there is no way to achieve meaningful recognition domestically, they are desperate for recognition from their international peers.

Of course, the Nobel prizes for the sciences are beyond most ordinary people's ken. As a result, the Nobel literary and economics prizes are very emotional issues. Few peoples have endured more tragedy and hardship than the Chinese in the twentieth century. Their experiences should have nurtured great writers, who should have won the Nobel Prize for Literature. Yet the only one to have done so is Gao Xingjian,* a writer who was forced into exile and has taken French nationality. At least we can comfort ourselves that the issue might be that Chinese is a very particular language. But the language of economics is international. In thirty years of rapid development, surely we should have produced one economist worthy of the Nobel Prize.

No one is prepared to acknowledge that, for the last sixty years, the regime in China has treated its best brains as enemies. Political power, ideology and censorship are all-pervasive and there is no space for free investigation. In these circumstances, how is creativity to flourish?

Generally, Chinese people feel much less emotional about the Nobel Peace Prize. The Dalai Lama, winner in 1989, is largely regarded as an outsider. And anyway, in comparison with physics, chemistry, literature and economics, 'peace' seems too abstract a concept. For a century, the Chinese have been too occupied with their myriad problems to focus on broader world issues. Our insensitivity towards North Korea, Myanmar and Sudan makes this clear. The Peace Prize is always connected with world conflicts, and we are only really concerned with our own conflicts.

* These words were written before Mo Yan won the Nobel Prize in Literature in 2012.

We are convinced that the people of the world value our economic growth and sports spectaculars, and are largely unaware that our domestic conflicts are equally significant to them.

Many Chinese like to say that we have taken only sixty years to cover the distance that the West took several hundred to cover. We are overwhelmingly proud of our leap forward from an agricultural society to a player in the era of global capitalism. This pride is not misplaced, but we also need to experience the process of building a modern system of democratic government, which protects freedom and human rights.

When Liu Xiaobo won the Nobel Peace Prize, it was not only a tribute to his moral courage and advocacy of non-violence, it also showed the lamentable reality of China today. Where else in this day and age can someone be condemned for speaking out and sentenced to eleven years in prison for proposing mild reforms? This country, in one sense, is undergoing continuous change, and in another sense, is alarmingly stuck in the past.

Yet at the same time, just as with Yang Zhenning, this Peace Prize ought to make many Chinese feel more confident because it rewards conscience rather than intellect. We not only need to build a prosperous and strong China, we need it to value justice, have a sense of right and wrong, and to respect the individual. It is only this kind of China that can fill each one of us with confidence.

YU JIE WEEPS FOR LIU XIAOBO

7 November 2010

'Awake all night, crying my eyes out' Yu Jie's text message to me a week ago read. He was in California, watching the Nobel Peace Prize Committee announce at their televised press conference that this year's winner was Liu Xiaobo, a man currently incarcerated in a Chinese prison. Yu Jie may have wept tears of joy when Liu Xiaobo won the Nobel Prize, but he had to admit that society itself seemed generally indifferent. It is impossible to underestimate the resilience of the Party and the amnesia prevalent in Chinese society.

I can well imagine that Yu Jie felt conflicting emotions, that his jubilation was matched by grief. He has been Liu Xiaobo's closest friend for the last ten years, and the pair were involved in the Independent Chinese PEN Centre, which provides temporary refuge for a small group of dissidents in this huge country.

While the cruelty of the government machine is appalling, the internal struggles among those who oppose it are equally worrying. The twin pressures are so great that it is almost impossible to find people who can maintain their independence *and* a constructive attitude. It is extremely depressing. China has plunged to an all-time low. Its dissidents behave no better than those in power; they are incurably dogmatic and forever fighting among themselves. At the same time, those who oppose the government are increasingly perturbed at international ambivalence towards China: the countries of the democratic West often criticize China for its human rights record, but they then queue up to do business with it. They praise the effectiveness of the 'Chinese model' and treat democracy, freedom and human rights as if they were simply historical relics.

'Just when you feel most hopeless, God suddenly gives you a gift,' said Yu Jie. The Peace Prize was a protest against an unfair trial and an encouragement to long-repressed and ignored dissident forces. Possibly just as important, it was an affirmation of the spirit of gentleness, gradualism and tolerant opposition. Liu Xiaobo and the other signatories of 'Charter 08' manifest a spirit rare in Chinese history; they are not into a zero-sum game, nor are they infatuated with power and violence.

There was jubilation over dinner. Yu Jie had just returned to Beijing and we met with a group of friends in a local restaurant. For several days, you could almost smell the joy floating in the air of Beijing. People got together in bars, as happy as if they were in love and anxious to spread the good news to others. 'You know what? The prize money is 10 million yuan (£900,000), enough to buy the nicest house in the best area of town!' That was how a friend tried to explain to a taxi driver who Liu Xiaobo was, and the value of the Nobel Peace Prize.

Joy floating in the air may be an exaggerated way of putting it, but that was how we psyched ourselves up, because the vast majority in this city of seventeen million had not the faintest idea who Liu Xiaobo was. Although in one well-known university, the teacher in charge of the student union warned students not to organize any politically sensitive activities because, 'A dissident author called Liu Xiaobo has won the Nobel Peace Prize.'

Following the campaign mounted against him by the official media, Liu Xiaobo's name has become better known. But has his winning the prize had any significant impact in China?

The jury's still out on that one. Historical analogies are not appropriate here, because Liu Xiaobo is neither Andrei Sakharov who won in 1975, nor Aung San Suu Kyi, the 1991 winner. These two Peace Prize laureates were already famous in their own countries, and enjoyed huge popularity. (Even so, the effect they had on the political situation in their countries was nowhere near as clear-cut as romantics like to make out.)

'It automatically brought the opposition together,' said a friend, commenting on the effect of the Peace Prize. Liu Xiaobo suddenly became the leader of those opposing the government. His challenge to Premier Wen Jiabao on the issue of political reform could also be construed as awakening the liberal faction within the Party. As far as my friend was concerned, the combination of these two forces would change China. I believe this is the major reason for many people's optimism.

I am not prepared to comment on this. I feel rather uneasy that we take such a utilitarian view of these issues, as if high emotions and convictions have no independent importance unless they can be transformed into concrete action and results.

On the sofa at the entrance to the restaurant sat seven or eight young people, despatched to monitor Yu Jie's movements, as if there was anxiety that this frail writer suddenly posed an incalculable threat. But there was a change in the atmosphere of this monitoring. The old Party ideology no longer held sway, and the youths could not honestly maintain that they were rendering their services to country and Party. They were just doing a job. It is usually futile to try and appeal to their humanity. This was no scene from *The Lives of Others*. You often feel that Chinese society has sunk into what Hannah Arendt called 'the banality of evil'. Everyone shrugs their shoulders helplessly and allows the system, weighed down by inertia as it is, to carry on. There is no prospect of immediate change.

A MOMENT OF ABSURDITY

12 December 2010

Two and a half years ago, a columnist in a British newspaper compared the Beijing Olympics of 2008 to the Berlin Olympics of 1936 (see page 144), noting a similar ugliness and evil lurking beneath the brilliant surfaces of the sporting spectacles. Many people have dismissed this comparison as nonsense because Beijing has no ambitions to impose a new world order, still less an issue with Jews. It is easy for the casual visitor to be taken in by China's façade of prosperity and openness, and to see the German analogy as scare-mongering. Such a visitor may also dismiss as irrelevant any comparison between Liu Xiaobo and the 1975 Soviet winner of the Nobel Peace Prize, Andrei Sakharov. People feel the term 'totalitarianism' is outmoded and too redolent of the Cold War, quite inapplicable to a China that is rapidly embracing global capitalism.

However, it must now be acknowledged that the Berlin analogy – while inappropriate in many ways – is not totally absurd. Liu Xiaobo is only the second winner of the Nobel Peace Prize since 1936 who has been unable to collect his prize either in person or via a family member. In 1936, the Nazi German government said that it would allow the winner of the 1935 prize, Carl von Ossietzky, a news reporter and pacifist, to go to Norway to collect it but did not issue him with a passport. Ossietzky died two years later in Berlin. Even by the standards of the many dictatorships of the last half of the twentieth century, Beijing's decision seems unforgiving. In 1975, Sakharov was unable to leave the Soviet Union but his wife went in his place; in 1983, the Polish military regime allowed Lech Wałęsa's wife to collect his prize; in 1991, Aung San Suu Kyi's son picked up her prize and delivered her speech.

This is a time of absurdity. For the last few years, Beijing has been trumpeting China's 'peaceful rise', yet on this occasion has shouted itself hoarse in condemnation of the world's most important peace prize. It has labelled democracy, human rights and freedom as Western constructs, and now 'peace' has become untrustworthy too. Chinese officials view the Nobel Peace Prize as a stick that is being used to inflict a vicious beating on China – as a plot to control it. Not content with expressing its view through the media, the regime has openly put pressure on the Norwegian government. When you add to this the fact that in the last year China has increasingly acted as regional strongman, coming into conflict with the countries it borders, you can easily see that this is an internally oppressive and externally aggressive state.

Thus the hypothesis of the last nearly twenty years – that economic development would temper the grip of the regime, and that a China that was increasingly part of the global process would gradually become a responsible great power – has been destroyed at a stroke. However, until the existing power structure changes, newly created wealth and techno-logical advances can only reinforce the logic of that structure. China, the country that in the frothy language of the media wants to become a new world leader, is now revealing its true face, just like a monkey climbing a tree and showing off its scarlet buttocks.

But that does not mean that China is the new Germany or Soviet Union, out to change the world order. Beijing does not promote its ideology overseas. Its policies are entirely prag-matic; it is a narrow-minded bureaucracy only concerned with immediate interests. It responds slowly and awkwardly to changes in the outside world, and its chief interests are inward-rather than outward-looking. Since it has no principles to speak of it has great flexibility externally. When a rising diplomatic tension threatens to get out of control, it can make a remarkable volte-face. Internally too, when social tensions are about to boil over, it can make a few concessions and calm things down. The regime did exactly that twenty years ago, abandoning its isola-tionist position to become the world's factory and an enticing market for consumer goods; while relaxing some of its controls on the domestic front, and using consumer production and spending to keep a whole generation happy.

Nowadays, China seems to be facing one crisis after another, as does the Party. The international situation is no longer as benign as it was, and there is increasing international disil-lusionment with China. Domestically, dissatisfaction is shown in the more than 90,000 civil disturbances that break out every year. But do not imagine that change will come quickly. The Party's regime is far quicker on its feet than were the

Communist parties of the Soviet Union or the satellite states of Eastern Europe in 1989. In no time at all, it can make itself look friendly again, and people are so forgetful they just assume that real change has occurred.

At the same time, the resilience of Chinese society is far greater than commonly imagined: the disturbances of 1989 largely centred on the intelligentsia and city-dwellers, and did not reach the wider Chinese population. Twenty-one years later, the Party has succeeded in corrupting the whole of society, destroying all forces that might have posed a serious challenge to its power. The difficulty facing most of its people is that they are dissatisfied with the current situation but they cannot imagine other possibilities and are afraid of the upheavals that might follow radical change.

That means that for a very long time to come, the Chinese state will continue to be both powerful, wealthy, and depraved. It mistreats its own citizens and despises universal human values; it then brings this cruelty and lack of principle into the international arena.

DOMESTIC TERROR

24 April 2011

No one believes in the Party any more, but the Party still decides everything. It has locked up the Nobel Peace Prize winner and sacked liberal editors like Li Datong and Di Minglei; it has shackled its netizen activists; and is now levelling accusations at Ai Weiwei, a world-famous artist and son of Ai Qing, the celebrated early Party revolutionary. The cost of maintaining domestic stability has outstripped the military budget. Essentially this demonstrates that it spends more money defending itself against its own people than it does against external enemies.

lena Bonner, an outstanding Soviet Union human rights activist, recalled what happened under Stalin. A friend of her parents was arrested, and her mother refused to believe that the friend had committed a crime. Her father, Bonner wrote, 'replied in a strange, pleading voice, "But... how can I not believe?"'* The Party is the arbiter of everything, laying down the law, deciding what is right and wrong, what is beautiful and what is ugly. It takes possession of you, body and soul, so of course it can make the judgment that you have committed a crime.

The China of 2011 is similar to the Soviet Union of the 1930s, not only because it occupies centre stage in world politics and is seen as offering another way of doing things, but also because its achievements are constructed on the human rights it has trampled underfoot. Of course, the persuasiveness and power of today's CCP to terrorize is nowhere near that of Stalin's Russia, and further still from China in the Mao Zedong era. Elena Bonner's father could only sigh in helpless self-mockery, while Gao Ying, mother of Ai Weiwei is quoted as exclaiming, 'If only I could go to the scaffold to support him!' (Of course, no one who is acquainted with Ai Weiwei will believe for a minute the charge of 'economic crimes' levelled at him.)

No one believes the Party, but the Party still decides everything, saying and doing anything it wants. Its spokesperson told a foreign journalist, 'Stop harping on about the law. . . no law can protect [Ai Weiwei].' When the journalist questioned the length of Ai Weiwei's detention, the answer came back that the investigation was in accordance with the law, and foreigners did not have the right to interfere in China's domestic affairs.

Twenty years ago, Wang Shuo mounted an offensive against Party ideological language with his motto, 'I'm a bad boy, I'm

---

* From Orlando Figes, *The Whisperers: Private Life in Stalin's Russia.*

not afraid of anyone.' Nowadays those words come from a Communist Party spokesperson.

The Party does indeed seem to be afraid of no one. 'We don't care about criticism from America or Europe, and you can't do anything about it,' seems to be the message. At the same time, it feels itself hemmed in on all sides; the cost of maintaining domestic stability has outstripped the military budget. Essentially this demonstrates that it spends more defending itself against its own people than it does against external enemies. The accidental death of a village head, the slightest show of independent thought on the part of a student, everything triggers a fearful overreaction.

Its own fear makes it terrorize others. Terror eliminates people's capacity to think, stifling their imagination and destroying their unity; each individual becomes a solitary atom. However great their suffering, all they can do is grin and bear it.

'We feel powerless,' a twenty-eight-year-old from Hunan province said to me when we were talking about Ai Weiwei. I understand what he means. You see, in China you can be picked up at any moment even if you are the idol of China's youth, the son of Ai Qing, have appeared in the *New York Times*, and have Western politicians appealing on your behalf. Imagine if you are just an ordinary person. You can see that society is unfair and you are idealistic, but once you've been carted off to the county police station, all your beautiful ideals will be extinguished and no one will know your miserable fate.

Lies and violence are the dual cornerstones of a totalitarian system and they have become more potent than ever in Chinese society over the last decade. Now new lies are being created around 'nationalism', 'the revival of the East', and 'the Chinese model'. Highly effective in foreign affairs, this web of deceit is, however, incapable of dealing with domestic problems, hence the frequent outbursts of violence. Since 1992, China has turned into a sort of 'gilded cage', where globalization, market reforms and city life are the gilding. Only now are the ice-cold iron bars beginning to show through the gleam.

As individuals, we're so fragile compared to these iron bars, and are gripped by fear despite ourselves. This fear sometimes shows itself in the pursuit of pleasure. All over China, you can see people indulging in consumer binges, or, with young people, a craze for fashion. It's all a kind of escape. It allows us to pretend that the repressive system doesn't exist. This fear is passed down through the generations, and follows us all over the world. A year ago, I was at Waterloo station in London and overheard a conversation between a young Chinese couple. They were in their early twenties and looked like students. When the young man said that he had read about Tiananmen on the Internet, the young woman hurriedly whispered, 'Keep your voice down, or you might not be able to go back to China.' When Wang Dan, a Tiananmen dissident, went to give a lecture at Cambridge University, hardly any Chinese students were willing to sit in the front rows in case their presence was noted, leading to problems on their return. And these, we should note, were young people full of curiosity about their visitor.

I don't know how to get rid of this terror, because it's part of me too. It pervades our history, our educational system and our society. But history sometimes turns the tables; just when you feel most powerless and despairing, it offers unexpected hope.

Shortly before he was arrested, Ai Weiwei was interviewed by the *Economist* magazine. In despair about the regime, he was quoted as saying that all young people should learn good English and move overseas. In Cairo in 2007, Egypt's most famous film actor, Youssef Chahine, said much the same thing to a British reporter, 'In the past, I used to tell young people not to emigrate, we need you, this is a beautiful country. Now I tell them, get out as quick as you can, this place is rotting. If you stay, you'll rot too.'

Analogies are frequently erroneous, but recent political changes in Egypt actually hint at how unexpected historical developments can be.

THE PLASTIC PEOPLE OF THE UNIVERSE AND AI WEIWEI

15 May 2011

What Ai Weiwei has been through reminds me of The Plastic People of The Universe rock 'n' roll band and Václav Havel. Any kind of totalitarian regime, whether of the 1970s or in the twenty-first century, whether in Moscow, Prague or Beijing, is locked into intellectual mediocrity. It criminalizes rock 'n' roll music, charges artists with 'economic' crimes, slanders them with powerful rumours, and applies to them moral standards that it does not itself believe in.

In 1976, the Czechoslovak authorities finally arrested the members of The Plastic People of the Universe and other long-haired young people linked to the band. The state-run media said they were a bunch of rogues, drunkards, drug-addicts and got ready to condemn them as criminals.

The playwright Václav Havel made contact with this band, and his sympathies were aroused by their honesty, distress and desire to resist. They had no political axe to grind; they just wanted to live life their own way. They sang about confusion and despair, and their unconventionality was a way of preserving human warmth and hope.

Eight years had passed since the Prague Spring, and oppression, and depression, weighed heavily on the Czechs. The relative openness and liveliness of the Dubček years had given way to the mediocrity of Gustáv Husák, with the authorities stifling people's imagination in the name of 'normality'.

Havel believed that a trial would create a bad precedent: it would allow the regime to detain at will anyone it regarded as capable of independent thinking, even people who just privately expressed independent opinions. If the trial went ahead, it would be a violation of the freedom of spirit and thought. It would also deceive the majority into believing the regime was cracking down on criminal activity. The trial would reveal the true aim of totalitarianism: to make life uniform, to eliminate anyone or anything that stands out from the norm or is in any way different.

Of course, the trial went ahead. Havel was well aware of the implications: 'Their trial was not a confrontation of two differing political forces or conceptions, but two differing conceptions of life.' It was more serious because it was totalitarianism's assault on life itself, a violation of the most basic human freedoms and conscience.

The arrest of the Plastic People made Havel extremely uneasy, but in China the reaction to the Ai Weiwei case was unusual – both more profound and far-reaching than the sentencing of Liu Xiaobo and his Nobel Peace Prize. Unlike the youthful Plastic People, Ai Weiwei is in his fifties, and has clear and incisive opinions on politics and society. He knows exactly what he is doing. But to the general public, especially to his youthful followers, he is an artist doing something new and original: not so much rebelling politically as reaffirming basic human values of freedom, dignity and justice. He has a great sense of fun and mockery, and has turned resistance into spontaneous, improvised games, very different from 'political behaviour' as normally defined. His way of working has been extremely successful, and he has acquired a worldwide reputation. He represents a brand new form of resistance – a lifestyle full of fascination.

People's lifestyles have once again become a battleground, a space where people are damaged and humiliated.

Totalitarianism is characterized by its pervasive control of body and mind, forcing you to conform in the public sphere, and also prying into your private life. Over the last thirty years, China has gradually emerged from a period of totalitarian rule over every aspect of life and entered a new era where individuals have their own space. Students are no longer expelled from college on the grounds that they wear jeans or have long hair, and 'a bad lifestyle' is no longer necessarily a form of condemnation. But the regime has not really relaxed control over its citizens' desires and abilities. When it senses danger, or a challenge to its authority, it makes another attempt to control your inner world and private life. Totalitarianism is the apex of a bureaucratic system, and diversity and individualism send it into a panic. It needs constantly to invent new enemies as a way of maintaining its hold. Its aggression conceals its inner confusion and weakness.

In the last two years, people have begun to feel the increase in controls not only over traditional political dissidents but also over their daily life. We've had the singing of old-style revolutionary red songs and Google's withdrawal from China, Hu Jintao's 2008 campaign against 'vulgarity' in popular culture, and the monitoring of university students' private as well as academic activities. But the Ai Weiwei case is the climax and the most serious in twenty years.

The Plastic People case triggered the 'Charter 77' movement. This was not a traditional political initiative, and was not looking for political power. Instead it reaffirmed the values of conscience and morality, and called on people to 'live in the truth'. If everyone lived in the truth, and said what they really thought, then a government built on lies would collapse. Many factors contributed to the collapse of communism in Eastern Europe, chief of which was probably the restraint shown by Gorbachev, but no one could ignore the force of the call to 'live in the truth'. Might the persecution of Ai Weiwei lead to another political awakening? Could different strata of society, leading intellectuals or hip young people, realize that if they do not resist, even the pitiful freedom that they currently have will be wrested from them? Impossible to tell.

SOMETHING ELSE THAT'S 'MADE IN CHINA'

1 August 2011

From Cairo to the Aswan Dam, every street peddler, guide, waitress and tourist bus driver says, 'Ah, China! Everything's made in China!' They can say two things in Chinese: 'Ni hao' (hello), and 'Jackie Chan'. Two that I met who were more sophisticated, added, 'China's going to conquer the world.' And another one, a well-educated man, commented, 'China has a good thing going in Sudan. Is this the new colonialism?'

China's influence, in the shape of sportswear, trainers, leather belts, lighters, mobile phones, vehicles and tourists, has reached every city in Egypt. Even the souvenirs of mummies and pyramids may well have originated in some nameless small Chinese factory. Apparently, China has even found a place on the political agenda of Hosni Mubarak's government, as an example of how to maintain a dictatorship while protecting economic growth.

Being a tourist is both an enriching and a monotonous experience. The tombs and temples left by the Pharaohs are unforgettably splendid and the Nile at sunset has a lyrical beauty. (Few people bother with the fact that these marvels were built by slave labour.) But tourists are normally limited to contact with hotels, guides and shop-keepers, and such exchanges are superficial, courteous and glib. In my case, my Chinglish and their Arab-English added a further stumbling block. So I went to some trouble to find the *International Herald Tribune* every day, and this English-language world became, at least temporarily, an intellectual relaxation.

On 26 December 2009, I read the news about Liu Xiaobo in the weekend edition of the *International Herald Tribune*, which lay discarded in a corner of the Sofitel Hotel bar. Other guests on their Christmas break had hardly even flicked through it.

After being locked up for a year, China's most famous dissident author had been given an eleven-year prison sentence. Even though he must have prepared himself psychologically for harsh treatment by the Chinese government, this was still an absurd sentence. For a few posts on the Internet and a declaration which could not have been more mildly worded, he was condemned for conspiring to overthrow the government. This government is in control of one-fifth of the world's population and is regarded as a future world leader.

All educated people in China picked up on the implications of the judgment; it was intended as a deterrent – slaughtering the chicken to scare the monkeys, as we say. These monkeys include not only China's intellectuals, but no doubt Westerners too. (We live in a country dominated by the Communist Party which, so the Party says, other people have no right to concern themselves with.) The sentence was a warning not to interfere in China's 'internal affairs', though quite how 'internal affairs' is defined is unclear.

This was the end of a drama which started in 1992, with the boom in China's economy and its entry into the global market, and which climaxed in 2008. That was the year when China not only hosted the Olympic Games and withstood the world economic crisis, but also held a grand celebration of the sixtieth anniversary of the founding of the People's Republic of China in 1949. All of this was proof that China had developed a unique development model: it had thrown out democracy, human rights and the rule of law, but had succeeded in creating a booming economy, with Chinese companies expanding to every corner of the world. Its citizens were filled with patriotic fervour and any dissent – such as Liu Xiaobo's – could speedily be swept under the carpet.

There is a new consensus which goes something like this: the Cold War is over and ideology is dead. The only criterion for success is whether or not a country is economically developed. 'Dictatorship' and 'despotism' are no longer appropriate labels for a Chinese government which has brought real material benefits to its people. And with the growth of China's influence abroad, the whole world needs to sit up and listen to China's views on global warming and the currency crisis. China is not another Soviet Union, and is not preparing to export ideology, nor does it have military ambitions. As for how it deals with internal dissent, it regards that as its own affair. We've all been taken in by this line, not just the outside world, but the Chinese people themselves. Chinese society is becoming more self-satisfied, apathetic, narrow-minded and unfeeling by the day.

When developing countries marvel at the plethora of goods sporting the 'Made in China' label, they rarely realize that this powerful country is also constantly manufacturing humiliated and damaged people; people who would rather set fire to themselves than be forcibly evicted as their homes are demolished; children who have drunk formula milk tainted with melamine; whole village populations contaminated by the chemical industry; and of course intellectuals like Liu Xiaobo, who have suffered terrible consequences simply for trying to uphold basic human rights. China and the world have absorbed the materialism of one 'Made in China', while completely ignoring the other kind of 'Made in China'. But the day will eventually come when pent-up anger and distress boils over, and no one yet knows what the consequences of that will be.

History always exceeds our expectations. The climax of the drama that is the 'Chinese model' may well signal the beginning of its decline. For the most part, historically, the ascent is slow and laborious while the descent is like an avalanche. The preposterous cruelty of the judgment against Liu Xiaobo could not be a clearer sign of the regime's weakness.

THE BIZARRE BRILLIANCE OF THE BLIND DEFENDER OF HUMAN RIGHTS

1 January 2012

As Judgment Day approaches, the saviour of humanity will not be Superman or Batman but a Chinese Noah's Ark. Such is the plot of the film *2012*, and it echoes the mood of an entire generation. As the financial crisis engulfed the world, only the government and economy of China showed the extraordinary fortitude needed to become the main hope for global revival.

One recent, real-life episode offered observers a new angle on how the Chinese regime operates: Christian Bale, Hollywood star and eponymous hero of *Batman* was playing the lead role in a prestigious new Chinese film called *The Flowers of War*. Bale drove eight hours to a village in Shandong to see a Chinese citizen called Chen Guangcheng. But he found that he was unable to achieve this simple goal. At the entrance to Dong Shi Gu village, 'Batman' was turned back by a group of people in dark-green coats. All he could do was keep repeating, 'Why can't I go and see a free man?'

This truly was a 'lost in translation' moment. The guards probably did not understand what this foreigner was saying or, even if they got the words, couldn't understand why he was so angry. They live in different worlds.

The guards had been ordered to block anyone trying to visit Chen Guangcheng, by military force if necessary. People have been trying to get into the village since September 2010. Yet it is very likely that the guards have never known why the man they are guarding is so important.

Chen Guangcheng is a blind, self-educated lawyer who used to file lawsuits on behalf of villagers who had neither power nor influence. Six or seven years ago, a small group of human rights lawyers, including Chen, represented China's conscience and hope for change. Direct political reforms seemed too hard to achieve, so the group found a more feasible route. Where possible, they used existing laws to defend individuals' rights and educated them in citizens' rights. But these lawyers were very soon either beaten up, sent to prison or otherwise silenced. Chen Guangcheng served four and a half years. Since his release, he has been kept under surveillance, prevented both from leaving his home and from receiving visits. Even his wife and child have had their movements restricted.

All the same, for the last year, a steady stream of visitors have turned up at Dong Shi Gu village – human rights workers, reporters, writers, diplomats, and ordinary people with a conscience, both Chinese and foreigners – but not one has succeeded in seeing him. The local government has allocated huge sums to enlist a vast army of spies in the hopes of making Chen Guangcheng disappear into a black hole.

But black holes have their own particular energies and the disappearing Chen Guangcheng has emitted his own bizarre brilliance. The more he has been put off limits, the more people have been attracted, especially foreigners. China is such a complicated place, so hard to unravel. Its sudden, relentless rise has aroused anxiety and incomprehension. But the persecution of Chen Guangcheng may have been followed so closely because it is so easy to understand. The story of China is a morality play where good battles against evil. When a blind lawyer who defends human rights is persecuted by the regime, the media have hit on a romantic narrative that fits their expectations. This is the case with Chen Guangcheng, just as it was with Aung San Suu Kyi. After his fruitless visit, Bale told CNN, 'What I really wanted to do was to meet [Chen], shake his hand and say what an inspiration he is.' Bale's words are admirable but somehow reminiscent of scenes from *The Quiet American*. What he says is right but a bit too simple.

Nevertheless, Batman's frustration does remind us of our moral stupidity: the majority of city-dwellers have no idea that Chen Guangcheng exists, or what has happened to him, because his name and activities have never been made public. He is far from well known even by those few intellectuals, and others, who are concerned with public affairs. Apart from the small stream of visitors, most of those who privately feel sympathy for him have not shown their support by making the journey to his Shandong village. Perhaps they (and that includes me) doubt whether a visit would really mean anything. Could it really help Chen or his family? Would it cause them more trouble? Or would it just be sanctimonious showing off?

Doubts like this remind us just how low society has sunk. To a very large degree, the China of today is sustained by a pervasive moral paralysis. People have lost the ability to see beyond their personal interests and understand and sympathize with the suffering of others. We are either indifferent, or we get over-emotional about basic good moral conduct. Either extreme prevents us from seeing the the real roots of the country's problems.

We oversimplify things by labelling the present situation 'totalitarianism', as we do by calling it a confrontation between 'corrupt government' and 'suffering people'. Some of those who have been recruited to monitor Chen are villagers for whom this has provided a job. Nor is the government monolithic; it is fragmented into competing factions, each fighting for their own interests. To the local government, Chen Guangcheng represents a huge source of revenue. His house arrest, as well as other fresh disputes, are crucial to their ability to raise money for policing.

Chen Guangcheng's predicament shows just how deep the rot has advanced within government and society, and how difficult it will be to rebuild them in the future.

FADING INSPIRATION

20 May 2012

When I heard that Chen Guangcheng had left the American embassy, I was sitting in a lakeside tea house in Shapingba Park, central Chongqing, with an awesome replica of the Statue of Liberty rising before me. She was about eight metres tall, made of grey concrete and standing on a redbrick plinth. She held the legal statutes in her left hand and brandished a torch in her right. It was too bad that she looked so gloomy; perhaps she was depressed by the lack of free expression in China. The boats bobbing around on the lake passed by her but no one so much as cast her a glance.

All over China there are replicas of the Statue of Liberty; in theme parks as well as adorning high-end residential estates. No one cares that the scrolls she holds are the legal statutes from the American Day of Independence, 4 July 1776, or what the torch she holds in her right hand actually means. As far as they are concerned, she is just a symbol of the good life, along with the Eiffel Tower in Paris and stately homes in the UK.

The Chinese image of America is constantly changing, and feelings run particularly deep in Chongqing. Seventy years ago, this city was Chiang Kai-shek's wartime capital, the symbol of free China. At that point, America was China's most important ally, supplying munitions, military technology, even advisors. Theodore White, then a reporter in Chongqing, discovered that the KMT was run almost entirely by American-educated college graduates, almost all of them imbued with American ideals and assiduous seekers of an American lifestyle.

Forty-five years ago, Chongqing was the scene of some of the most intense confrontations of the Cultural Revolution. Young people chanted quotations from Mao Zedong and anti-American slogans, and turned the whole city into a war zone. These youths wanted to export the Chinese revolution all over the world. They wanted to fly the red flag over the White House.

When Deng Xiaoping instituted the reforms of the 1980s, America once again became a model to emulate and a source of inspiration. The climax was reached in the early summer of 1989 in Tiananmen Square, where students created their own Statue of Liberty out of Styrofoam to symbolize their aspirations for American-style freedom and democracy. At that point, America not only symbolized economic and military power, but was a huge moral inspiration too, something that marked it out from the other great powers.

In the succeeding twenty years, America's power to inspire the Chinese has rapidly faded. The US has continued to criticize China's record on human rights, and to offer asylum to Tiananmen dissidents like Wei Jingsheng, Wang Dan and Yu Jie – but largely speaking this has begun to feel more and more like posturing. China's rapid rise has had two consequences. The government has become increasingly arrogant and unheeding of pressure from the outside world, and there has been a commensurate rise in nationalism. The public has no interest in these dissidents and is resentful of foreign criticism. In their eyes, America is becoming just like any normal country; young people still long to go and study there, the new rich try to emigrate, and corrupt officials want to move their ill-gotten gains there, but there is little discussion any more about the political ideals it represents.

This situation is worth understanding, and is worrying. It represents a gradual narrowing of the gap between the two countries. As China understands America better, the romance wears off; America has deliberately toned down its rhetoric on human rights and freedom in order to embrace the huge Chinese market; at the same time, there is a new complacency and moral corruption in Chinese society, and curiosity about the outside world has been lost. The Chinese feel they no longer need to learn anything from anyone. The result of China's pervasive moral degradation is a general conviction that, between people and between countries, there is only the struggle between interests, not between moral rights and wrongs.

'Has he just gone to the embassy because he wants to go to America?' asked a friend of mine. He was not convinced that Chen Guangcheng's motives in working as a human rights lawyer, making him an enemy of the state, were entirely pure. Cheng must have been doing it in order to gain asylum in an even greater power, the United States of America. I did not know how to argue with him, because I knew pitifully little about Chen Guangcheng.

Posts about Chen went viral on Weibo, but most of what I had gleaned came from English-language news sources. We should be clear about the urgency and indignation displayed in the Western media, especially the American media. The drama of Chen Guangcheng seemed not only to be about the tussle between good and evil, it also reflected the power struggle between China and America. Faced with a rapidly emerging China, America has ever fewer cards to play.

A Chinese human rights lawyer sought safety in the American consulate, a symbol of America's moral principles. But, for the sake of international cooperation on security and business, America suppressed those principles, consciously toning down its emphasis on human rights and freedom. When future historians write the history of the twenty-first century, will they hold up Chen Guangcheng as an example of America's moral decline? And how powerful will China be then?

FROM SHAOYANG TO HONG KONG

29 July 2012

At demonstrations, Li Wangyang's image is ubiquitous, printed on T-shirts, on flags that the demonstrators wave, in newspaper advertisements, and painted on hoardings. It is a face so etched with helpless anxiety and anger that it looks exactly like Munch's painting, *The Scream*. He is filled with terrible pain, and has no one to tell it to.

P eople say we live in a global village nowadays, yet the divisions between us seem to be getting ever deeper. We are flooded with so much information, it is impossible to take it all in and digest it. The effect is that everyone stubbornly shuts themselves off in their own little world. Censorship has a role but it is ineffectual and there is another factor at play: if people have so much information at their disposal, why should they bother to go out and look for things they do not know?

I did not hear about Li Wangyang until I got to Hong Kong. His name is blocked in China, but everyone in Hong Kong knows about him. Demonstrators shout his name, write poems about him, and paste slogans in the windows of tower blocks about the injustice he suffered. Li Wangyang, a glassworker from the town of Shaoyang in Hunan who spent years in prison, has attained in Hong Kong almost the same symbolic significance as Liu Xiaobo, Ai Weiwei and Chen Guangcheng.

It is possible that Hongkongers relate to his plight even more than they do to Liu's and Chen's. When the news channel 'i-CABLE' (Hong Kong) broadcast the interview with Li Wangyang on 2 June 2012, Hongkongers were appalled by the cruelty he had suffered. As a democracy campaigner, he had spent the last twenty-three years in prison. He had been beaten up and confined in a tiny cell – 6 feet 5" (2 m) long, by 3 feet 3" (1 m) wide, by 5 feet 3" (1.6 m) high – where he could only sit or lie. He had neither light nor bedding, only one hole from which he got food and another for excreting. In this coffin-like space he spent anything from one month to three months at a time, on at least twenty occasions. It had made him a physical wreck, given him serious heart problems and hyperthyroidism, made him blind in the left eye and almost deaf in both ears, and damaged his cervical and lumber vertebrae. His height shrank from 6 feet (1.82 m) to 5 feet 8 inches (1.73 m). In spite of all this, Hong Kong reporters said that he still had enormous vitality. Not only did he not regret anything he had done, he also declared, 'Even if I were beheaded, I wouldn't regret it.' Yet four days after his TV interview, the Shaoyang police announced that he had committed suicide.

In Hong Kong, his death provoked an outpouring of emotion. Those not from the island might find it hard to understand this city's empathy with the pro-democracy movement and with the 1989 Tiananmen incident. But the tragic events of 4 June 1989 were separated by only eight years from the return of Hong Kong to China. Many residents of Hong Kong are there because they have fled turmoil and cruelty in China, only to find that the modicum of security, prosperity and freedom they had won might be taken from them once again. How could they believe a government that turned its guns on its own citizens? Tiananmen was a political awakening for them; they could not ignore the fact that their fate was intricately bound up with China's existence, and its problems.

For the last twenty-three years, on the night of 4 June, Hong Kong's Victoria Park has filled with crowds commemorating the tragedy of Tiananmen. Not a single year has been missed. The crowds vary in size, depending on how vivid people's memories are and how anxious they feel. At the beginning of the 1990s, memories of the tragedy were still fresh; people were very uneasy about the outlook for themselves and emotions ran high. By the end of the 1990s, memories had begun to fade, the handover was more peaceful than had been imagined, and the number of people at the vigil dropped off.

Memories fade and alter. They assume new forms under different circumstances. During the last few years, as China has sped up the process of re-integrating Hong Kong, new anxieties have arisen. Hong Kong fears being wholly swallowed up as China grows more powerful, and thus losing its uniqueness. At the same time, the Chinese political system has not developed and opened up at the same speed as its economy and society; indeed restrictions have tightened. Hong Kong has seen an increase in domestic conflicts, which are profoundly connected to government and the economy and are an unavoidable result of the post-handover process. Political enthusiasm, regionalism, the search for identity, social movements and the spirit of rebellion – all were suppressed in this migrant society under pre-handover colonial rule. These feelings, suddenly released, worked on each other. Now, as China seeks to impose control, Hong Kong wants self-determination. In the ensuing standoff, people have simplified a whole collection of different issues into a single core conflict between China and Hong Kong.

At this point, any highly symbolic event or person, whether it is 4 June or Ai Weiwei or Li Wangyang, assumes a particularly great significance in Hong Kong. Hongkongers see in these figures a reflection of their own resistance.

The candles at the vigils have also passed into new hands. This generation never saw the corpses of those who died during 'struggle sessions' floating down the Pearl River, nor have they felt the direct impact of Tiananmen. Stories like Li Wangyang's have become a shortcut to their understanding of China's dark side, telling them that China's cruelty has not diminished and that Hong Kong cannot stay safely on the sidelines. On the front page of the *Apple Daily*, I saw a picture of four Hong Kong youths who had travelled to Shaoyang, Li Wangyang's birthplace, to mourn him. For their trouble, the local police arrested them.

There is a new feeling that Shaoyang and Hong Kong share a common destiny. If Hong Kong wants to continue to enjoy its freedoms and achieve the democracy its citizens have wanted for so long, then they can't ignore China's domestic struggles.

ANGER AND ABSURDITY

LOSS OF PERSONAL INTEGRITY

12 November 2007

Over the last decade, stories of officials and their lovers have peppered the news, arousing more public curiosity even than the astronomical figures for official corruption. But the case of the top Shandong official, Duan Yihe, who blew up the mistress who was about to denounce him, still has the power to shock.

D uan Yihe has regular, square features and looks how one would expect an official of his age and status to look: his hair is neatly brushed back, and he is neatly dressed in a suit and white shirt. The photograph is of the Shandong delegation taken at the tenth session of the China National People's Congress (CNPC), and Duan Yihe is head of the Jinan City delegation. Up until 9 July 2007, Duan Yihe's career had progressed smoothly: he was born in Qihe county, Shandong, graduated from Xi'an Communications University in 1970, and worked for six years in Tianjin. He then returned to Qihe county, becoming deputy head of the young cadres section of the Organization Department of the Provincial Party Committee, rising to be departmental head of the Intellectuals Works Office, deputy head of the provincial Electronics Industry Bureau, and deputy secretary of the Jinan City Party Committee and head of its Organization Department.

From 2001, Duan Yihe was head of the Standing Committee of Jinan's delegation at the CNPC, and secretary of the Party Leadership Group. He was sixty-one years old, and had reached a level where it appeared he could look forward to a secure retirement.

But at 5pm on the afternoon of 9 July, an explosion finally propelled this official into the limelight. After the bomb went off, it was reported that, 'A young woman was blown in two, with her upper half landing more than twenty metres away, on its side, by the roadside, and her internal organs below the breasts exposed to view. The lower half of her body was not found. It was a grisly scene.'

The case was quickly solved. Just four days later, the perpetrator, Duan Yihe, was arrested. The dead woman had been his mistress of thirteen years. Duan himself had not wanted to get his hands dirty, so he had enlisted the help of his niece's husband, who worked as deputy team leader in the city's Public Security Bureau. The photograph of the charred black skeleton of the car, a Honda, went viral on the Internet.

Over the last decade, stories of officials and their lovers have peppered the news, arousing more public curiosity even than the astronomical figures for official corruption. I remember I happened to read a news item from 17 January 1983 about Wang Zhong, the deputy head of the politics and law section of the Prefectural Party Committee in Shantou, Guangdong province, was who was executed for accepting 69,749 yuan (£4,565) in bribes. Fourteen years later, the stories of Wang's embezzlement sounded like something out of the *Arabian Nights*, and the sums involved still seemed off the scale. Reading the news from this period is an anaesthetizing process. At first, you are shocked at a million yuan's (£65,000) worth of graft, then you read that someone else siphoned off tens of millions, and finally even the embezzlement of hundreds of millions loses the power to shock. Then there are cases involving the sex trade, the inevitable companion of corruption. It is also true that as these cases come to light and to court, they become disconnected from the corruption *per se*. As one of the wives put it to a reporter of the *Wall Street Journal*, 'What is important is not the amount of money he embezzled, but the fact that it was incorrect politically.'

Nonetheless, the Duan Yihe scandal is probably the most shocking of recent times. (It went almost unnoticed that he was also being investigated for accepting bribes worth more than a million yuan (£100,000).)

Such a loss of integrity is surely the most profound and intractable problem faced by Chinese society. In the last 150 years, we have twice faced a crisis of faith. The first was at the end of the nineteenth century, when traditional Confucian values came under attack from Western ones. The second followed the death of Mao Zedong, when the inward-looking values and system of collectivization he had set up disintegrated completely. The effects of the latter were exacerbated by the demonic onslaught of commercialization after 1989. People abandoned attempts to create a better society and plunged headlong into consumerism.

This collapse of faith has led to a loss of personal integrity. When people don't believe in any principles, all that matters to them is outcomes that best serve their personal and material interests. Duan Yihe's decision to blow up his mistress because she was about to denounce him is an extreme example of this, but it represents Chinese society in a nutshell nonetheless.

I remember once meeting a crippled tricycle driver in Baicheng City, Jilin. He was over fifty and had been a chauffeur until, twenty-five years ago, his legs were broken while he was trying to save his bureau chief. 'If I ever faced a situation like that again,' he told me, 'I'd jump out of the car. I wouldn't push him out first. I'd let him take the brunt of the impact, even if he was the Jilin mayor!' Yet he was rueful about the way social mores have degenerated. He told me that the one ambition of his son, who was a newly appointed prison warder, was to become prison head, because then all those under him would have to 'give gifts, whether it's his mother's birthday or his son getting into university, or whatever'. His son's words were, 'When I'm prison head, it'll be them giving me presents.' Nowadays, people are so fed up with corruption and injustice that they no longer want to change the system, they only want to become beneficiaries themselves, shifting the hardships they suffer onto someone else.

Such is the climate of opinion that any attempt to construct a system to resist corruption of the powerful has become extraordinarily difficult and verges on self-deception. You set up an organization to tackle corruption but that institution soon becomes corrupted itself. One look at how China's bureaucracy has ballooned shows that only too clearly.

As politics and society become ever more complex, personal integrity becomes increasingly important, even more important than the system itself, because no matter how carefully constructed our political and social systems are, they rely on human beings to implement them. If people's integrity cannot be relied upon, then no matter how strict the system, the rapacious will use it and it will become the best excuse for passing the buck. In China's current political climate, morality and integrity are part of an outmoded ideology. The result is that individuals are increasingly hypocritical, and flippant about life. In these circumstances, any discussion about reforming the system is futile, and China's innumerable laws have had absolutely no effect on lowering the crime level.

RELAX, WE'RE A GREAT POWER

4 May 2008

On 9 April 2008, when asked to comment on the United States' relationship with China on CNN's *The Situation Room*, the commentator Jack Cafferty remarked: 'I think they're basically the same bunch of goons and thugs they've been for the last fifty years.' In response to protests both in the US and in China, Cafferty later said: 'I was referring to the Chinese government and not to Chinese people or to Chinese-Americans.' Thousands of Chinese-Americans nonetheless protested in front of CNN's headquarters in Atlanta and San Francisco on 26 April.

Since CNN was founded by Ted Turner in 1980, the TV station has come under widespread attack for the superficiality of its reportage. But this does not detract in any way from the ground-breaking contribution it has made to the news business. Foreseeing the coming of a globalized age, it deluged its viewers with information from all over the world, continuously, 24/7, prompting numerous imitators at home and abroad. When Al Jazeera was set up in 1996, it wanted to become the CNN of the Middle East. When China's CCTV was preparing CCTV News, it took CNN as a model, although of course it would never admit to that.

CNN is undoubtedly a symbol of American influence. When a country leads the world, or attempts to, its thinking and its ethos has at least as much power to inspire and influence as its military bases and the goods it produces. We might draw an analogy with the pride associated with becoming a citizen under the Roman Empire, which was no less important than Rome's military might.

Of course, becoming an influential great power or organization brings not just privilege but also responsibility. If you are too strong, even your inadvertent movements can damage others, and if you lack self-discipline, such damage will happen often.

I watch CNN very little. After it was taken over by the giant corporation, Time Warner, it lost the sharp edge it once had, and it never did have much depth. BBC news coverage is far more objective and thorough. But no one can deny the huge influence CNN has had. I remember the uproar it caused in 2007, when the then-Venezuelan president, Hugo Chávez, sued it for linking his name with Al-Qaeda. Internationally, influential media outlets are often the subject of such lawsuits. Italy's Silvio Berlusconi sued the *Economist*, and Indonesia's Suharto sued *Time Magazine*. What is media independence to one is slander to the other.

Before Jack Cafferty expressed the opinions on China that caused such a stir here, I had never noted any particular presenter's name. After all, CNN presenters all speak with the same accents and express the same shallow, emphatic opinions. But what we should focus on is the reaction of the Chinese government and the Chinese public, rather than Cafferty's lack of common sense. In the last week, Cafferty, along with Carrefour, has become a household name in China. For nationalists, these are the obvious and easiest targets, because they show that the West harbours sinister motives towards China and is trying to humiliate it.

I understand why the Chinese public feel so utterly outraged. The feeling is that we Chinese have made so much progress, have put such enormous efforts into the Olympics, and have extended welcoming smiles to the whole world. So why are you all so critical and prejudiced? And why are you using Tibet (which is a domestic issue) as a stick to beat us with?

Yet if you want to investigate further, you will discover that behind the Chinese outrage lies a deep-rooted sense of superiority. This is something we Chinese have had for a very, very long time, but in the last 150 years, we have lost the material basis and the ethos which gave rise to it. The feeling never disappeared, it just went into temporary abeyance. In fact, suppression over a long period only added to its vigour, and, as soon as the time was ripe, it re-emerged fiercer than ever. However, it is based purely on a vague, historical memory. As far as Chinese people today are concerned, China's former glory may have disappeared but it still acts as a powerful charm; we use it as a talisman but have forgotten the words of the spell. Too often, whenever we find ourselves criticized, we overreact but can't muster arguments in our defence. Our usual response is either to hurl abuse at our opponents, or to relapse into silence.

Looking back over the last month, even accepting that the West is full of prejudice, the only refutation of any force has come from the Chinese ambassador to the UK, who wrote an article for the *Daily Telegraph*.* Other opinions, including attacks on Cafferty, sound as if we are reassuring or encouraging ourselves, or winding ourselves up into a fury.

To rebut these prejudices with any force, it's necessary to understand the real world. When all these Chinese attack Cafferty's views, how many of them refer to the fact that he is notorious even in his own country for shooting his mouth off? After the US invaded Iraq, he openly branded the Defense Secretary, Condoleezza Rice, as a 'war criminal'. And when the Department of Homeland Security published its report on the response to Hurricane Katrina, he declared that, 'The public is not going to buy any of this stuff that comes out of Washington. They're not going to believe anything that comes out of these partisan reports or stuff that was done from within the White House. It just isn't going to wash. The game is up with John Q Public. They're not buying this stuff anymore!'

The very fact that we pay any attention at all to Cafferty's ravings reveals us not as a nation with self-respect, but as one that knows nothing of the world today and which cannot hold its nerve. An emerging great power should expect misunderstanding and criticism, as well as praise, from the rest of the world. Blame grows along with a country's importance. I often

* Ambassador Fu Ying wrote a piece in the *Telegraph* on 13 April 2008, during the build-up to the Olympics, criticizing negative portrayals of China in western media, entitled 'Western media has "demonised" China'.

find myself wanting to say nowadays, 'Relax, this is just a sports competition. Relax, we're a great country.'

If we look a little deeper, we will discover that our fury at such criticisms is an emotional reaction to decades of being trapped in a closed society rather than an expression of genuine patriotic fervour. It has its roots within China, not abroad.

PROSPERITY AND ANXIETIES

18 May 2008

A pall of smoke hung over the bustling centre of Shanghai. It was about quarter past nine on the morning of 5 May in Huangxing Road, when the number 842 bus exploded in flames. The explosion resulted in three deaths and twelve injured. Two friends separately texted me the news, both of them adding words along the lines of, 'Cause not known, though official version is spontaneous combustion.'

This piece of news, so short, so instantly forgettable, encapsulates Chinese society in a fascinating way. Everyone is worried about increasing social instability, with terrorism no longer just a remote concept. And the word 'though' in my friends' texts could not show more clearly the public's attitude to government – mostly they find it not worth believing.

Big cities like Beijing and Shanghai are rather like islands in China. They are prosperous, exciting and safe. Their policing is meticulous, plenty of important people live there, and there is little aggressive criminal activity to challenge the government. But every now and then, rumours and fears trouble big city dwellers. I remember at the end of the 1990s, Beijing residents were very concerned about a series of attacks where people were hit on the back of the head with a sharp instrument, and then robbed. Rumour had it that the perpetrators were a gang from the north east of the country. It was just before the Chinese New Year, and people hung onto their wallets even more tenaciously than normal. Meanwhile, the residents of the south China metropolis, Guangzhou, were having palpitations about the Arm-chopping Gang and the Biker Gang, and Guangzhou station was said to be a no-go area for the police. These fears arose in large part from suspicions of the influx of huge numbers of migrant workers into the city, and unease at the growing gap between rich and poor. Every newly built residential estate was surrounded by high walls and patrolled by guards to keep strangers out, and to segregate residents from the rhythms of city life.

Prosperity and anxiety existing side-by-side seems to have been a characteristic of Chinese society since 1989, and is inseparable from China's strategy and policies. In the turmoil that engulfed China, and half the world, between 1989 and 1991, the Chinese government took a lesson from the collapse of the Soviet Union: political reforms could not take precedence over economic reforms. It prioritized economic prosperity as a way of bonding society together. (The Soviet Union's aggressive military expansion, with the invasion of Afghanistan, also speeded up its political demise.)

So the Chinese government made a bargain with its citizens, relaxing controls over part of the economy so that they could enjoy the fruits of economic growth. At the same time, the sphere of influence of the ruling elite gradually expanded, occupying any area where there was no resistance. The ideology of the Communist Party lost its vitality. The Party became merely an organization bonded together by mutual interests.

China's foreign policy thus far has been clear. To keep a low profile so as to create conditions for domestic economic development. It wants to attract global funds, resources and markets. As far as the Chinese people are concerned, however, the influx of goods and ideas from abroad has not aroused their curiosity and desire to understand the outside world. Their heads are stuffed with memories of past national traumas and the current pursuit of rampant consumerism. At work here is a sort of instinct for expansion – your home can be even bigger, your car can be shinier, your job more important, your entertainments more enjoyable. Consumerism, stifled for many years, has broken its shackles and as a result people are temporarily willing to forget other desires. In this way the government achieves temporary stability.

Even though domestic disturbances are on the increase, the last eighteen years in China really have been stable and prosperous, compared with the constant upheavals of the country's more distant past. People have focused on things which are sometimes real, sometimes illusory, and in the process have forgotten other feelings. For example, in the last few months of 2006, the frenzy for buying stocks and shares reached fever pitch, and society quietened down. Even the crime rate dropped somewhat, because everyone was so busy watching the share prices.

But people often forget the challenges posed by consumerism. It demands a constantly expanding economy which, in turn, means that China must be able to draw on a constant supply of the world's capital and resources, other countries must continue to be willing to throw open their markets, global stability must be maintained, and there must be no global disasters.

But China in 2008 is not the same place as China in 1990. Back then, it was not only self-sufficient in oil, it exported it. Now, it needs to import oil from the Middle East, Africa and Latin America, iron ore from Australia, and timber from the Amazon before it can manufacture all those Made in China goods that it sells worldwide.[*] This means that China's pursuit

* Anyone who is interested in this epic process will find it worth reading James Kynge's *China Shakes the World: The Rise of a Hungry Nation* (2006).

of material wealth is not only played out on the domestic stage, it also offers opportunities to other countries. And those countries may find China competing for their own resources. At the same time, the refusal to carry out political reforms and the repression of civil society means that economic growth is overshadowed by political power. China today faces ecological and moral crises that are inseparable from its mode of economic development. Even more importantly, there is no guarantee that the outside world will continue to furnish China so generously with the conditions it needs for that development.

America and Europe have accused China of a 'new colonialism'. Since they are old-style colonialists themselves, this is hypocrisy on their part, but, without doubt, China *is* getting more deeply involved in world affairs. With its size, every deliberate or involuntary movement it makes may be enough to upset other countries. By the same token, China is attracting increasingly heavy criticism, and even direct attacks.

The close attention people have paid to the Shanghai bus explosion must surely be because they are secretly worried that it is a dummy run for future terrorist actions, just as the attacks on the Olympic torch by human rights and other protesters during its global journey must have made many Chinese feel beleaguered. Interference from external elements, has intensified the problems in Tibet, Xinjiang and other ethnic minority areas of China.

China may well be entering a period of increased political turmoil. The rules of the game that have operated since 1989 are playing themselves out. China must look afresh at its domestic situation as well as its relations with the rest of the world. For many years, we have ignored both of these, but that is only a temporary measure; the problems will not go away by themselves.

RUMOURS IN A PROSPEROUS AGE

12 June 2008

It started with a preposterous rumour that, in order to build a new highway from the towns of Fengjie to Yunyang in the municipality of Chongqing, construction workers were looking for eighteen boys and girls under twelve years old, whom they were going to bury under the bridge supports to increase the viaduct's stability. A week passed and the rumours became more colourful and more specific: a precise time and place were mentioned; the going rate the builders were offering for a child was 400,000 yuan (£30,000); some children had narrowly avoided being abducted; and others had been carried away in jute sacks.

The rumours plunged the whole of Zhuyi township into a state of consternation. Teachers informed the local paper that parents had been calling the school to ask if they were true. Parents turned up at the town primary school's front gate to take their children home. The director of the Gujia Kindergarten heard the following 'precise' account of an abduction: 'Last Thursday morning, the Li family, who live in the old state-run stores building, sent their nine-year-old son to school and he was chased by a man whose face was covered by a broad-brimmed hat. The kid only managed to throw him off by running away as fast as he could.'

Two weeks after these rumours started, the local police told a reporter from the *Chongqing Evening News* that they had not filed any reports about pupils disappearing, and were certain that there had been no attempted abductions. Xia Xize, chief engineer of the organization in charge of building the stretch of the highway in question had laughed off the rumours, calling them preposterous.

The story spread far and wide on the Internet. Zhuyi township has nearly 60,000 people, and is 20 miles (32 km) from Fengjie county town. The latter, on the eastern edge of the Sichuan basin, is also where the Three Gorges of the Yangtze River begin. During the Three Kingdoms period (AD 220–80), Fengjie was a key military stronghold. Its other claim to fame is the line in a poem by the Tang dynasty poet Li Bai: 'In the morning one departs from [Fengjie], amid rosy clouds.' In the last ten years, the gigantic Three Gorges Dam has transformed the area, and the old town will eventually be completely submerged.

I saw the fantastically beautiful Three Gorges scenery in Jia Zhangke's film *Still Life* (2006), with the old county town crumbling away on one bank and the new county town rising on the other. I was trying to guess what it felt like to be someone living in those circumstances. The reporter from the *Chongqing Evening News* wrote of Zhuyi township that, 'Towering cranes stick up from the mountain slopes and great holes in the valley bottom await the piers of the viaduct supports.' As far as the inhabitants of this once-remote county town are concerned, all this is alien and beyond their control. And now Zhuyi township, like so many small towns and villages all over China, has lost most of its youth to migrant labour, leaving behind only the elderly and school-aged children, precisely the ones least able to defend themselves against calamity.

I cannot describe how peculiar this news item, which appeared in mid-January 2007, seemed. My first reaction was to think of the book by Harvard sinologist Philip A. Kuhn called *Soulstealers: The Chinese Sorcery Scare of 1768*, which also takes the building of a bridge as its starting point. People believed back then that in order to ensure the stability of the bridge, the stonemason needed to write the names of living people on a piece of paper, stick it on the bottom of a wooden pile and sink it into the river bed. This way the bridge took with it the spirits of those named. The practice was known as 'stealing souls'. The story then took a different turn, as itinerant monks secretly cut off strangers' queues (plaits of hair worn at the back) in order to 'steal their souls' and their wealth. In less than three months, the panic had spread all the way from Deqing county in Zhejiang province, to Han Yang prefecture on the upper reaches of the Yangtze River, (1,000 km distance). This all happened at the end of the reign of Emperor Qianlong, China's golden age, in the seventeenth and eighteenth centuries.

In Kuhn's impressive history, this rumour, which ultimately spread nationwide, reflected a deep unease which infected courtiers and ordinary people alike. The emperor treated it as a political affair and used it as a pretext to purge an increasingly unwieldy bureaucracy, but it also revealed the ordinary people's heightened anxiety about survival. Between 1700 and 1794, China's population rose from 150 million to 313 million. Resources became dangerously scarce, and a trade boom exacerbated the gap between rich and poor regions. Ordinary people felt their lives were being controlled by some alien force, and they felt helpless. Rumours are a way of coping with helplessness; people often need to make things up so that they have something to blame for their anxieties.

In the last thirty years, China has been the world's most spectacular laboratory, not only because of the material wealth it has created, but also because we have compressed several hundred years' worth of history into the space of a generation. People often wake up in the morning to find that the familiar world around them has collapsed. Individuals are extraordinarily powerless to resist such huge, abrupt and often chaotic changes.

As I was reading this news, rumours of a different kind, about tainted pork meat, were flying around Beijing, picking up on a popular unease about the quality of food products, which has been around for a few years. Intriguingly, this loss of confidence has melded with a similar distrust in medical care, education, the law and bureaucracy. It is easy to imagine that, no matter how strenuously the government issues denials, rumours of this kind will happen more and more often, not only because of developments in the means of communication, but because society has become so unequal. A common faith in the system has been destroyed and no one knows what they believe any more. To a large degree, we all share the anxieties of the Zhuyi township parents. Sometimes I feel that today's China is a giant with enormous limbs but an empty head and a heart riven with anxieties.

PRIDE AND PREJUDICE

27 July 2008

Two cases, both involving fatalities and taking place in the space of three days, have given us another way of understanding China today: the death of a seventeen-year-old girl in Weng'an county, Guizhou province on 28 June 2008, and the killing of six police officers by a young man with a knife on 1 July.

The girl's death produced a storm of protest, with angry people burning police cars and attacking the local police station, as well as the county town government building. No one believed that the girl, a pupil at No. 3 Middle School, had drowned. There were suspicions of a cover-up on the part of senior officials in the local government.

The Chinese government had been anxious to show the world a brand new image, with the most spectacular Olympic Games in history demonstrating how much prosperity and progress it had achieved. The Sichuan earthquake of the same year aroused great sympathy and, when public suspicions and accusations of corrupt building practices were brushed under the carpet, Chinese society seemed to be in a state of harmony, at least for the time being. Then the Weng'an riots shocked the world.

But the riots showed us the real situation: domestic conflict is worsening. People gathered in the streets not just to show sympathy for the dead girl but, even more, to give voice to their long-pent-up frustrations with the government. If you travel to any small county town in China, you often find that the local government and the public are two sides of the same coin: one side full of arrogance, the other prejudiced and intensely distrustful. As far as the public is concerned, anything the authorities say and do is (a) a lie and (b) self-interested. To local officials, the mass of the people are uneducated and bigoted, not worthy of decent treatment. The officials' main aim is to please their superiors.

The legitimacy of the Chinese regime is built on violent revolution, not on election. With normal modes of communication between the government and its citizens blocked, the regime is intrinsically vulnerable and anxious. The overwhelming priority of the government is stability, and the greatest achievement of local governments is to maintain that stability. At the same time, people's understanding of stability is extremely narrow – there must be unanimity of thought and action, with no dissent or argument. This often leads to officials using high-handed tactics to deal with public dissatisfaction. Under pressure, the public starts out as powerless and acquiescent, and then resentment builds up over a long period before finally boiling over and getting out of control.

The Weng'an riots are a perfect example of this. To start with, the local government ignored the demands of the family of the dead girl, Li Shufen, treating them with arrogance and brutality. The public not only had absolutely no faith in the official investigation into the incident, they also harboured long-pent-up grievances about local government violence. When they showed their displeasure, the officials reacted as they always do, by suppressing the protests so they wouldn't reflect badly on their personal records. Far from calming the situation, crushing the protests only aroused more public anger which, because it had no other channels of expression, exploded in arson and other violence.

At this point, the provincial government, to whom the Weng'an county authorities answered, got involved. In an attempt to appease public opinion, a third autopsy in less than ten days was performed on the corpse of the seventeen-year-old girl, in order to yield a more authoritative report; and a number of junior officials were relieved of their duties. At the same time, 'criminal elements', which had supposedly instigated the public unrest, were rooted out. 'Ineffectual officials' and 'criminal elements' are the usual scapegoats in such situations.

As for the central government, on the one hand it has become so rigid with the passage of time that it has lost the ability to judge the public mood. On the other, its own anxieties about its power base, and the loss of its political convictions, have caused it to be oversensitive to that mood. Because it is trapped in a continuing struggle with the local authorities, it was also keen to use the Weng'an incident to punish local officials and win public approval.

A couple of days later, on 1 July, a youth armed with a knife broke into the police station in Zhabei district, central Shanghai, and attacked nine police officers and one security guard, six of whom died. The initial public reaction was not of anger and shock, but incredulity. How could a police station, which represented the power of the state, and individual police officers who were part of this system, have proved so vulnerable?

How should we interpret these two incidents? Merely as absurdity and weakness on the part of a declining regime?

Such a contemptuous view is pervasive in China. Many people voiced support for the people of Weng'an county quickly and succinctly, condemning the authorities and appealing for democracy as the only way to resolve the problem.

But I anticipate that people will perceive an even deeper national problem. The Chinese state has become proud, while its people have become prejudiced, biased against the system. Both sides are at an impasse, in terms of their feelings and their reasoning, meaning there is no chance of fair-minded reflection, rational analysis, or empathy for the other. People simply give their own angry opinions and rarely take time to reflect.

This situation is so complicated that it can only be improved gradually over many generations. There is no magic solution, that much is obvious. I remember the comparison that is sometimes made between football and rugby: in a game of football, the action on the pitch is intense and hard fought, but the real fighting takes place between the fans in the stands. In a rugby match, by contrast, the players battle like barbarians on the field, while the spectators never come to blows. Why can't a benevolent government be like a rugby game, with open debate in public, in the media and in politics, bringing differences and disagreements out into the open? Then a peaceful compromise and resolution can be found, and life can go on as normal.

At the moment the opposite is true: in Chinese society today, all is harmony and stability in official speeches and the media, and public opinion appears to be in complete agreement; while in the real world, dangerous tensions are bubbling under the surface.

A HAPPY IDEA

6 March 2009

From Jiang Zemin inviting capitalists to join the Party to Wen Jiabao posting on Internet forums, everything shows how Chinese politics, while superficially undergoing dramatic changes, remains stubbornly resistant at a deeper level. Chinese bureaucrats are skilful at adapting to new circumstances, but no amount of posturing can conceal their deep-seated resistance to change.

On 1 August 2001, Jiang Zemin made a famous speech in which he introduced his philosophy of the 'Three Represents', proclaiming that the Party should stand for the dynamic triad of economic production, cultural development and political consensus. He was sending a clear and enthusiastic invitation to private business in China to join the Communist Party.

Even though around the dinner table people commonly joked that 'communism is dead', Jiang's speech still aroused huge controversy. The most noteworthy feature of Chinese society since the start of the reforms in 1978 is that while the economy and society have changed out of all recognition, the prevailing ideology has remained astonishingly fossilized.

China today has entered the era of Windows, McDonald's, nightclubs and large numbers of unemployed workers, but if you flick through the *People's Daily* or watch the news on Central China Television (CCTV), what you get is the language of thirty years ago. Even when so many workers have lost their jobs and whole villages have gone bankrupt, the Party still proclaims that it represents the workers and the peasants. It is as if the speakers on the podium at the National People's Congress are simply delivering the same speeches, but thirty years late.

But on this occasion, Jiang Zemin broke new ground. His Three Represents speech was immediately taken as a declaration that the reforms would run deep. Entrepreneurs whose businesses had taken off in the 1990s had not only gained a voice in the economy but could now have a direct entry into the political arena. It showed how political reforms would be driven by economic growth. In Marx's formulation, the economic base determines the superstructure. So, in China the economy has changed, but what about the superstructure? As a symbol of the CCP's flexibility, it could enable nearly 700,000 Party members to throw off the fetters of ideology, gather their strength and meet the challenge of reforms.

But the doubters said that it was all smoke and mirrors. In their view, the Party and its bureaucracy had no intention of implementing any thorough-going changes. It no longer represented the interests of the workers and the peasants, nor of the newly wealthy and the middle class. It had become a gigantic interest group on its own, which others must serve. The voices of intellectuals had long since faded out, except for the technological elite who supped with the regime, while also making space at the table for the entrepreneurs.

After 2003, however, political leaders were no longer so committed to honouring business people, discussing the importance of the market economy and globalization, and entertaining the CEOs of transnational corporations. Instead, they went to the mines and the villages demanding better wages for migrant workers and abolishing the agricultural tax. Migrant workers could become city folk, they promised. They went online and discussed China's diplomacy and economy with anonymous netizens who used handles like Ugly Fish and Summer Wind. These high-ranking politicians even tolerated the nicknames people gave them on Facebook. This, we were meant to believe, showed increasing openness, a victory for public opinion and a return to the spirit of the common people.

When Wen Jiabao posted a comment online on 28 February, commentators on the Xinhua News Network said that netizens had expressed approval of the premier's style in his online debut: very down-to-earth and realistic.

In fact, everything from the Three Represents to the down-to-earth and realistic shows that Chinese politics, while superficially undergoing dramatic changes, is stubbornly resistant to change at its core. It is easy to see the last eight years as a shift away from the elite and back to the ordinary people, from the unilateral drive for high-speed economic growth to a re-balancing of the whole of society and a search for social harmony, from a closed dictatorship to a stress on the importance of public opinion. But has there been any real change? Or does the perception of change simply reflect wishful thinking on our part?

With regard to the expectation that entrepreneurs will join the Party, that is an extension of 'economic determinism', the belief that economic growth necessarily leads to democratic government, and that increasing wealth must transform into social progress. But these hopes have remained unfulfilled. Eight years have gone by. There is no longer the same enthusiastic talk about business people joining the Party. In fact, there is altogether less focus on the business community. Not only have entrepreneurs not become a force for political change, their position seems to have weakened. They have become far too humble in the face of authority, and even of a newly vocal public opinion.

So we have placed our faith instead in 'technological determinism'. Those lively netizens, the public opinion of the Internet world, the product of emerging online technology, are inevitably anti-authority, multi-centred, open and free-moving. Thus they could be seen as the most effective tool for checking authority and driving reform.

But the leadership's eager participation in online forums, rather than reflecting political openness and the public's enthusiasm for politics, starkly reflects Chinese society's paucity of opportunities for political participation, and of public spaces for expressing opinions. It also shows how politics has been reduced to a talk show, and how easily the public is mollified by fine words and a fleeting warmth from its leaders. The populace is disgruntled but the Internet is incapable of creating an effective, well-organized voice of opposition. The multiple levels and multi-centred complexity that politics needs simply have not formed. Instead, politics has turned increasingly into a show.

Compared with eight years ago, China's giant Party apparatus and bureaucracy is now expert in manipulating the new environment but, at the same time, it seems to have become more inert. No amount of posturing can conceal its deep-seated resistance to change. We may not be able to alter this immediately but at least we should not allow ourselves to be taken in by it.

SENSITIVE MEMORIES OF TWELVE ANIMAL HEADS

8 March 2009

In 1860 an Anglo-French army looted and sacked the glorious palace and gardens – the *Yuanmingyuan* – of the Old Summer Palace in Beijing. Countless treasures – including twelve bronze animal heads, supposedly designed by Giuseppe Castiglione for the emperor Qianlong (1711–99), who regarded them as the supreme blending of Chinese and Western cultures – were scattered across the world. For a long time thereafter, it seemed as if history had obliterated the heads, but then, in the early years of the twenty-first century, a series of public auctions brought them back into view.

Rat, ox, tiger, rabbit, dragon... the twelve bronze statues with human bodies and animal heads were arranged in a half-moon shape around a fountain, representing the twelve two-hour periods of the day, telling the time with successive spouts of water. Every day at noon, they would all spout together. They must have delighted the emperor, who reigned for more than sixty years and continued to expand and embellish the vast gardens in the Old Summer Palace begun by his grandfather, the emperor Kangxi. It was his father, the emperor Yongzheng, who gave them the name, Gardens of Perfect Brightness, or *Yuanmingyuan*.

The scale and style of *Yuanmingyuan* reflect the fact that the Qing dynasty was then at the height of its powers. Apart from the Chinese-style courtyards, the gardens include a large number of western-style buildings and displays, and hint at the complacency of a Middle Kingdom where all nations came to pay court.

Looted during the destruction of Old Summer Palace by an Anglo-French expeditionary force in 1860, the bronze heads that once delighted the Qing emperor have, in recent years, reappeared at public auctions: in 2001, a state-owned conglomerate, the China Poly Group, bought the tiger, ox and monkey heads; in 2003, the Hong Kong entrepreneur, Stanley Ho, bought the pig and the horse heads on the open market and presented them back to the nation. The restitution seemed to show China as on the rise again, and to wash away past humiliations.

A third auction is about to bring more of the bronzes to public attention. The Christie's auction, scheduled for 23–25 February 2009, will sell 700 antiques belonging to super-rich Yves Saint-Laurent and his long-time partner Pierre Bergé, including the rat and the rabbit heads.

The Chinese government have protested, on the grounds that these objects had been looted, and that auctioning them would 'not only hurt the Chinese people's feelings and infringe their rights to their cultural heritage, but also contravene international treaties'. A huge consortium of Chinese civil lawyers is preparing to fight to get them back.

The very weekend that the Chinese Foreign Ministry voiced its strong opposition to the auction, the G7 Summit was being held in Rome. The *International Herald Tribune* commented that China's image had grown more positive with the world economic recession. China's four trillion yuan (£260 billion) economic stimulus package seemed to set new standards globally. Timothy Geithner, US Treasury secretary, softened his previously critical tone when he said in a press conference that, 'We very much welcome the steps [China has] taken to stimulate domestic demand...[and its] continued commitment to move to a more flexible exchange rate.'

These two simultaneous events are likely to provide two different angles on China for some time to come. In the first piece of news, China's fury and sensitivity reveal that it still bears the scars of past humiliations, and is unable to throw off the memory of distressing historical events. Even China's great revival serves as a reminder of its painful past. And the second piece of news shows the world taking a new view of China as an emerging power, destined to become the next world leader.

One paradox of China today is that it feels both strong and weak. Its powerful economic growth gives it a strength the world recognizes, but at the same time, its feeling of weakness runs deep, stemming from historical memories as well as contemporary experiences. Deep-seated feelings of being backward and humiliated have never really disappeared. So when a *Times* newspaper reporter interviewed ordinary people in Beijing during the Olympics, they expressed intense pride and, at the same time, let slip remarks like, 'I feel that now the Chinese people have stood up.' Such a simple but significant comment. After all, Mao Zedong said the very same thing back in 1949.

In reality, China's power is a function of the scale of the country. What foreigners see is its massive 1.3 billion population, while domestically people realize that even the greatest of achievements is tiny, when shared among 1.3 billion people. China has reached the status of a great power with startling suddenness and is still not sure how to present itself as it joins in the game. For a number of years, it has been China's boast that it is deliberately keeping a low profile. But in its reticence, it has neglected to study the rest of the world and so is unprepared, both intellectually and psychologically, for the new role it must play. Sometimes China appears so confident it verges on arrogant; at other times it appears over-sensitive, and prone to flinch away from criticism. The rest of the world's fear of China – in the face of China's constant assertions that its rise is peaceful and that, historically, it has been invaded rather more often than it has invaded other countries – is, in many ways, perplexing. On the other hand, China can sometimes appears to be unaware of the view, expressed by the political scientist Robert Gilpin, that, 'Throughout history a principal objective of states has been the conquest of territory in order to advance economic, security, and other interests.' How to heal the painful memories and understand the new world is the most pressing problem that China faces. One day, China may be back in possession of the twelve bronze animal heads. But even more important than their symbolic significance is the fact that, through the process of regaining them, China must grow up quickly and develop a more mature understanding of its relationship with the world.

ANGRY URUMQI

26 July 2009

Sorrow, terror and a profound anger have overwhelmed Urumqi. On the night of 5 July 2009, the city was the scene of a premeditated massacre. Photos and stories have leaked out, showing that many of the dead did not die from street violence but were killed at home, old and young alike, sometimes whole families, and most of these were Han Chinese. The clashes in the streets were insignificant compared to the tragedies that played out in the back alleys.

The Western media instinctively take the side of the Uighurs, whom they have persisted in seeing as a vulnerable colonized people facing the formidable dictatorship of Beijing and outnumbered by the Han Chinese, just like the Tibetans of the high plateau. But from the point of view of the rest of the population of China, it was only too easy to believe stories of a massacre. In many central Chinese cities, Uighurs have a bad reputation. They are seen as violent thugs and thieves, enjoying privileges that Hans do not. The police even sometimes stand by when they commit crimes, as if enforcing the law might harm ethnic sensitivities. But it has to be said that few Hans have really bothered to try and understand the Uighurs' grievances, their faith, their customs, their history, their hopes and fears. Most of the time, the Hans are racist without knowing it, rarely appreciating communities which are different from theirs, especially those that are weaker.

On the surface, the reaction of the local government during the present disturbances has been different from in the recent past. Officials have been more open-minded than they were in Lhasa in 2008, allowing the media, especially foreign reporters, to enter the region and carry out interviews. But the intrinsic logic of their behaviour has not changed. As the massacre spread, local officials were completely wrong-footed. Desperate phone calls pleading for help went unanswered. For a few hours on the night of 5 July, their city was plunged into madness. The officials decided the tragedy was completely unrelated to the government's own policies and actions, and blamed it on manipulation by external terrorist forces. In other words, they passed the buck. They refused properly to consider the root causes of the riots, and started a campaign against the activist Rebiya Kadeer, elevating her to super-terrorist status. And this is a woman who is not terribly competent; she even confused photographs of clashes in Urumqi with separate ones in Shishou, in Hubei province.

At the same time, there has been a clumsy attempt to paper over the cracks with propaganda: more troops, the restoration of order, more food in the supermarkets. People began to walk in the streets again and different nationalities who live in Xinjiang went on record as saying that the ethnic groups were unified, it was only a small minority who were violent, and that development could only be achieved with stability.

Of course only a small minority are violent and stability is crucial. But to ignore the social factors that gave rise to the violence, to read repression as stability, can only bring greater problems in its wake.

Ethnic conflict is something the whole world finds hard to resolve. The trigger for every movement for independence (or secession) is the desire for recognition of a community's special identity. But the immediate reasons for such conflict are more often the powers of a dictatorship, violent policies and an out-of-kilter economy.

Let us put aside for the moment restrictions placed on religious freedom by Beijing's ethnic polices post-1949, and the fact that the so-called autonomous regions have never really achieved autonomy. In the last fifteen years alone, two major political and economic changes have foreshadowed the tragedy of today. Wang Lixiong, the Han Chinese husband of the Tibetan dissident Woeser, believes that 'Document No.7', published in March 1996, clearly indicated a hardening in the government's stance. Crucially, it stated that the key element threatening the stability of Xinjiang was 'separatist forces and illegal religious activities'.* After the document's publication, there were increasingly fierce attacks on 'separatist forces and illegal religious activities'. Wang Lixiong believes that compared with the six years leading up to its publication, 1990 to March 1996, the five years that followed, March 1996 to 2001, produced far more intense terrorist activity, with the death toll rising more than threefold and the number of injured rising fourfold. In other words, a hard-line government stance has nurtured hard-line rebels.

Starting in the year 2000, the west of China was opened up for development on a massive scale, which brought in its wake a huge increase in investment and business opportunities, as well as an influx of Han Chinese. As far as these small traders and migrant workers from Henan, Sichuan and Zhejiang provinces in the interior of China were concerned, Xinjiang was just another place to try and make a living. It was never going to be their home, they just wanted to earn some money and get out. Ever since the time of the Qing dynasty, the government has looked on Han Chinese migrants as the best way to stabilize the border regions. But because the Uighurs were originally occupied by force, they fear Han immigration and see it as a threat. Not only have key posts in government and the economy been taken over by Hans, they have also taken ordinary jobs. The large numbers of Hans make the Uighurs feel afraid of being overwhelmed in their homeland.

The Uighurs have therefore turned on the Han immigrants, although both communities are actually victims of a giant,

---

* In March 1996, the Standing Committee of the CPC Politburo – the seven most powerful men in China – convened a special session to discuss the 'Xinjiang question'. The official record of that meeting, issued as a 'top secret: classified document, called "Document No. 7"', is indicative of the Beijing leadership's current theoretical perspective on, and its practical policy response to, the challenges confronting Chinese rule in Xinjiang in the post-Soviet era. http://www.hrw.org/legacy/campaigns/china-98/sj_xnj2.htm.

out-of-kilter political machine. In Urumqi, race and religion have just added to an already complex problem.

CHINA SWINGS BETWEEN EXTREMES

14 October 2009

When the parades marched through Tiananmen Square in 1949, people thought they were witnessing the rise of a new China, but what they were actually seeing was the grandiose re-emergence of the old era, complete with a vacuous commentary, totalitarian aesthetic, and a personality cult. Underlying this relentless process was the regime's passion for monopolizing political and economic power, and even individuals' private thoughts.

The sixtieth anniversary celebrations of National Day on 1 October 2009 demonstrated the political changes of the last few years, years in which the whole world has been plunged into speculation (and hopes and fears) that China will become the next world leader. They hope that China will solve the financial crisis, combat global warming, and that Beijing will not only behave responsibly but also inject new dynamism into global cooperation. As for Beijing's repression of human rights, free speech and democracy, that's a domestic problem which can be overlooked for the time being: US Secretary of State Hillary Clinton talks only about the environment, and Obama refuses to meet the Dalai Lama.

However, recent developments in China are hardly in keeping with the idea of a society moving towards a bright, shiny future of free speech and democracy: the official media has dubbed the Dalai Lama a 'wolf in sheep's clothing'; after the disturbances in Xinjiang, it was claimed that two of the children of the Uighur activist Rebiya Kadeer had publicly denounced their mother; and university students have accused their professors of teaching them 'reactionary history'. The novelist Mo Yan pronounced at the 2009 Frankfurt Book Fair that 'China enjoys relative freedom of speech'. Yet the latest news is a notice from the Education Ministry that students are being mustered to post patriotic messages on the Internet over Chinese New Year. China is deluged with ideology, with the state remorselessly taking over the lives of its citizens. It's all reminiscent of The Carpenters' song 'Yesterday Once More'. Underlying this relentless process is the regime's passion for monopolizing political and economic power, and even individuals' private thoughts. Ironically, while the world overestimates China's strength, the regime underestimates it, seeing dangers lurking in every corner. It even sees mobile phone 'sexting' as a potential threat.

The ever-perceptive Lucian Pye[*] has summed up Chinese politics as bouncing between the two extremes of ideology and pragmatism, in contrast to America where the struggle is between liberals and conservatives. The ideological end of the spectrum stresses containment, compliance and central control, while pragmatism is more tolerant and free, and delegates powers. We can see many examples of this. The successive eras dominated by Mao Zedong and Deng Xiaoping saw China swing between the two extremes. Even within Deng's period in office there were many swings of this sort. A year after the Third Plenum of the 11th National Party Congress, in December 1978, which marked the beginning of the 'Reform and Opening Up' of China's economy, Beijing put the dissident Wei Jingsheng on trial. Immediately after experimental local elections came condemnation of the play *Bitter Love*, which described a painter's ardent love for his country, and how that

* Lucian Pye (1921–2008) was a distinguished American sinologist and political scientist who taught at the Massachusetts Institute of Technology for thirty-five years.

country trampled on it. Even in the 1980s, a decade which came to symbolize personal freedom, there were broad-ranging campaigns against 'spiritual pollution' and 'capitalist liberalization'. This all demonstrated that the regime wanted to control what people saw, talked about and read, even if its youth wore jeans. Beijing's conflicting attitudes towards the West are clear: it needs its capital and its technology, but it worries that Western influence may undermine its control.

Nowadays, the regime seems to stand at the peak of its strength, bolstered by the power of money and the terror of its police force. The West seems to have lost all its bargaining power, and liberal factions within the regime have simply faded away. But Beijing, which continually stresses nationalism, forgets the ancient Chinese wisdom – that pendulums always swing back the other way. Splendour and decline go hand in hand. This regime has a terrifying ability to pose as lenient, liberal, open, pragmatic and progressive, deluding people that this is the dawn of a new era. And its people forgive it so easily. Stability and progress in today's China can only be achieved by means of popular amnesia.

A VICTORY FOR ORNAMENT

13 December 2009

Everyone is talking about Wang Zifei, a research student at Shanghai's Communications University. On 6 November, she happened to be sitting behind Barack Obama among a 500-strong audience in the Shanghai Science and Technology Museum. The American media like to stress that this was the first time that an American president had conducted a Town Hall-style meeting in a communist country. Like all political leaders, Obama had expressed a fervent desire for a meeting with young people. However, on this occasion, the personal charisma and eloquence that has charmed the world fell flat. After some dull, reserved exchanges with the students, he deliberately raised the question of the Great Firewall and Twitter. He is firmly convinced of the power of information to bring about change.

Chinese netizens watching Obama online seemed to have no interest in what he was saying. It was the student behind him that attracted far more attention. She was young and beautiful, and very composed, and while Obama was speaking, she took off her scarlet coat to reveal a black dress underneath.

The reason why she took off her coat is inconsequential. The fact is it immediately earned her the nickname 'Obama girl'. By the third day of Obama's state visit, most young people were thinking about Wang Zifei, even though she had not spoken a word. The Internet – quite contrary to the dull questions of the young audience with their identical expressions – was abuzz with excited speculation.

Welcome to the new China. A China getting more rigid and stupid by the day. (Even its youth, who ought to be the most lively, are prematurely set in their ways.) The Hong Kong journalist Rose Lüqiu Luwei recalls two previous American presidents visiting Shanghai. In 1984, Reagan gave a talk in Fudan University's Xianghui Hall, an unforgettable experience for the university's graduates, not so much because the American president represented power but because the exchanges were open and spontaneous. She was also present in 1998, when Clinton visited China and appeared at the Shanghai Library. On that occasion, there were eight Chinese on the platform and Bill and Hillary Clinton put the questions to them. The eight each gave their views of what was happening in China from a different angle. One of them was Wang Hai, the famous consumer rights advocate, regarded as representing a growing awareness of civil society. Compared with Reagan and Clinton, Obama had a highly formalized encounter with China's youth. It was as if we had gone back to the Nixon era, with everyone, from president to teachers, parroting the exact same lines.

But this is also a China full of noise, confusion and mockery. A country of terrifying cynicism, with no ideals worth respecting, and no goals worth pursuing. Everything can be scoffed at, in fact, can *only* be scoffed at. Fudan students remember Reagan fondly, not just for his personal charisma, but because of the values he believed in. Of course, they took too rosy a view of America, but they knew what they aspired to. This was especially because China had just been through a long period of repression and isolation, and these young people were full of curiosity about how things could be different. They liked the sound of the freedom, openness and democracy that America represented. And of course there was the equality – no Chinese leader could talk to them as equals, the way Reagan did. The same went for Clinton, whose relative youth no doubt made the American dream even more attractive. China in 1998 was opening up and going up, and people believed that these were ideals worth pursuing.

But by the time Obama arrived, the mood in China had changed radically. The country has grown much stronger. There is much mindless banging of the nationalist drum, a phony arrogance, and people no longer feel that China has anything to learn from outsiders. China's educational system has gone completely bankrupt in the last decade, and young people's powers of independent thinking and willingness to stick their necks out has atrophied. Political isolationism has brought repression, warping the mood of society so that ridicule has become the only weapon of resistance and, indeed, an aim in itself. People have now turned their energies to frivolous entertainments; the Internet is not just an instrument of progress. By making people's feelings bigger, it has magnified repression and mockery, and it has huge power to reduce everything to a single common denominator. This mechanism of social dialogue has not only not evolved, but has become more repressive and extreme.

Obama may be the most inspirational president since Kennedy, but he obviously lacks the ability to arouse the curiosity of young Chinese. Doesn't the news keep telling them that the Chinese model is a winner? Why should they think beyond that? And in this era of instant entertainment, people have lost the ability to go deep into issues. Serious explorations of foreign relations and political concepts have disappeared from public discourse. As a result, young people only understand the entertainment value of anything. Wang Zifei taking off her coat is far easier to discuss than Obama's politics.

The new reality of China is one nightmare after another. What Orwell most feared was the banning of books, the suppression of information, the concealment of truth, the controlling of culture. Huxley's nightmare was that no one would be willing to read books, that a deluge of information would overwhelm people's ability to reflect, that the truth would be submerged by the tediousness of worldly affairs, that culture would be debased to superficial entertainment which overstimulated the senses and the appetite... Orwell's nightmare has not yet come to pass, but Huxley's has, in many different forms. Obama had stepped, unwittingly, into a Brave New China.

PITCHFORKS IN THE PLAYGROUND

23 May 2010

Five years after Hu Jintao first coined the slogan 'social harmony', the crowd-control pitchfork has arrived in the primary school playground. A series of attacks on schoolchildren has plunged parents and teachers alike into panic.* Anxiety has spread from riots in Shanxi coal mines and in Xinjiang, all of which felt safely far away, to killings at the school gate.

In one news item, about Shenzhen, I learned that the police were training with pitchforks, in the hope of subduing future opponents. In Beijing, many schools employ a policeman or a security guard of some sort. In Shanghai, children are not allowed to run and play freely in the playground, and are kept in the classroom. You might be forgiven for thinking that the whole of society is under military lockdown. The Lhasa and Urumqi models are no longer far away; when people live in fear, they want the streets to be full of police. But can the police really protect us in our daily lives?

Chinese society has got itself into a vicious circle. On the one hand, the expansion of bureaucracy is the main reason for our social ills, stifling commercial creativity, undermining the education system, creating endless waste, swallowing up most of the wealth that the Chinese people have produced, destroying cultural traditions, suppressing freedom of speech, and driving those whose homes are forcibly demolished to do things like set themselves on fire. On the other hand, bureaucracy is the only way that people feel safe. They want bureaucracy to drive share prices up, drive house prices down, attack corruption and protect their children.

The politicians are proficient at playing this game: they connive at rampant bureaucratic interference in commerce, society and culture while constantly making new pledges to

---

* On 23 March 2010, eight children were murdered by a knife-wielding assailant, Zheng Minsheng, at a shool in Nanping in Fujian province. In late April, sixteen children and a teacher were wounded in a similar attack at Leizhou in Guangdong province. Further attacks followed in Jiangsu and Shandong on the 29th and 30th of that month. Wu Huanming, a school landlord, then killed seven children at a kindergarten in Hanzhong, in Shaanxi province, on 12 May.

give people a democratic and dignified life. A lot of contradictory thinking has taken hold in Chinese society. One minute, people criticize power-for-money deals and systemic corruption; the next, they praise the dictatorship for its effectiveness and attribute to it China's rapid rise to power. People also blame all society's ills on local officialdom; saying that the central government wants to take charge of its people but its decrees never get beyond the walls of Zhongnanhai.* Or they believe that China is so huge, that of course government controls must be strengthened. School shootings and stabbings doubtless exacerbate these contradictory beliefs, because fear has turned the government and the police into symbols of security. But will government controls have the desired effect?

It is almost as if the louder we shout Hu's slogans 'social harmony' and 'eight moral maxims', the more rapidly society degenerates. In the last five years, 'harmony' has existed only in the newspapers and on our TV screens, and the 'eight maxims' only in official speeches. Let us face up to this reality: China has an ever-deepening social crisis, rooted chiefly in the ballooning of a bureaucracy which is incapable of providing a solution. Murders of schoolchildren in Nanping (Fujian province) and Taizhou (Jiangsu province) have enraged the public but so has the official response. In an attempt to hide what had happened, officials refused to allow parents to pay their last respects to the dead children because it might endanger 'social harmony' and cause the officials to lose their jobs.

Belief in bureaucracy is nihilistic. It says that there is nothing in this world more important than authority; life, dignity and freedom have no value. So how can we expect bureaucrats to protect anyone?

In the last five years, a renewed emphasis on ideology

---

* Zhongnanhai is a compound in Beijing (next to the Forbidden City), and the central headquarters of the Communist Party of China and the State Council (or central government) of the People's Republic of China.

has aggravated the spread of nihilism and cynicism. 'Social harmony' has become a pretext for controlling freedom of speech, further reduced the media's ability to investigate and expose, and made the bureaucracy more arrogant. A wave of nationalization has turned the bureaucracy into the embodiment of power and money, and has created an ever-increasing dependence on it. Politicians have whipped up populism, defusing the pressure for political reform, and turning it into fanatical nationalism or even Han Chinese chauvinism. At the same time, all non-official and community organizations have come under serious attack, making it impossible for a multiplicity of cultural and social values to be established. This has forced a situation where the buffer between the people and the government has been eroded and all that remains is the individual and a vast bureaucracy. There are no community organizations to ease the pressure on the ordinary people and bring them together to confront their problems. You can only rely on the government. So, fleecing the state system any way you can, or expunging your loneliness with a brief glorious moment of fanatical nationalism, are the natural choices.

However, as part of the same process, bureaucratic logic is beginning to dominate the whole of society and each individual. Spontaneity and independence have disappeared, and no one feels they have to be responsible for their own actions anymore. Society has become ever more insecure, more boring, more lacking in creativity and human sympathy. This has created a social desert in which extreme opinions and actions flourish. It is as if there are only two things you can be in this life – the oppressed or the oppressor.

We find ourselves now in a vicious circle where desperate remedies are adopted regardless of the consequences. Society has become more and more bureaucratic and people are less able to fend for themselves. Social cohesion and faith in the system are at an all-time low and people expect the government to solve every problem for them. So the government becomes more inflated, more bureaucratic and more arrogant, and the only thing it can do is stick labels like 'Xinjiang lone operator' or 'Tibetan lone operator' onto rioters, denounce murderers as 'mentally ill', produce more crowd-control pitchforks and put more police onto the streets, thus suffocating society even more.

If people really want to protect themselves, then we need to embark on a long and difficult journey of rebuilding our society. The media needs to demand more freedoms, and to expose more injustices, to uncover the deep-seated reasons for this social crisis. Individuals need to form into a variety of community organizations to help each other. We will only have security, democracy and individual freedoms if everyone fights for them. Freedoms that are bestowed never really belong to us.

A FAILED SOCIETY ON FIRE

9 January 2011

The taxi stopped and the driver pointed in an easterly direction. 'It's that black building,' he said, 'charred like roast duck.' Some sections of Jiaozhou Road were still closed off to traffic. It was a Sunday afternoon, I was in Shanghai and I thought I would go and see the building destroyed by a fire that, four weeks previously, had shocked all of China. After a World Expo vaunted as the most extravagant in history, the Shanghainese discovered that their lives could be snuffed out just like that. In the space of four hours, the fire took fifty-eight lives.

The speed of the authorities' response to the fire was in inverse proportion to the speed with which it spread. The fire engines were only a block away but still managed to arrive late; the firefighters were helpless because their hoses only provided a feeble flow of water.

A week went by, and public anger grew as more details leaked out. From the fact that the building was being renovated with eco-friendly materials, to the endless subcontracting of different levels of the project, to the Shanghai media's collective silence, and to official indifference to the disaster. Every detail pointed to a bureaucratic system roundly condemned by the public as being ever more grossly inflated, grandiose and greedy, as well as extraordinarily arrogant, and indifferent to the point of stupidity.

The fire also put paid to the complacency of the Shanghainese, and we saw another side of them. Traditionally, they have been known for their propensity to haggle over minutiae and count every cent they spend; when they come across outsiders, they generally behave with a superiority only they know how to assume. They inhabit the wealthiest, most modern and most fashion-conscious city in Mainland China. After the fire, I remember a Shanghainese colleague, who previously could only talk about Prada and house prices, posting comment after comment on Weibo. She eventually decided to emigrate. Insecurity and indignation even drove the Shanghainese onto the streets. At the memorial ceremonies held on the seventh day of mourning, crowds estimated to number 100,000 assembled around the building, holding white flowers. Some perched on cardboard boxes and formed a makeshift orchestra to perform 'Time to Say Goodbye'. Some of the families of victims refused compensation for the deaths, saying they wanted to see people held responsible. The scenes of protest were very encouraging. After all, this was Shanghai. Further inland, protests in Weng'an in Guizhou and Shishou in Hubei had been violent and ended in riots. But the Shanghainese know how to use reason and restraint and put forward their demands in a civilized way.

Yet in my taxi driver, I met a reaction I had not expected. 'I can't feel any sympathy,' he said 'The dead were all wealthy people with connections.' The driver was in his forties, with a South China accent, and as voluble as a Beijing taxi driver. He said that this block was so centrally located that only the wealthiest could live there, and yet each family had received government grants of 50,000 yuan (£4,800) for the additional eco-friendly renovations. One of the victims, he said, was someone in their twenties, living on the first floor, who died after taking refuge in the bathroom. How stupid not to be able to find a way out. He reckoned the relatives were only protesting so they could get more money. If the former city head, Chen Liangyu,* was still in office, he said, something like this would never have happened. He spoke in mocking tones, as if the victims were wholly separate to him. Class animosity, it seemed, had suppressed in him the normal human impulse to feel sympathy.

This short conversation in the taxi went round and round my head. It reminded me that when the fire had just broken out, I was watching pictures on the Internet being filmed by a young person on their mobile phone in a nearby building. Apart from the burning building you could hear the person talking, 'Ai-ya! There's not a chance they'll escape, they'll all be burned alive!' What made me uneasy was not what they were saying but their complete indifference and the detachment in their tone of voice, as if they were watching a film.

Many years ago I read of a conversation between the Qing dynasty general, Zeng Guofan and his top advisor, Zhao Liewen, during the Taiping Rebellion. The year was 1867, and

* Chen Liangyu (b. 1946) was Shanghai party secretary from 2002, but lost his job in 2006 after accusations of illegal activity and corruption. It is believed that he was the victim of intra-Party struggles. Shanghai under Chen experienced rapid development, which won him the general approbation of Shanghai's citizens.

the general was describing a scene in the capital, 'The situation at the gates to the city is terrible and there have been fires and fighting. The city's beggars have gathered, even half-naked women in rags. The people have absolutely nothing left. I am afraid that great changes are about to happen. What is to be done?' To this Zhao Liewen responded,

> Imperial rule has lasted so long that it is tending towards disintegration. But the current emperor's virtue is still greatly respected and disaster has not yet struck. So long as our will does not fail, then society will not fall apart. However I foresee catastrophe; imperial power will be overturned, the empire will be leaderless, the people will govern themselves, and this will happen within fifty years.

I was very struck by the idea of failure of will. In the last few years, there have been scandals such as melamine-tainted milk, factories exploiting workers with learning disabilities, and the massacre of primary school students, while corruption has grown to eye-popping levels. Nowadays nobody has the will to confront moral problems, and the whole of society seems oblivious to the difference between right and wrong.

If you do not like Zhao Liewen's karmic despair, there is sociologist Sun Liping's concept of the 'collapse of society', which he used to interpret the modern age. We live in a time infatuated with systems. Many friends of mine believe that if we can only change the current political system, society's ability to rebuild itself will exceed all our expectations. Unfortunately, I think they are overly optimistic.

OLD FRIENDS OF CHINA

13 March 2011

China has made an unexpected appearance in Middle Eastern politics. In his most recent and possibly his last TV speech, Colonel Muammar Gaddafi stated that he will defend his power at all costs. He spoke in resounding, urgent tones, and wore a ferocious expression, snarling like a cornered beast. In the speech, which lasted seventy-five minutes and completely lacked any logic, he proclaimed that he would defend his position 'to the last drop of blood'. He also mentioned China, comparing Libya today to China in 1989. According to him, it was the suppression of the Tiananmen protests on 4 June in that year, which stabilized China and made it prosperous. 'Absolute unity is more important for China than the Tiananmen demonstrators,' he declared.

I don't know whether our leaders should laugh or cry at this. They have always hoped that China would influence the world not only through trade and finance but also through its values. The 'China model' has risen to the occasion in many guises, and now a modern-day tyrant has drawn on it for his valedictory speech.

Gaddafi has been an 'old friend' of China for a number of years, in an alliance against the Western powers, and he is a proponent of the concept of the 'Third World'. China has in the past given Gaddafi funds and inspiration: his 'Green Book' is a clumsy imitation of Mao Zedong's 'Little Red Book'. He shares a fervent belief with Mao that the only thing worth fighting for is power. However, Gaddafi is a more masculine figure than Mao. He lives in a tent, surrounds himself with tall, sturdy female bodyguards, and can give a speech lasting several hours without drawing breath.

Over time, as ideological bonds have weakened, cooperation has changed into the protection of mutual interests. Libya's oil has fuelled China's growth. Chinese companies have sent workers to the North African country in large numbers, to extract oil, and to build roads and railways to transport Chinese goods for sale there.

Money has been a driver for corruption, and has also given new life to moribund thinking. In the spring of 2007, the Arabic language department at Wuhan University set up the Gaddafi Institute for the study of Libya's Green Book. In 2004, the former ambassador to Libya praised Gaddafi as a fervent revolutionary idealist, a legendary hero who 'could not be overlooked'. He professed himself moved by Gaddafi's pure Islamic faith, his shutting down of dance halls and brothels, and his abstention from 'killing living beings'.

Perhaps in Gaddafi's eyes, humans are not worthy of the name 'living beings'. After all, he refuses to eat prawns and fish but doesn't fret about killing people. Twenty years ago, in 1988, he manufactured the bombing of Pan Am Flight 103 over Lockerbie* to target the Americans. Now he has turned his guns against his own people, calling them 'rats' that should be purged.

Both China's ambassador and the Wuhan professors would appear to approve of Gaddafi's values. This is a perfect demonstration of another characteristic of the emerging China: no matter how strong it becomes, it retains a terrifying moral insensitivity. From top leaders to ordinary people, this insensitivity permeates the whole of Chinese society.

Why stop at Libya's Gaddafi? China has a whole string of loathsome 'old friends', including Cambodia's Pol Pot, North

---

* Pan Am Flight 103 was destroyed by a terrorist bomb on Wednesday 21 December 1988, killing all 243 passengers and sixteen crew on board. Large sections of the aircraft crashed onto the town of Lockerbie in southern Scotland, killing eleven people on the ground.

Korea's Kim Jong-il, Myanmar's military junta and Zimbabwe's Robert Mugabe. Ideology, strategic needs, economic collaboration can all cause China to turn a blind eye to evil. You could put it that national interests always trump moral principles; America, a state that regards itself as righteous, has also supported one dictatorship after another. But American public opinion still makes itself heard, while in China, few people have examined their conscience. The massacres carried out by the Khmer Rouge, the famines in North Korea, the humanitarian crisis in Darfur, Sudan, have never impinged on China's social consciousness. This has something to do with state control of the media, meaning that we have little knowledge of what is going on in the outside world. Or could it be that we ourselves face so much hardship that we simply have no space to sympathize with the hardships of others? Either way, this stupidity and moral relativism has an impact on our own interests: if you cannot empathize with other people's suffering, how can you understand your own?

Crazy dictators can always be overthrown and even put to death. In the last thirty years, the Chinese have witnessed many of their 'old friends' being toppled from power. Every time this has happened, it has no doubt reduced the Chinese leadership to fear and trembling, and perhaps allowed some Chinese people a sigh of relief. But in essence nothing has changed. We still do not make moral judgments about the world. The Chinese government has despatched military ships and planes to bring Chinese workers home. Photographs have appeared in the Chinese newspapers, on the Internet and on TV, showing the evacuees elated to have escaped disaster and to be on their way home. China's Propaganda Ministry has skilfully turned the crisis into a victory. 'Look how your government takes such good care of its people,' is the message. 'Your powerful motherland is protecting ordinary people.' Indeed, if Gaddafi had not reminded them, no doubt many

Chinese would have forgotten about the terrible events in Beijing twenty-two years ago.

A GHOST FROM THE GRAVE

10 June 2011

One day, a few months ago, I was staying in a guesthouse in Hebei province. It was cold and cheerless and the bed linen was soiled, but its name – the Emperor's Lodging House – was resonant with glorious historical associations. From the middle of the eighteenth century until 1912, this grand-sounding hotel in Liangge village, Yi county, about 75 miles (120 km) from Beijing, was a royal lodge. Emperors used to journey here to offer sacrifices to the ancestors. The body of the emperor Guangxu (1875–1908) rested here for four years.

During the day, I visited the Western Qing imperial tombs; the emperors Yongzheng, Jiaqing and Daoguang, as well as Guangxu, were all buried here. They are exquisite, and on a huge scale, emblematic of the rise and fall of the Qing dynasty. Now the glory and the awe has faded somewhat, and the tombs have become just another tourist attraction. Outside the mausoleums, hawkers flog indiscriminate heaps of poorly printed bestsellers; from accounts of Yongzheng's rule to Mao Zedong's philosophy of power, cheek by jowl with biographies of the empress Cixi, and of Mao's third wife Jiang Qing, all lightly coated with dust. What has not faded in China today is the allure of absolute power.

In the evening, I retreated to my hotel room. Beijing TV was running a lecture contest on the topic of the 'Party Spirit'. The contestants were a bunch of young men and women smartly turned out in Western-style suits, village officials, political cadres from state-run industries, office workers. They all stood there, dignified and impassioned, spouting the kind of thing that reminded me of my childhood political education classes, full of elaborate parallel phrases and clichés, brimming with enthusiasm, but completely meaningless, indeed, illogical. It seems hard to believe that their words bore any relation to what they really thought. It was all a performance. They were acting their loyalty, and the audience was acting its applause.

I suddenly realized that the ideological movement that began with Bo Xilai in Chongqing had finally reached Beijing. Three years ago, when I first heard about the red songs, revolutionary stories and 'red text messages' being sent to people's mobile phones, it had just seemed like a joke.

These people are self-serving so-called Marxists, but they haven't read Marx's famous essay, 'The Eighteenth Brumaire of Louis Napoleon', where he wrote: 'Hegel remarks somewhere that all great world-historic facts and personages appear, so to speak, twice. He forgot to add: the first time as tragedy, the second time as farce.' When Louis Bonaparte tried to restore the empire, assuming the glory of his uncle Napoleon's name, it wasn't only about personal ambition. French society was in turmoil and the French embraced the 'Bonaparte myth' and supported Louis' claim to the throne, out of anxiety that they would otherwise be left leaderless.

In present-day China, something similar has happened. People have borrowed the mantle of Mao Zedong, invoking the imagined spirit of his era: more just, less corrupt and bureaucratic. In the last three years, this fiction seems to have come true, with a crackdown on crime and the singing of red songs proving popular not only in Chongqing, but all over China. The General's Children Choir has toured the country and delegations from every province have arrived in Chongqing to pay their respects. Other cities have run their own red songs events, cheered on by the country's intelligentsia who lend theoretical respectability to the new model.

Other aspects of the Mao period have taken hold too: some county towns have conducted public trials, and study courses on the Party are flourishing.

Is the farce turning back into tragedy? From the start of Bo Xilai's campaign to promote Maoist quotes and red songs, it was possible to hear internecine political struggles going in the background, with supporters of the revolution fighting over who were its true heirs. The louder the singing, the more bitter the struggles over the Party line. But subsequently, they seemed all to be singing from the same songbook. Top-level leaders, no matter how intense their struggle to defend their own interests, have all approved this experiment. It is as if with the worsening of social tensions, the difficulties in maintaining economic growth, and the bankruptcy of ideology, this dubious wave of nostalgia has re-energized the top leaders (and pacified the public and briefly united Party members) in their attempt to entrench themselves in power.

You can bring back ghosts from beyond the grave but they are still ghosts. Louis Bonaparte never succeeded in restoring the glory of the French empire, as his backers very soon found out. He proved an extravagant but weak ruler, swinging helplessly between empire and republic. Similar 'restoration' attempts were made in the Soviet Union in the era of Brezhnev, who tried to recreate himself in Stalin's image and strengthen his control over society. However, after a superficially stable eighteen years, the Soviet Union abruptly collapsed. It was Brezhnev's weakness and not Gorbachev's reforms which put paid to the Soviet empire. That was the fundamental reason.

These leaders tried to reinstate a defunct Communist totalitarianism because they were under the mistaken impression they could manipulate history for their own ends. Eventually history humiliated them.

CHINA'S ROBBERS

18 December 2011

At the end of the year, the Chinese government at all levels discovered that there was 3.5 trillion yuan (£350 billion) left unspent in the budgets. Spending that much money in one month has become an absurd challenge, and regional expenditure has, accordingly, become preposterously inflated.

In Shenzhen, the local government spent 1.6 million yuan (£160,000) to rebuild pedestrian overpasses that were never received and installed. In Changchun, the police department splurged on laptops worth nearly 30,000 yuan (£3,000). In almost every city, people open their front doors to find highways being dug up unnecessarily, and the rising dust clouds herald nothing more than the digging up of old road surfaces to replace them with new ones.

The rise of China as a power has astonished the world, and the expansion of its government has been even more dramatic. It is the greatest beneficiary of economic growth. For the last three quarters of the year, China's GDP grew 9.4%, while government income grew 29.5%. Figures have been comparable for a good many years, and keep growing. The government keeps discovering that it cannot match expenditure with income. Thus, at the end of 2007, there was a sudden rush to spend 1.2 trillion yuan (£120 billion). At the end of 2008, it was 1.5 trillion (£150 billion). And at the end of 2009, it was 2 trillion (£2 billion). There is nothing that characterizes China's government more clearly than these figures. The government no longer guides economic development but simply acts like a barefaced robber. Moreover, a robber that no longer only operates at central government level but has its fingers in the till of every regional government.

Anywhere you travel in China, you can see concrete evidence of the way local government is fleecing the people – in the buildings. Even the poorest county towns have the most splendid municipal buildings, with spacious plazas and huge office blocks. In stark contrast, you will hear dispossessed families voicing grievances about having their homes demolished, and ordinary people telling you how worried they are about the state of education, about food safety and about falling ill and not being able to afford the medical bills. Feelings of insecurity are everywhere. The main impression given by the bloated bureaucratic institutions is not that they can solve these problems, but that they are causing them.

Some people believe that because no Budgetary Law has been promulgated, it is impossible to curb government spending at different levels. But internal checks and balances have never been effective. Behind the existing structure of anti-corruption offices, corruption runs rampant. Until there is monitoring by NGOs, all talk of democracy within the Party is just so much idle chit-chat.

China today brings to mind the judgment of the US-based political scientist, Professor Pei Minxin. Five years ago he said that China is 'trapped in transition'. In my opinion, those people who praise the 'China model' and the 'Beijing consensus' lack not brains but a heart. And if you try to treat China as if it were Japan, Korea or another East Asian country, you will quickly find that the main role of the Chinese government in the last few years has been to fleece its people rather than to guide them.

Pei's comment could not show more clearly how illusions about China have been shattered. We used to think that economic progress would bring with it a degree of political liberalization but, in reality, economic growth has also had negative consequences, bringing more benefits to the ruling elite who then firmly reject calls for political reform. Additionally, they have vast resources at their disposal with which to buy off possible resistance.

We used to believe that gradual reform was better than shock treatment. But nowadays, I have come to the conclusion that gradual reform actually produces its own plethora of problems. The more sluggish the reform, the more difficult it is to kick-start it. At the same time, the social and environmental costs have become more apparent.

I would like to believe that a highly effective authoritarian regime could be good for economic growth but now I know this is just wishful thinking. If we lack the concept of the rule of law, civil society, media freedom and political opposition, then the government quickly degenerates into a robber government.

In this situation, China's economic growth is poor quality growth. As an ordinary Chinese person, you not only do not enjoy its benefits, you feel as if you have been ripped off. And the growth gives birth to worse corruption.

Ten years ago, when political scientists envisaged China's future, this was one scenario: corruption would become more serious, and a robber government would stunt economic growth, affecting China's international image and strength. A chaotic and corrupt authoritarian system would be established and officials would only be concerned with their own narrow interests. In this scenario, there would be constant low-level disturbances and order could only be maintained by a powerful police force. China would have no interest in playing an important and constructive part on the international stage. Its actions would be short-sighted and vacillating, just sufficient to enable it to get by.

To a very large degree, China is now on this grim road.

THERE'S ONLY ONE WUKAN

1 April 2012

You can meet all sorts of people around Wukan's* street stalls: newly elected Village Party Committee members, volunteers from Guangzhou, 'petitioners' from Zhejiang appealing against local government decisions, students from Beijing with proposals, documentary filmmakers from Tokyo. But the majority are reporters working for various news outlets – from the French newspaper *Libération*, to Qatar's Al Jazeera TV station.

P eople introduce themselves, and discuss the election results, the latest happenings or the latest rumours. As the drama in Wukan plays out, some people have paid several visits and have built up friendships with the villagers, and have even found themselves drawn into the emerging struggle.

The most enthusiastic visitors are always from Hong Kong. 'They have it so much better than us,' they say, in their Guangzhou-accented Mandarin, spoken slowly and clearly so I know what they mean: these villagers have one person, one vote, while fifteen years after Hong Kong was returned to Chinese control, its people still only have 1,200 representatives to elect the head of their Special Economic Region. In a certain sense, the Hong Kong media's enthusiastic praise of Wukan is a way of sublimating the resentment they feel about their own situation.

* In late 2011, anti-corruption protests in the village of Wukan, in Guangdong province in southern China, led to the expulsion from the village of local Communist party officials. Following a siege of the village by police, a peaceful agreement was reached between village representatives and provincial officials, in which the villagers' demands in relation to the transparency of financial records, the conduct of local elections and the redistribution of land were largely met.

Wukan crops up regularly in the news because the situation is ongoing. Visitors have come at different times, and interpreted it in different ways. But what everyone is curious to know is: Why has Wukan succeeded? Can the Wukan experience be replicated?

Everyone, whether they live in China or experience China through the eyes of the media, knows how frequent farmers' protests over land disputes are. After the central government abolished the agricultural tax in 2005, paying taxes was no longer the big problem it once was. Land sales became the main source of revenue for local governments, and thus the chief source of conflict between local government and farmers. In Guangdong, where development has been extremely rapid and pressure on the land particularly intense, such disputes are common. But protests, although begun enthusiastically, are often suppressed with violence and quickly forgotten.

Wukan is not particularly remarkable for its spirit of resistance or its experiment with democracy. Petitions and appeals over the heads of local government have been going on for many years. There have been village elections for thirty years, and local elections have been held at township level too. Wukan's democratic experiment has gone no further than Taishi village near Guangzhou, where villagers succeeded in getting local officials dismissed a few years ago.

There are a series of factors, however, which have heightened the drama in Wukan: the energy of the young people involved, the highly organized ways in which people have mobilized, the use of new technology and the fact that the whole business has lasted a long time. This is largely due to the fact that Wukan is big enough, with a population of 13,000, to sustain an ongoing movement. The developments at Wukan have also taken place at a critical time in China's development. Everyone is aware that China needs new reforms. Everyone senses subtle signs of competition among the top leadership. As a result, what happens in this village has suddenly become a weathervane of national politics. Additionally, interest on Weibo and the involvement of the international media have turned Wukan into a sustained drama.

When you are involved in the drama, it is always hard to reflect on it. Sometimes when I look around me at my new friends in Wukan, I am surprised that I do not feel more enthusaism. I have been to Wukan twice and each time I was underwhelmed. Perhaps at some deeper level, I am unsure how to interpret the much-discussed concepts – the peasantry and democracy.

Around the time when I matured intellectually, any responsible educated person regarded China's agriculture, the villages and the farmers as key issues that would determine China's future. Even considering China's rapid urbanization, the peasants were still the major national topic of discussion. Not only were they numerically dominant, they were also morally persuasive. When you read such books as *Premier, I'm telling the truth** and *Will the Boat Sink the Water?: The Life of China's Peasants*, the overwhelming sense of suffering makes an indelible impression.** There is an irony here: throughout Chinese history, it is quite clear that literate people have controlled the state and heavily over-romanticized the peasantry, turning them into the wellspring of politics and morality. The stability of the peasantry has meant the stability of the dynasty; if they revolted, the dynasty had to change. Then, in twentieth-century China, the peasantry were regarded as the core of the revolution, and the CCP was most successful in areas where it established a revolutionary alliance that gave direction and significance to traditional-style peasant revolts. The

* *Wo xiang zongli shuo shihua*, by Li Changping, Shaanxi Renmin Chubanshe Publishers, (2009).
** Translated as *Will the Boat Sink the Water? The Life of China's Peasants*, by Chen Guidi and Wu Chuntao, 2004.

revolution failed in the cities but maintained its vitality in the villages. But once the regime came to power, the new China fleeced the peasants mercilessly. They lost their land and their basic freedoms. The *hukou** tied them firmly to land that did not belong to them, and forced them to grow crops they did not want to.

The reforms at the end of the 1970s brought some changes: the Household Responsibility System gave the farmers back some rights, villages were energized and prospered, rural incomes swiftly caught up and even, for a time, overtook city incomes. But the honeymoon was soon over. By the beginning of the 1990s, the effect of the Household Responsibility System had begun to dwindle, the outlook was bleak for the village economy, and farmers migrated to the towns in search of work. China's rural migrants became the world's largest community of factory workers, and a key factor in China's growing position in world manufacturing. The gap between town and countryside widened, rural areas declined once more, and the outflow of farmers in search of work left only the elderly and children in the villages. A hugely complicated tax system left local governments in the red, and exacerbated tensions between officials and farmers.

Can the victory at Wukan last, and spread? Or is it just an isolated incident like so many others that have preceded it? In its progression from mass protests to village elections and then the defence of land rights, does it have any meaning for contemporary democracy? Is it just the usual story of unseating corrupt officials and replacing them with honest ones? Or perhaps it is just an experiment, graciously permitted by the government in the short term, but destined to be swallowed up by the system in the usual way? In a country with so little

---

* The household registration system officially identifies every person as a resident of a certain area using identifying information such as name, parents, spouse and date of birth.

democracy, people were understandably keen to celebrate what happened in one small corner of Guangdong province, but the reality is that praise for Wukan has been out of proportion to the actual scale of what was achieved there.

As the night draws in, silence descends on the streets, and empty beer bottles litter the ground. I see an advertisement for Hutu *baijiu* liquor on the wall. The brand, which advertises itself as 'Woozy [*hutu*] for a hundred years!' suddenly reminds me that it was exactly a hundred years ago that the Republic of China was founded, Asia's first republic.

A CALLOUS MACHINE

15 July 2012

A young mother and her aborted infant lie side-by-side in a hospital bed. The photograph is filled with a feeling of despair and death. Feng Jianmei's plight has aroused intense public sympathy because everyone feels that, after so many years of high-speed 'progress', there has been no let-up in the cruelty of the bureaucracy, and individuals are too weak to defend themselves against this kind of organized barbarity.

'Do we want to be barbarous?' I hear the local officials protest. 'In China's villages you can talk to the peasants about reason and policy till the cows come home, and walk till your shoe leather's worn out, but who's listening? What can we do? We have to have population control, and central government orders have to be obeyed, don't they? So what are we supposed to do?'

In his unforgettable novel *Frog*, Mo Yan created Auntie Wan Xin, a woman of extraordinary determination. In order to fulfil the government's family planning targets, she cuts down families' trees, knocks down their houses, and hunts down any woman pregnant with her second child, until she ends up sending her nephew's wife to her death.

Among contemporary writers, Mo Yan is known for his epic stories of desire, fantasy and cruelty. The last century of Chinese history has provided plenty of material. In *Frog*, he addresses the Chinese government's family planning policy. Policies have varied, but whether the state has been encouraging large families or enforcing small ones, it has treated the individual as a tool to be manipulated. In order to realize its aims, it has resorted to ruthless violence.

Reality is often more fantastic than fiction. Consider again the young mother in the photograph. Her name is Feng Jianmei and she comes from Zhenping county in west China's Shaanxi province. She was going to be forced to abort the child she was pregnant with, because it would have been her second. Instead she ran away. She was on the run for more than seventy hours before the local government recaptured her and forced her into a car. In the hospital, she was forced to sign a consent form and injected with drugs to cause the abortion of a child she had been pregnant with for seven and a half months. As she suffered, her sixty-year-old father-in-law was prevented from entering the hospital. Her husband was still hurrying home from Inner Mongolia.

This is not the first time an incident like this has happened, and it will not be the last. The locals told reporters who arrived in the county town that seven-months-pregnant women were often forced to have abortions. Throughout China, it sometimes happens that the woman dies as well as the infant.

On the surface, these desperate mothers are victims of the family planning policy, which has been in force for over thirty years and permits only one child per family. The basic idea of the policy is rational and in line with Malthus's population theory. With steadily increasing pressure on resources, we have to control the increase in our numbers. However, the local officials who drive numberless women like Feng Jianmei to their hospital beds are not in the slightest bit interested in Communist ideals or national policy. What drives them is their own interests. If Feng Jianmei's family had handed over 40,000 yuan (£4,020), she would have been allowed to keep the child. The fine is officially (and bafflingly) called a 'social support fee'.

Enforcing family planning targets has become very lucrative. There is a common saying in Shaanxi province, 'Whilst county and city governments feed off land rents, township and village budgets feed off "belly rents".' In other words, fines levied on families who want a second child have become a major source of income for local authorities. In Feng Jianmei's case, the Family Planning Committee workers, the hospital doctors and the local officials had combined to form a giant net, from which she could not escape. The fines support a vast bureaucracy, which puts food on people's table, builds useless highways and tower blocks, and keeps the lid on social unrest. As far as the local government officials in Zhenping county, Shaanxi are concerned, violence is the lubricant that makes the wheels of 'rent collection' turn smoothly. With Feng Jianmei as an example, more families wanting more than one child will meekly hand over the 'rent'.

In Chinese academia, there is an ongoing discussion about abolition of the family planning policy, no doubt encouraged by the terrible thing that happened to Feng Jianmei. Demographers note ruefully that China is getting old before it is getting rich, and one unforeseen result of population control has already become plain – a shortage of labour. China has become an example of a rapidly aging population. Other people argue that the population will not expand without limits in any case. In the wake of economic and social development, people will change their attitudes and control their family size in their own way.

But the tragedy of Feng Jianmei is not simply an example of policy, but also of the intrinsic nature of political power. Since 1949, the Party has religiously implemented top-down control over everything from the natural environment, the direction of the flow of rivers, the size of cities and the movements of people, to economic models, personal thought, and even life itself. Of course, extreme rationality here often ends up as extreme irrationality. And in the process, individuals either become fodder for political movements or producers and consumers. Their dignity and values are not and have never been respected. Between the individual and the government, there is a serious imbalance.

We were wrong to think that economic development would diminish the power of the government or the barbarous cruelty of the bureaucracy; in the last few years we have seen how economic interests have actually reinforced its powers. Feng Jianmei has aroused intense public sympathy because everyone is moved by the fact that, after so many years of high-speed 'progress', there has been no let-up in the cruelty of bureaucracy, and individuals are too weak to defend themselves against such organized barbarity.

TEETERING ON THE BRINK

12 August 2012

With Gu Kailai, a fascinating woman has once again brought calamity in her wake. She is the latest in a long line of infamous Chinese beauties. There was Yang Guifei, the beautiful concubine who committed suicide on the orders of her king after the Anshi Rebellion which brought catastrophe on the Tang Dynasty in the eighth century; the Empress Cixi, whom many believe hastened the end of the Qing Dynasty; and Jiang Qing, who has taken the blame for the ten-year-long Cultural Revolution.

In Chinese politics, crises are often simplified as moral crises, and the weakest link, whether a woman or a eunuch, is often made a scapegoat. Scapegoats can allow people to avoid the real problem, whether that problem lies in politics or morality. When writing about the rise and fall of Chinese dynasties, historians are not slow to blame individuals, yet the country's political system has somehow lasted for an astonishingly long time.

Now, new names are being added to the list of scapegoats. After disappearing for three months, Bo Xilai's wife, Gu Kailai, suddenly reappeared and became front-page news. In one very short item, Xinhua reported that investigators had charged her with murder. Analysts all over the world concluded, although they knew little about the case at that time, that the charge was politically motivated in preparation for the 18th National Party Congress which was about to open. The way the analysts reached their verdict was superficial, but they may well be correct. The authorities were doing their utmost to separate Gu Kailai from her husband in order to pre-empt a deeper schism at the top of the governing hierarchy.

As Premier Wen Jiabao said at a press conference on 14 March 2012, 'It is quite possible that a historical tragedy like the Cultural Revolution will be repeated.' His emotional words were an oblique reference to Bo Xilai's Chongqing. Most people believe that what was ending was not just Bo Xilai's political career but a struggle over the 'Chinese road' that had gone on for a number of years. A sluggish government system has given rise to widespread social conflict, with some forces believing that the only thing to do is to continue to push forward reforms, and take China onto the road to freedom and democracy; while others are attempting to take China back to what they see as the glorious days of the revolution, using methods from the Mao era to deal with social injustices, moral bankruptcy and bureaucratic corruption. Bo Xilai is a representative of the latter.

Wen Jiabao was clearly stating his position that more hopeful times are on the way and much-postponed reform will eventually happen. In the politics of the elite, the 'liberal' faction represented by Wen Jiabao has, it seems, gained the upper hand, while at the bottom level of society, the Wukan democratic experiment has given rise to widespread romantic fantasies that the inside story of the battles at the top will be revealed, the Tiananmen protesters will be rehabilitated, and restrictions on press freedom will be lifted. Groups who want political reform are happy to believe that the turmoil of the Bo Xilai case will go beyond a drama, that it will shake the entire regime to its foundations, exacerbating internal schisms. The restless mood in Chinese society will, so the groups hope, compel those in authority to react.

A few months passed and this optimistic mood and excited conjecture vanished without a trace. Enthusiasm for the Wukan experiment had dissipated and it seemed unlikely to be repeated elsewhere. The Gu Kailai trial showed the leadership at the top level adopting a common consensus, and in-fighting stopped for the time being. In order to prevent the whole boat from capsizing, action had to be taken while it was still possible. The entire blame was heaped on Gu Kailai, showing that in moments of crisis, the leadership adopts old methods.

Many people believe that these mechanisms of deceit will no longer yield results, that the government in Beijing has lost all legitimacy and that it can only carry on through the use of violence and through using the economy to buy support. The slowing down of economic growth and the rising costs of maintaining social stability will cripple the system once a critical point has been reached. Riots from Shifang to Nantong, as well as political storms in Beijing, are all proof of this.

But the way in which the Bo Xilai case was dealt with shows

that China's rulers, while having changed into an oligarchy, still retain a common rationale and, at a critical juncture, will act together. Oligarchs they may be, with the power and wealth of oligarchs, but they still accept being ruled by the political machine. The Beijing authorities may commit endless mistakes but they still have effective means of control at their disposal.

A China observer once described the Mao era as guerrilla politics. Back then, you could see two completely different characteristics at work: despotism whose authority could never be questioned and, below that, total chaos from whose impact no individual or organization could escape. The Party apparatus could at any moment sacrifice people's lives in order to protect the stability of the apparatus itself. The methods of the regime were characterized by a high degree of flexibility, opportunism and cruelty. In the absence of any checks and balances, the rulers could choose to do as they pleased.

Today, a powerful dictator has been replaced by a mediocre collective leadership. There is no longer a madman to take the system to the brink of collapse, and so the system has attained a new stability. Economists talk of 'rescuing capitalism from the hands of the capitalists', and here is Beijing currently implementing a new line, 'rescuing dictatorship from the hands of the dictator'. Everywhere it is as if no one is responsible and the country is hurtling towards chaos and darkness, yet the system retains a certain stability. The rulers still have a grip on vast natural resources and their ability to rule opportunistically gives them a great deal of room for manoeuvre.

If the precondition for change is a transformation in ways of thinking, then it is clear that China has still to reach that consensus for change. China has experienced an alarming number of public protests, running into the hundreds of thousands, but all of them have been 'protests with Chinese characteristics'. In other words, local protesters have not lost faith in the central government; they just want provincial or central government to show its concern. While for their part, the local government increasingly show themselves willing to give concessions of one sort or another, putting the brakes on many controversial policies in the face of resistance. The CCP still enjoys another legacy from Mao Zedong. During his thirty-year rule, in which China reached an all-time low, any community organizations that might have developed a collective strength were destroyed and, even more importantly, memories of fear and suffering were planted in every heart. Public anger is a potent force in China but no community organizations at any level or of any complexion are strong enough to channel this anger, and without these organizations it is hard to sustain pressure.

A general dissatisfaction, localized protests, pressure-cooker-style repression, the shunting of migrant workers back to their home villages, all this seems set to persist for a long time. People have said for years that we are on the brink of a transformation, but we may teeter on that brink for many more years yet.

A PARTY THAT TRIES TO DEFEAT HISTORY

1 November 2012

'Resolutely fight to protect the Party's 18th National Congress.' So reads the white lettering on a red banner hanging over the door of a shop in Wangfujing Street, one of Beijing's most flourishing commercial streets. With its string of shopping centres, bars and restaurants, and crowds of shoppers, it is an amazing show of China's economic prosperity.

The banner's look and its message are in stark contrast to its surroundings. It brings back shades of the Mao Zedong era, when slogans like this were plastered all over China, and everyone was caught up in political fervour; as if just a few slogans could transform China and save the world. But China has changed, and these crazy times are long gone. Revolutionary China is now the factory of the world. Socialism with Chinese characteristics has turned into something closer to capitalism with Chinese characteristics, but the political culture that produces a slogan like this clings stubbornly on.

There are foreign visitors who are fascinated by these contradictions. In the rest of the world, communist experiments have proved to be a cruel joke now consigned to history, but in China, the Party system has assumed a different form and gained new vitality. When people come to study China as a newly emerging power, they find the country hard to classify. It fits neither the totalitarian model of the former Soviet Union, nor the development model of the Four Asian Tigers and Japan.

This is the world's largest Communist Party, with eighty million members and still expanding. It has long since lost any ideological glamour but is in firm control of a violent machine and vast interests. Even more importantly, it has destroyed or bought any civil organization that might offer the slightest challenge to its power.

This Party has a total monopoly, and tentacles everywhere. Whenever you mention the word 'Party', it means the Chinese Communist Party. Like when you say 'emperor', no further explanation is needed. This is the reason why the five-yearly National Party Congress is so important, because it elects new leaders and determines the direction of China's future development.

The Party wields such power, yet appears to feel it is under siege. The slogan adorning the Wangfujing shopping centre says it all. It needs protection, and it uses military language to say so.

In the last twenty years, the Party seems to have shattered all predictions made about it. The China that it leads has not only not fallen apart, it has experienced a dramatic rise. However, it has not led China towards democracy, and under the bright and shiny surface lies a political and social crisis: corruption is pervasive; bureaucracy has taken hold of the market, squeezing the economy; the banking sector is ineffective and wasteful; and the environment, education and healthcare are stuck in the same bad old ways. There are constant social disturbances. I am sometimes reminded of the Harvard professor Roderick MacFarquhar's comments at a 2005 conference, that communism may well collapse within years not decades, and that when the CCP arrests social activists, it is playing with fire. In his view, the Party is capable of controlling the new reality and dealing with local protests, but the resulting sparks may one day set all China alight, and thus cause a collapse of the entire system. The only question is where the fire will start.

The Party responds to the difficulties it faces with repression. It uses every means at its disposal to maintain the status quo, and as a result exacerbates internal decline. The CCP organization has closed in on itself, and now devotes itself solely to protecting its power and interests. It has become an entirely self-serving political conglomerate. In so doing, it has triggered all sorts of social conflict. Maintaining social stability through repression has locked the Party and society into a vicious circle, and the fact that the Party's budget exceeds military expenditure shows that China has been drawn into an invisible civil war – the Party versus the people.

No one is clear yet whether the new leadership can bring about real change, despite the fact that Beijing's dinner tables, salons and private parties feed on endless speculation, and that some top Party officials have been heard to say privately, 'Without change, the 19th Party Congress may not happen.'

However, the Party has a surprising ability to recreate itself, often by employing means that are cruel and partially self-denying. An example is the ongoing case of Bo Xilai. People thought that such a fierce struggle conducted so publicly would lead to a split in the Party but it is very possible that the Party will simply absorb the incident.

In the face of internecine Party struggles, cliques, princelings* and the Shanghai Gang** have all shown a remarkable consistency of outlook that far outstrips their differences of opinion. Society's anger and dissatisfaction at the CCP, by contrast, is still impromptu and fragmentary. The Party's opponents are incapable of sustaining the pressure and of stiffening the resolve of the general public.

Will these games between the sparks and the firefighters continue? Xinmin Pei, an outstanding China analyst, warned on the CCP's ninetieth anniversary that the Party had been in power for sixty-two years and its leaders would do well to note that the record for a Communist Party is held by the Soviet Union, at seventy-four years. As the CCP leaders raise their glasses to their ninety-year-old Party, they should not be under the illusion that it will be forever victorious.

It may seem like a joke to predict a political party's future prospects on the basis of a numbers game, but history is full of such jokes.

CITY OF RESISTANCE

February 2015

I walked from the Mandarin Hotel down Connaught Road Central to the central government offices in Admiralty. I had never see anything like it. The street was lined with tents and placards. People were walking in the middle of the road and there was not a car to be seen. Hong Kong's customary hustle and bustle had vanished and the whole city had gone completely quiet, as if it was a huge school whose young

---

* A common term for sons and daughters of Party leaders.
** The Shanghai Gang was the name given to a group of officials in the Communist Party of China who rose to prominence under Jiang Zemin.

people had all dispersed, its tension temporarily relaxed. There was a feeling of exhaustion but expectation too, as if everything hung in the balance. The glass-walled tower blocks, snaking upwards like pythons, formed a silent backdrop to the performance.

'Nothing like this has ever happened in Hong Kong,' I recalled the words of my hotel doorman. He looked Indian and was over sixty, a symbol of Hong Kong's multi-ethnic heritage. This lush little island in the South China Sea was ceded to Britain 170 years ago in a treaty which symbolized the humiliation of China in modern times but which, against all the odds, produced a marvellous city, an amalgam of East and West, a melting-pot of people from different dependent territories of the British Empire and Chinese migrants.

The doorman's astonishment was understandable. For many years, Hong Kong has been known for being apolitical, utilitarian and orderly, a bargain-basement shopping mall, an exotic 'pearl of the East', a reliable and super-efficient financial centre. Hongkongers gave the impression that their love of money came above everything else. They were capable of producing economic miracles and a world of entertainment, but had no interest in politics or public life. There is much that could be written about just how such an impression was formed. From Kipling, writing at the apogee of the British Empire, 'How is it that everyone smells of money?' to the warning given to the last governor of Hong Kong, Chris Patten before he took office, that he would soon be mixing with people who could only talk about money, and on to China's elite today who lament that, 'Hongkongers have no understanding of politics.'

Yet now, Hong Kong's youth are occupying the streets, demanding real democracy. They have employed everything from civic resistance to non-violent action... and Hong Kong has suddenly transformed into a city of resistance and of politics.

As I walked down the street on the afternoon of 30 September 2014, I found it difficult to suppress my excitement. For my generation, Hong Kong is special. After the Reform and Opening Up on the Mainland in the 1980s, it was Hong Kong pop songs, TV dramas and martial arts novels that moulded our imaginations. For a long time, people believed that Hong Kong offered a vision of China in the future – clean, prosperous, free, even if not very democratic.

Travelling there on a fairly frequent basis over the last thirteen years, I have gradually begun to discover another Hong Kong, a Hong Kong in revolt. The late Qing dynasty reformer Kang Youwei (1858–1927) found inspiration here; Sun Yat-sen regarded Hong Kong as the birthplace of his revolutionary thought; and in 1989, when students in Beijing occupied Tiananmen Square, their most fervent supporters came from Hong Kong. After the massacre and crackdown, it was Hong Kong democrats, Mafiosi and media stars who organized a rescue network and succeeded in getting student leaders and academics safely out of China.

Starting with the July marches of 2003, Hong Kong has gradually transformed into a city of demonstrations and protests. Their increasing frequency is open to a number of interpretations: they are connected to the widening gap between rich and poor; to the incompetence of Hong Kong's leaders now that it has been returned to China as a 'Special Economic Zone'; to the upset caused by a flood of investors and tourists from the Mainland; and to Hong Kong's loss of status and privileges as a result of the economic rise of Shanghai, Shenzhen and Beijing.

But the most important reason is structural: how can Hong Kong preserve its former freedoms and gain the democracy it has never had, under China's totalitarian rule?

When the Joint Sino–British Declaration was signed in 1984, what Hongkongers most hoped for was a preservation of the status quo and a 'return to democracy'. At that time, almost every Hong Kong family had bitter experience of the cruel face of Red China and dreaded the CCP's totalitarian rule. But Deng Xiaoping promised that there would be 'no change for fifty years' and that 'Hong Kong will be ruled by Hongkongers'. The implication was not only that the people of Hong Kong could retain the freedoms, rule of law and the way of living they had enjoyed under British colonial rule, but also that they could win new political freedoms – to elect their leaders and exercise democratic rights. The formulation 'One Country, Two Systems' laid to rest the anxieties of many.

But after Hong Kong returned to China in 1997, those rosy expectations quickly evaporated. The feeling of disillusion became more marked as China became more powerful and important. Hongkongers discovered that instead of achieving autonomy, they had swapped rulers from London with rulers from Beijing. And because these new rulers had only just acquired huge wealth and power, they were ignorant, vulgar and arrogant. They simply transferred the authoritarian methods they were applying in the Mainland, to Hong Kong. Not only were Hongkongers still deprived of genuine democracy, they also faced grave threats to their former freedom of the press and the rule of law.

Hongkongers' feelings of having been cheated came to a head in the summer of 2014. In a White Paper, Beijing bluntly rejected their call for democratic rights, and made it clear that the election for chief executive of the Special Economic Zone in 2017 would be subject to manipulation.

And so, a mass protest movement unprecedented in the history of Hong Kong gathered momentum. Young people occupied Central, an area that represents the financial and business heart of Hong Kong. As distinct from the protests of former years, these demonstrations were not only on an astonishing scale, they were led by high school and university students who used social media as a tool for rapid and flexible mobilization. Joshua Wong, aged seventeen, was the symbolic head of the movement.

This generation of young people was born around the time of the handover to China. As they grew up, they witnessed the resurgence of Beijing's authoritarian powers. They are a generation deeply influenced by the technological revolution and globalization, instinctively opposed to totalitarianism and class divisions, who care about their own dignity and feelings. In a certain sense, they are spiritually akin to the young people in Egypt during the Arab Spring, the young New Yorkers who occupied Wall Street, or the Ukrainians of the Orange Revolution. They no longer acknowledge their origins in Mainland China, as their parents' generation do, nor do they regard Hong Kong as a temporary stopover, as migrant workers have done for over a century. They are rooted in this city, it's their home turf, and they will defend it with their lives. They may regard resistance to Beijing's power as useless, but they are going to protest all the same, because expressing dissatisfaction is a basic requirement for human dignity.

It is more than half a year since my visit to Hong Kong last September. The Occupy Central movement lasted until December, longer than anyone expected. It must be the most orderly and peaceful movement in the history of mass protest, with almost no disturbances or looting. On the surface it does not seem to have succeeded in its aims: Beijing offered no concessions and the rules governing the 2017 election have not changed. But anyone in Hong Kong will certainly sense that its atmosphere has changed irreversibly. There is a pervasive desire among Hongkongers to control their own destiny. Hong Kong has become increasingly self-aware, no longer a 'floating city' squeezed between China and Britain. After a period of disruption, Hong Kong is reverting to being a normal city. It needs to reaffirm its dignity and its rights, and stand up for its opinions.

The significance of Occupy Central does not stop at Hong Kong. From Beijing's point of view, this is the biggest popular challenge to its authority since Tiananmen in 1989. The tighter controls Beijing has imposed on Hong Kong, demonizing its people's actions through censorship and propaganda, is a fore-taste of the future for Mainland China. Hong Kong's economic importance may have diminished but it looks likely that its political and social importance will continue to grow.

THE LURE OF ISOLATION

February 2015

If Manuel Castells was in Wuzhen, what would he feel? Castells, a sociologist born into a conservative Spanish family, was forced to flee Spain because he opposed Franco's dictatorship. He is the most important thinker of the Internet age. His Information Age trilogy – *The Rise of the Network Society, The Power of Identity*, and *End of Millennium* – is considered to be as seminal as Max Weber's work. Regrettably, I never met him when I was at Berkeley though I did hear that he was a formidable bon viveur and talker.

Castells believed that the Soviet Union came to an end because its gigantic bureaucracy could not adapt to the demands of the new information age:

In the last quarter of the twentieth century, a technological revolution, centred around information, transformed the way we think, we produce, we consume, we trade, we manage, we communicate, we live, we die, we make war, and we make love. A dynamic, global economy has been constituted around the planet, linking up valuable people and activities from all over the world, while switching off from the networks of power and wealth, people and territories dubbed as irrelevant from the perspective of dominant interests.

This was written in the year 2000. He observed that there was 'a new brand of leaner, meaner capitalism alone at last in its planetary reach.' In this new age, the Soviet Union failed but China achieved astonishing success.

In the new global economic structure, China's economic development, and the modernization of its science and technology, has been implemented under the leadership of the Communist Party. This has become an indispensable tool for an emerging state power, and a new way for the Communist Party to obtain legitimacy.

Fourteen years have passed since Castells made these judgments. The success of the CCP has outstripped people's wildest predictions; it has not only embraced the information age, it has even started rewriting its principles.

At the end of November 2014, in Wuzhen, a small town 140 kilometres (90 miles) from Shanghai and famed for its beauty and culture, the first ever World Internet Congress opened. It was co-hosted by the Zhejiang Provincial Government and the newly established Cyberspace Administration of the People's Republic of China. The latter is universally regarded as the Chinese government's most important propaganda organ, more important even than the long-established Propaganda Ministry.

With more than 1,000 participants from over 100 countries, the congress attracted business executives, strategists, reporters and information analysts. The organizers clearly had ambitions to make the gathering the Davos of the online world. If Davos, from the 1970s onwards, came to represent the globalized era's thinking on economics and politics, why could not the canal town Wuzhen become another such centre in this flourishing Internet age? It fitted perfectly with China's rising global influence. China was already the country with the biggest number of Internet users, and the centre of production for electronic devices. It had earned the right to speak in the online world, but that right was currently firmly monopolized by America.

However, the conference participants at the World Internet Congress were stymied by the Chinese government's highly effective 'firewall': they discovered that they could not access their Facebook and Twitter accounts, or read the *New York Times* or the BBC online. In effect, they realized, China is one giant intranet. The congress organizers were most interested not in the Internet's huge opportunities for promoting equality and developing content, but its worrying potential to undermine traditional government power. They became apologists for China's censorship system.

At the congress, the biggest celebrities all came from China. In addition to Jack Ma, founder of Alibaba (just floated on the New York stock market), there was Pony Ma of Tencent Holdings* and Robin Li Yanhong of Baidu.** They are all regarded as representative of the Chinese Internet, having started in the Chinese market and gone on to create global-scale companies. It is as if they are showing that, even though the Chinese Internet faces all kinds of restrictions, Chinese entrepreneurs can have huge success. If China created 'socialism with Chinese characteristics', then it can also create an 'Internet with Chinese characteristics'.

The participation of these Internet giants also shows how weak they are in the face of Chinese state power. No matter how many customers they have, and no matter how great their

---

* Tencent Holdings is a Chinese investment holding company whose subsidiaries provide media, entertainment, Internet and mobile phone value-added services, and operate online advertising services in China.

** Baidu is a Chinese web services company based in Beijing.

market value, they need to be obedient and docile. Does this also mean that they have adopted the same modus operandi as Hu Xueyan, a famous late Qing dynasty merchant, also from Zhejiang province? His enormous wealth was wholly dependent on the favour of the government, and he had to accept being fleeced by it.

The Wuzhen World Internet Congress was a highly ironic occasion, full of metaphor and symbolism. It was a world congress that expelled the world, so that the rebellious, decentralizing Internet evaporated, to be replaced by a highly centralized, monopolistic version.

It seemed to indicate that China's immense state machine, after subjugating the middle class, capitalism and civil society, could also subjugate the information revolution. Was this a new China-centred world order in the making?

As John King Fairbank describes it, the nineteenth-century Chinese created ports and international settlements to keep out Western technology, business, and political, cultural and religious influences. This was a defensive strategy, designed to bolster China's self-sufficient world view. Now the Chinese have discovered that they can have Youku instead of YouTube, Weibo instead of Twitter, Baidu instead of Google, WeChat instead of Facebook, Alibaba instead of eBay and Walmart, and because their number of users is big enough, the substitutes may actually set new standards, not just within China's borders, but worldwide. China is on the offensive.

But no matter whether defensive or offensive, these are isolated phenomena. China refuses to understand the rest of the world, it just wants to act in its own way. Wuzhen shows that China has plunged into isolation once more, this time precisely because of its huge success and wealth.